"There are thinkers and doers and John Spencer is both. When this warrior-scholar has something to teach about conflict, we all need to listen."

—MAX BROOKS, *New York Times* best-selling author of *World War Z* and *Devolution*

....

"John Spencer's story is valuable for leaders in military organizations and beyond. *Connected Soldiers* provides unique insight into the experiences of a military family in which both parents served their nation, one another, and their fellow soldiers. This memoir not only describes wartime experiences; it also explains how real combat power derives from effective leadership and disciplined, cohesive teams in which soldiers are dedicated to the mission and to each other."

—LT. GEN. H. R. McMASTER, U.S. Army (Ret.), former national security advisor

....

"John Spencer has provided us with far more than a normal military memoir. He ties his personal experiences of combat and of staying home to care for his children during his wife's deployment to a wide array of examples and anecdotes from military history, as well as to his extensive readings in social science on group cohesion, military effectiveness, and the impact of new technologies. At once comprehensive and intimate, it is an original and invaluable book on modern war, as well as a frank and unflinchingly honest portrait of leadership and family life in the current military."

—PHIL KLAY, National Book Award–winning author of *Redeployment* and *Missionaries*

....

"*Connected Soldiers* provides a wonderfully stimulating, thoughtful, and thought-provoking examination of how the increase in connectivity between those on the frontlines and those on the home front affects the all-important bonds between our soldiers carrying out tough missions overseas. As John Spencer relates—sharing compelling personal examples from his and, later, his wife's deployments—the pluses and minuses of ubiquitous connectivity bring realities with which military leaders, families, and the bands of soldiers who are now so connected must grapple."

—GEN. DAVID PETRAEUS, U.S. Army (Ret.), former commander of the surge in Iraq, U.S. Central Command, and Coalition Forces in Afghanistan

....

"John Spencer is the real deal: a seasoned veteran who has experienced the intense group cohesion of battle firsthand. But his generation has also dealt with the incredibly disconnecting effect of the internet. His insights about how twenty-four-seven connection to home affects a platoon in combat is vital to any modern understanding of war."

—SEBASTIAN JUNGER, *New York Times* best-selling author of *War* and *Tribe: On Homecoming and Belonging*

....

"A personal and truly compelling exploration of war, *Connected Soldiers* illuminates the humanity and inhumanity of conflict and the critical question of how constant electronic communication is changing the experience of combat for soldiers and their families."

—GAYLE TZEMACH LEMMON, *New York Times* best-selling author of *Ashley's War* and *The Daughters of Kobani*

....

CONNECTED SOLDIERS

CONNECTED SOLDIERS

Life, Leadership, and Social
Connections in Modern War

JOHN SPENCER

POTOMAC BOOKS
An imprint of the University of Nebraska Press

Library of Congress Cataloging-in-Publication Data
Names: Spencer, John, 1975–, author.
Title: Connected soldiers: life, leadership, and social
connections in modern war / John Spencer.
Identifiers: LCCN 2021038178
ISBN 9781640125124 (paperback)
ISBN 9781640125162 (epub)
ISBN 9781640125179 (pdf)
Subjects: LCSH: Spencer, John, 1975–| Iraq War,
2003-2011—Campaigns—Iraq—Baghdad. | Iraq War,
2003-2011—Personal narratives, American. | Unit
cohesion (Military science)—Case studies. | Command
of troops (Military science)—Case studies. | United
States. Army—Officers—Biography. | United States.
Army. Parachute Infantry Regiment, 508th—Biography. |
United States—Armed Forces—Military life—History—
21st century. | Social media—Government policy—
United States. | Soldiers—United States—Social life and
customs—21st
century. | Soldiers—Family relationships—United
States—History—21st century. | BISAC: BIOGRAPHY
& AUTOBIOGRAPHY / Military | HISTORY / Military /
Afghan War (2001–)
Classification: LCC DS79.764.B35 S64 2022 |
DDC 956.7044/373—dc23/eng/20211012
LC record available at https://lccn.loc.gov/2021038178

Set in Minion Pro by Laura Buis.

To Isaac, Isabel, and Maggie

CONTENTS

ILLUSTRATIONS

ACKNOWLEDGMENTS

This book is a by-product of an article, "From Army of One to Band of Tweeters," I published in the *New York Times* in November 2015. It would take an entire manuscript to list all the people who helped me get from that article to this book; however, there are two individuals I cannot thank enough—John Amble and Lionel Beehner. Both of these men spent countless hours helping me not only refine my writing abilities but frequently encouraging me to just create. Without their patience and persistence over the years, this book would not have become a reality. Several other people merit special recognition for their never-fading support, assistance, and words of belief that I could one day finish such a major undertaking: Leon Hall, Liam Collins, Max and Michelle Brooks, Jessica Gallus, Mike Jackson, Vinnie Viola, Ed Coss, and David Johnson. Most importantly, thank you to my wife, my best friend Emily Spencer. With her love, advice, and patience I have been able to thrive not just in this project but in life overall.

INTRODUCTION

One of the hardest questions I have had to answer about this book is why. Why this topic? Why now? I am not sure I can ever fully answer those queries, but my journey for this book did start with asking questions.

I served twenty-five years in the U.S. Army. I spent a majority of that time doing, not thinking. By that I mean when I entered the military at age seventeen, I was set on a path to focus on learning to be a good soldier, leader, and warfighter. I was taught to continually develop skills that were important to leading men in combat. I sought out and excelled in positions that were valued by my community of infantry soldiers, noncommissioned officers (NCOs), and officers. I served as both an enlisted soldier and an officer.

The mindset for continuous skill development and job progression were to prepare me for combat, and in 2003 I got my chance. With only a few months' experience as an officer, I conducted a parachute jump into northern Iraq as a platoon leader responsible for forty soldiers. My soldiers and I were a part of an invading army with the mission to overthrow a ruthless dictator in Saddam Hussein, liberate an entire country's population, and then build stability in what would become a new Iraq. For twelve months I experienced the true complexity of being a new leader adapting to the daily challenges of leading soldiers in war, searching for an elusive enemy, carrying out an evolving mission, and facing battle on a personal level.

After my first twelve months in combat, I returned to the army life of building skills and seeking out future jobs. Five years after that first deployment, I found myself back in Iraq—this time as a captain taking on a company of over a hundred and fifty soldiers in a different type of war—and frankly a different army. I struggled on many levels with my new responsibilities. I struggled with the burden of command; the magnitude of tasks required to fight a counterinsurgency while helping build a nation that had just overcome a period of near civil war; and, most importantly, leading a formation of soldiers inundated with their own sets of problems—from dealing with the divide between home and combat to maintaining cohesion under extreme distress.

After my cumulative twenty-four months of combat, I again returned to the path of military upward progression and continuous motion. In 2010 I attended a military school for majors, known as the Command and General Staff College. At this point I had served in the army for over sixteen years. In this school, like others I had attended in the past, we had courses on history, tactics, ethics, and other topics. The history lessons were instructed by Dr. Ed Coss. I had sat through plenty of military history classes in the past, but this time something was different. I am not sure if it was because I was different or if it was Dr. Coss's unique teaching style; it was probably a combination of both. Dr. Coss did not drown us in PowerPoint instruction or monotone lecture. He gave military history readings as usual, but classes were centered on questions for us to answer in front of the rest of the group. These questions consisted of exploring history to reveal the challenges, changes, and similarities in the military profession over time. We covered everything from tactics, weapons, and small unit cohesion to soldier motivation. By having a question to answer, it caused me to not only think about what a soldier or leader hundreds of years ago dealt with but it also made me hold those ideas up to my own fairly recent combat experiences.

After each history class, I could not stop thinking about what the books or scholars said about close combat. I had been oblivious to the body of works looking at how soldiers dealt with or responded to enemy action, how soldiers from ancient Greece to Vietnam relied on each other to survive combat, and how a soldier is conditioned to overcome fear. As a warrior I had taken it all for granted or assumed away many any of these underlying connected issues.

I coupled the in-class experiences with hours of talks with Dr. Coss outside of class. He listened to my own stories of dealing with combat during my two deployments. We discussed the depth of studies on topics such as the psychological and physiological response to combat, small unit cohesion, morale, and many other related areas. I was surprised that after centuries of recorded warfare there were still many gaps in knowledge or research about the subjects. The entirety of Dr. Coss's influence ignited an intellectual curiosity in me, a desire to learn, that I had never had. From that point on, I consumed any book or study about how soldiers and teams dealt with combat that I could get my hands on. I continually asked myself how the different writings or theories related to my own experiences.

I left Dr. Coss and that military school to enter a series of assignments at the Pentagon. As fate would have it, one of the first projects I was assigned was to be a part of a group developing an army-wide program to address the growing national issues in soldier suicides, post-traumatic distress disorder (PTSD), and many other military personnel issues. I was introduced to numerous psychologists, sociologists, medical professionals, and fields of study, such as industrial and organizational psychology, resilience, positive psychology, post-traumatic growth, and holistic health. Our group met frequently to discuss the stresses on soldiers and units in the army. I was honored to share my experiences in Iraq with this group and to see them listen earnestly. They allowed me to ask them hard questions about what assumptions regarding combat life they were leaving unasked. It was here that I first thought about how today's soldiers and their families face unique stresses while deployed in battle, as in my 2008 deployment, because they are connected daily through the internet and other electronic means. This access to virtual connections and immediate exchange of information between forward deployed soldiers and their friends, families, and loved ones was unlike any time in the history of war.

For my next assignment I was selected to be a part of a group of soldiers and civilians brought together to do cutting-edge, unconstrained research for the army's top four-star general, the chief of staff. While in the organization, called the Chief of Staff of the Army's Strategic Studies Group, I learned how to do research using multiple methods and approaches. I also learned multiple styles of critical thinking. Most importantly I learned that the U.S. Army is a massive institution that for many reasons will carry forward ideas and practices without question. We learned to ask the army why it was doing something and then to do our own research into the history, rationale, and reasoning for that practice, policy, or equipment. Sometimes there were many good reasons, while at other times it was because the practice or policy was simply the way the army had always done it.

While in the program I again found a leader in the group's director, Dr. David Johnson. Dr. Johnson, like Dr. Coss, spent hours of off-duty time listening to my stories about fighting in Iraq as well as my questions about how to prepare soldiers, leaders, and small teams for the unique challenges of close combat. He exchanged his stories of the challenges of commanding soldiers in the post-Vietnam era. The more I talked about my stories the more questions I had. Sharing these experiences with others was truly a process of cathartic introspection.

After my work with the Strategic Studies Group, I landed at my final assignment in the army, teaching at the United States Military Academy in West Point, New York. As an instructor there, I was in front of cadets everyday. They wanted to hear my stories whether I offered them or not. I found that the cadets craved any stories of leading in combat, where topics like leadership, cohesion, ethics, and stress were presented in current context rather than as history or theories. I was surprised to learn that there was not only a gap in current narratives but there was also a large segment of the population both inside and outside of the military who wanted to hear them.

I served as an instructor at West Point and also cofounded a research center there called the Modern War Institute. This allowed me to continue to do research and develop my ability to write. While teaching, researching, and continuing to think about the individual and small group demands of close combat, I began to think about how the cadets communicated. I knew from my research that there are not major differences in generations. A nineteen-year-old joining the military today demonstrates many of the traits of a nineteen-year-old who joined during generations past. Yet I did notice how electronically connected the new generation in the military were. I observed that at times they would rather text than talk to each other. They sought group justice in anonymous online platforms, carefully curated their social media personas, and spent an enormous amount of time on their devices. I started to use these observations to ask myself questions about how such a connected life or social practices might impact individual and group norms, bonding, and performance in combat. Then I began to remember what in Iraq I had not questioned in 2008: the constant access of my soldiers to the outside world while we struggled with the day-to-day challenges of the war.

I started a draft of this book in 2015. I knew I wanted to write about my deployments to Iraq so that people could read about the realities, leadership challenges, joys, fears, love, fellowship, and other human aspects of the modern battlefield experience. I also knew I wanted to focus the book on the observations I had made after thinking about the impact of connectivity on the individual soldier and small groups in war. I had done the research, interviewed others who were in Iraq with me in 2003 and 2008, and outlined a structure of the book that would highlight the difference in stresses, living conditions, and social structures between the two tours. I wrote rough drafts of the sections about the two separate tours but then could not mentally see the book in full form. I ultimately let the drafts sit and retired from the military in 2018.

Less than a year after I retired, my wife, an active-duty officer in the army, deployed on a nine-month tour to Kuwait. I became the stay-at-home parent of three young kids aged three, five, and seven. I became the outside world to the soldier in combat who I had written about in my drafts. My kids and I were the everyday life presented to my wife every night on FaceTime, social media, or live texting. I came to realize what I had not before as a platoon leader or company commander. I understood that each soldier is dealing with internal struggles between the mission in combat and the life they left back at home. Each situation is clearly different, but as I experienced in 2008, the new era of instant connections between the frontline and home can create both positive and negative situations for the soldiers and their teams. These final experiences of transitioning out of the military and into the role of a family member of a deployed soldier gave me the perspectives to bring my book together.

Ultimately this book is a memoir of three distinct episodes along my journey as a soldier, scholar, veteran, and father. It is made up of my memories. I relied on extensive notes taken while deployed, as well as interviews with soldiers that served with me, but I fully acknowledge that my own memory is essentially fallible, dependent on what I saw in the moment, including how I interpreted what I saw and who I was with at the time. I have tried to be diligent in relying more heavily on my notes than on my memory. I have changed most of the names of the people involved to protect their privacy.

Like many other authors of memoirs, I hope the telling of my stories explains some details of life—in my case, a military one—that are helpful to others. I also hope my questioning of why and how soldiers fight, how they handle combat in the moment as a member of a cohesive team, and how they live with their experiences will encourage others to think critically about these most vital issues. There are lessons to be learned from my mistakes, struggles, and studies. My wish is that others continue to ask questions about the effects of constant communication with the outside world while serving in combat. It follows that if this is a new type of war experience, there must also be new types of leadership and soldiering considerations for those individuals deployed in combat.

U.S. ARMY FORMATIONS AND RANK STRUCTURE

Formations

Squad: 9 soldiers
Platoon: 40 soldiers
Company: 140 soldiers (this and other numbers vary, depending on the type of unit)
Battalion: 800–1,000 soldiers
Brigade: 4,000–4,500 soldiers
Division: 20,000 soldiers
Corps: 45,000 soldiers

Combatant Command: an organizational structure that has command and control over units from multiple branches of the military. It controls anywhere from tens of thousands to hundreds of thousands of military personnel, depending on the situation or mission. The chain of command has the commander of a unified command reporting directly to the secretary of defense. The U.S. Central Command (USCENTCOM, often referred to as CENTCOM) includes Army, Air Force, Navy, and Marines and its area of responsibility is generally the Middle East, ranging from Egypt to Afghanistan. As the name suggests, U.S. European Command (USEUCOM) has responsibility for all of Europe in addition to the entirety of Russia to the Bering Strait. CENTCOM had command and control over the wars in Iraq and Afghanistan.

These numbers represent the full authorization of each unit, despite the fact that units are often understaffed, even in wartime.

Rank Structure

Enlisted Ranks

Private: PVT (includes the pay grades of PV1 and PV2)
Private First Class: PFC
Specialist and Corporal: SPC and CPL
Sergeant: SGT
Staff Sergeant: SSG
Sergeant First Class: SFC
Master Sergeant: MSG / First Sergeant: 1SG
Sergeant Major: SGM / Command Sergeant Major: CSM

Officers

Second Lieutenant: 2LT
First Lieutenant: 1LT
Captain: CPT
Major: MAJ
Lieutenant Colonel: LTC
Colonel: COL
Brigadier General: BG
Major General: MG
Lieutenant General: LTG
General: GEN

ABBREVIATIONS

AD	accidental discharge
ASP	ammunition supply point
AQI	Al-Qaeda In Iraq
BFV	Bradley Infantry Fighting Vehicle
BN PA	battalion physician assistant
BOLO	be on the lookout
BOSS	Better Opportunities for Single Soldiers
BPT	be prepared to
CENTCOM	U.S. Central Command
CIA	Central Intelligence Agency
CHU	containerized housing unit
CO	commanding officer
COMMEX	communication exercise
COP	combat outpost
CP	command post
CNN	Cable News Network
DUSTWUN	duty status–whereabouts unknown
DZ	drop zone
EOD	explosive ordnance disposal
EFP	explosive force penetrator
FOB	forward operating base
FRG	family readiness group
GSG 9	Grenzschutzgruppe 9
HAZMAT	hazardous materials
HMMWV	high mobility multipurpose wheeled vehicles
HVT	high-value target

IED	improvised explosive device
IRAM	improvised rocket-assisted munitions
JAM	Jaysh Al-Mahdi
JDAM	joint direct attack munition
JMPI	jumpmaster personnel inspection
JSS	joint security station
KIA	killed in action
KH	Kata'ib Hezbollah
MEDEVAC	medical evacuation
MOS	military occupational specialty
MRE	meal-ready-to-eat
MWR	morale, welfare, and recreation
NATO	North Atlantic Treaty Organization
NCO	noncommissioned officer
ND	negligent discharge
NTC	National Training Center
OCS	Officer Candidate School
OPORD	operations order
PID	positive identification
PTSD	post-traumatic stress disorder
PX	post exchange
RI	ranger instructor
ROTC	reserve officer training corps
RPG	rocket-propelled grenade
RTO	radio-telephone operator
SAS	Special Air Service
SATCOM	satellite communications
SEAL	sea, air, and land (commonly used to denote a member of the U.S. Navy Sea, Air, and Land Teams)
SETAF	Southern European Task Force
SF	Special Forces
SOF	Special Operations Forces
TBI	traumatic brain injury
TOC	tactical operations center
UNESCO	United Nations Educational, Scientific and

	Cultural Organization
UCMJ	Uniform Code Of Military Justice
USAF	U.S. Air Force
USCENTCOM	U.S. Central Command (aka CENTCOM)
USEUCOM	U.S. European Command
USO	United Service Organization
VFW	Veterans of Foreign Wars
XO	executive officer

CONNECTED SOLDIERS

1

What We Believe and Know about Combat Cohesion

"From this day to the ending of the world, but we in it shall be
remembered—we few, we happy few, we band of brothers; for he to-day
that sheds his blood with me shall be my brother; be he ne'er
so vile, this day shall gentle his condition."

—William Shakespeare, *Henry V*

I would like to say I joined the army for some heroic reason, but
honestly I just had no plans after high school. I was fascinated by
the adventure outside of small-town Indiana that our local army
recruiters promised. I would go to the recruiter's office to watch pro-
motional videos of elite military units like the U.S. Special Forces
and U.S. Army Rangers and imagined myself as one of the best of
the best. Because of the army's recruiting needs, a ranger contract
was not available when it was time for me to enlist. In other words,
the rangers had enough privates at that time; instead, the recruiter
told me to choose the Military Occupational Specialty (MOS) of
11X (unspecified infantry) airborne. "It's basically the same thing,"
he said. ("Airborne" is army lingo for paratrooper.) Then I would
be able to enter ranger training after basic training. As a kid with
no army experience, I believed the recruiter, as all recruits do. And
like all recruits, I would learn that recruiters are not always entirely
straight with their newbies, despite their smiles and confident assur-
ances. Recruiters are basically the used car salesmen of the army. I
did not care. I was so ready to start the army that I signed the papers
before I even graduated high school in 1993. In the end, my journey

to becoming a ranger eventually did happen, just in a completely different way from what I had been promised.

I started off with basic training, advanced individual training, and airborne school, but I heard no mention of the rangers until years later. As a private in the infantry, you just do what you are told. Infantrymen are the riflemen, the ground pounders. We affectionately refer to ourselves as "grunts." More officially the infantry is called the "Queen of Battle," based on the queen's dominance of a chessboard, where she has the most freedom of movement of all the pieces. I definitely did not feel like royalty most of the time, but I did feel like a soldier. It may not have been exactly like the recruiting videos, but it was more adventurous than community college in Richmond, Indiana.

The army of 1993 was a peacetime army. Armies are always preparing for war: training, exercising, and developing soldiers and teams into what leaders believe is needed for the next war—and there will always be a next war. Gen. Douglas MacArthur said in his farewell address to cadets at West Point in 1962, "Only the dead have seen the end of war." (The original source of the quote is Spanish-American philosopher and writer George Santayana in his 1922 *Soliloquies in England and Later Soliloquies*, although it is often misattributed to Plato.)[1] So we prepare. Much of what is done to prepare for war or to develop a civilian off the street, like I was, into a soldier is passed down from generation to generation. Everything from the way we speak to each other, to how we eat, and to how we move is passed down over time. Some things have direct combat implications, such as putting two soldiers in a foxhole, instead of one. There are many reasons why you need a soldier—a battle buddy—beside you, as I would observe firsthand many years later.

The army sent me to a variety of assignments and locations. My first duty station as a private was at Fort Kobbe, Panama, in the 508th Parachute Infantry Regiment. As the recruiter promised, I got to be a paratrooper. From there I went to Fort Polk, Louisiana, and then I finally joined the rangers in 1995 in Fort Lewis, Washington, as a member of the 75th Ranger Regiment. This was the assignment

I had looked forward to since signing my enlistment papers. We were the ultra-infantrymen. The ranger lineage can be traced to the colonial period, while officially sanctioned by the army in World War II. Even civilians know the term "army rangers," although they may not really understand its significance. So I was happy to have arrived; being a ranger would be a part of my self-identity for the next twenty-plus years.

After about a year of being in the 75th Ranger Regiment, my ideal life as a ranger took a drastic and unplanned turn. In May 1996 in a dark alley in Kent, Washington, I was involved in a street fight with a civilian who bit off most of my left ear. Unfortunately as a junior soldier in the ranger regiment, I was not allowed to be absent from duty for more than a short amount of time, even if due to a medical issue. I tried everything I could to stay in the unit, including waiving a doctor's offer to perform a surgery to fix my ear by using my rib cartridge to create the missing piece. I told the doctor I could not have the surgery; I had to get well as soon as possible to stay in my unit. I was scheduled to go to the U.S. Army Ranger School in two months, but there was a four-month limitation for not wearing a helmet. Even without the additional surgery, it meant my time in the ranger regiment had come to an end. I was told to come back when I fully healed, but that never happened.

I did attend the U.S. Army Ranger School later that year, but becoming a ranger through school is different than being a ranger serving in the 75th Ranger Regiment. Neither has less value; they are just slightly different. Ranger school is the army's preeminent leadership course of three months (sometimes longer depending on individual performance during the course) of simulated combat stress that includes reduced calorie intake and sleep deprivation. With zero to four hours of sleep a night and only one or two meals a day for the three months, of the soldiers who attempt the school, only 50 percent pass, remember the experience, and tell stories of the suffering of ranger school for the rest of their lives, much to the regret of their family and friends. Graduates of the school are officially called rangers. They wear the ranger tab on their left shoulder for the rest of their military career. After graduating ranger school in February 1997, I considered myself a ranger from that point forward.

Shortly after graduating ranger school, I was moved to Italy, again in the 508th Parachute Infantry, which had been relocated from Panama. If I had to leave the ranger battalion, I was happy it was at least to an airborne unit. I served in Italy for three years and then moved to Fort Benning, Georgia, to be an instructor at the infantry school. By that point, having served eight years in the army, I had reached the rank of sergeant first class (SFC). I decided to advance along a different career path and become an officer. I made the decision mainly because as an SFC I was no longer directly involved in the planning of operations or directing mission. That is not to say I did not consider the difference in pay or other army opportunities, but as an officer, even a junior one, I knew I would be directly leading troops. I applied to attend Officer Candidate School (OCS) and received my acceptance in the summer of 2001 with a start date of early 2002. As we know, during that wait time 9/11 occurred, and overnight I was about to join a wartime army as a newly minted officer.

I had been training for war for eight years, but all I really knew of war was what I brought into the military. Most people hold a vivid idea of war in their minds. These ideas are gained from popular culture, movies, books, and watching the news during wartime. As a seventeen-year-old boy just out of high school in suburban Indiana, I had my own images of war. My first impressions were while visiting my grandma at the Veterans of Foreign Wars (VFW) and American Legion in our hometown. She was a staple at these places because all three of her ex-husbands had served in World War II. I was always fascinated by how all the old guys seemed to know each other on a different level than just sharing where they lived. At any of the holiday parties we attended, there would be small groups of grizzly men wearing hats and shirts linking them to military units, battles, and shared experiences that bonded them for the rest of their lives. They had lived through D-Day, Operation Market Garden, the Battle of the Bulge, Iwo Jima, Midway, Anzio,

Okinawa, northern Africa, the invasion of Italy, Luzon, and many other fights that shaped American beliefs toward war and soldiering that survive even today; these men were part of the proverbial Greatest Generation.

I also watched shows like *G.I. Joe* and *The A-Team*, where groups of cartoon characters or actor soldiers risked their lives for other members of their group. Later I watched old war movies like *To Hell and Back*, which starred the most decorated soldier in American history, Audie Murphy, playing himself. In World War II, Murphy received every military combat award available for valor from the U.S. Army, as well as French and Belgian awards for heroism. He received the Medal of Honor for actions he took when as a nineteen-year-old second lieutenant company commander his company was attacked by Germans. He ordered his men to move back into the woods while he single-handedly held off the attack for an hour, first with his rifle, then with a machine gun atop a burning armored vehicle, killing or wounding fifty of the enemy. Wounded in both legs, he then led a successful counterattack.[2] After the battle, he insisted on remaining with his men while his injuries were treated. When asked why he fought and overcame an entire company of German soldiers, he replied, "because they were killing my friends."[3] These stories and images speak to the romance of cohesion among combat soldiers, where they are so bonded that they will die for each other if needed. One of the many things I've learned from combat is that this type of bond does not just happen. It has to be fostered by circumstances and leadership.

My war experience includes three separate combat deployments to Iraq: two of my own and one where I was the stay-at-home father of three kids while my wife was deployed. As I couple my experiences with much of what has been researched or has been proven over time on the theories of how soldiers build cohesion, I ask myself three key questions: What did I believe about cohesion before combat? What did I learn about cohesion after experiencing combat? Why does knowing about cohesion matter? These questions also have to be asked in the context of the evolving realities of today's combat environment for American soldiers where I found unintended consequences of modernity were degrading the ability to build cohesive and effective combat teams.

My experiences explore how groups form bonds and work to maximize effectiveness, how technology can alter cohesion and team building, and how warfare is being reshaped by modern distractions and practices, from looking at Facebook to creating boutique individual living spaces.

Many things change in war: the locations of battles, the missions, tactics, equipment, and weapons, just to name a few, but throughout the history of warfare, much has remained the same. Combat remains a human endeavor fought at close range by small groups of men and women. The first-order question of combat remains how and why soldiers fight. *How* being a question of overriding human biology and rational thought to set aside fear and face danger, and *why* being the individual soldier's motivation to do so.

Combat motivation and cohesion have been studied in many wars and in many different armies. In emphasizing the impact of morale and the will to fight, on warfare Napoleon said, "Morale is to the physical as three is to one."[4] Research has established strong linkages between cohesion and performance. But a group of combat soldiers comprises a complex system of interwoven factors that determine the quality of their performance. Surprisingly there have been few holistic assessments or analyses to identify the factors that determine quality of performance and the relationships of each factor to others. We know that leadership, discipline, training, cohesion, morale, soldiers' personal interests, and other factors all combine to determine the quality of a unit's performance and allow these groups of men and women to perform amazing feats in the most stressful and dangerous human activity imaginable: war. At a glance, war is an individual endeavor, but more accurately it is a group activity.

A military formation, fighting in combat is a complex set of systems that add up to a unit's combat effectiveness or ability to function as a team under the stress of combat. One of the best explanations of this complex system is found in John A. Lynn's analysis of the

French military of the late 1700s. Lynn's system is as applicable to a modern military formation as it is to a Napoleonic formation. Lynn's model included three interconnecting systems: interests, motivational system, and the military system.

John Lynn's Model of Combat Effectiveness

INTERESTS[5]

—Compliance (coercive, remunerative, normative)
—Self-interests (well-being, survival)

MOTIVATIONAL SYSTEM[6]

—Moral (basic class and societal attitudes, indoctrination, wartime opinions/appreciation, reactions to conditions of service, esprit de corps)
—Primary group cohesion (group dynamics, conduit of shared values and attitudes)
—Motivation (initial motivation, sustaining motivation, combat motivation)

Military system[7]

—Disciplinary system (coercion, standards, justification)
—Tactical system (weapons, doctrine, training, experience, tactics)
—Administrative system (logistics, services, maintenance, manpower policy)
—Organizational system
—Command system (officer/NCO selection and promotion, command structure, communication, and political officers).

Each part of these systems is important.[8] It is hard to say which system is the most important, but the motivation system is certainly at the top as the one most related to teams that work together effectively. Within that motivation system, primary group cohesion has historically been the focus of military fact and societal folklore.

One of the leading management hypotheses is the open-system theory, and it is applicable to the army. This theory states that any

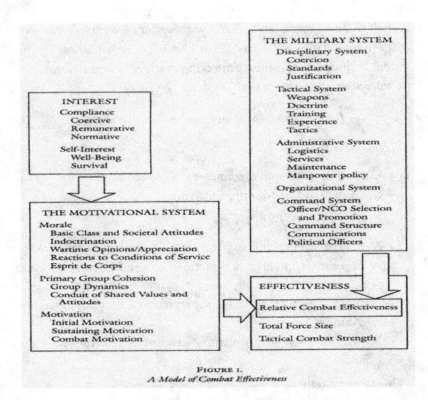

INTEREST

Compliance
  Coercive
  Remunerative
  Normative

Self-Interest
  Well-Being
  Survival

THE MILITARY SYSTEM

Disciplinary System
  Coercion
  Standards
  Justification

Tactical System
  Weapons
  Doctrine
  Training
  Experience
  Tactics

Administrative System
  Logistics
  Services
  Maintenance
  Manpower policy

Organizational System

Command System
  Officer/NCO Selection
    and Promotion
  Command Structure
  Communications
  Political Officers

THE MOTIVATIONAL SYSTEM

Morale
  Basic Class and Societal Attitudes
  Indoctrination
  Wartime Opinions/Appreciation
  Reactions to Conditions of Service
  Esprit de Corps

Primary Group Cohesion
  Group Dynamics
  Conduit of Shared Values and
    Attitudes

Motivation
  Initial Motivation
  Sustaining Motivation
  Combat Motivation

EFFECTIVENESS

Relative Combat Effectiveness

Total Force Size
Tactical Combat Strength

FIGURE 1.
A Model of Combat Effectiveness

1. John Lynn's Model of Combat Effectiveness. From John A. Lynn,
*The Bayonets of the Republic: Motivation and Tactics in the
Army of Revolutionary France, 1791–1794.*

changes to one of the internal or external elements of an organization's system, such as those listed above, will cause changes to the other systems in the organization.[9] As it relates to the theme of this book, external changes in technology that give the soldiers greater connectivity to the world outside of the war will impact the internal systems, like primary group cohesion, which in turn affects relative combat effectiveness.

There are few historical studies that truly and holistically analyze how combat effectiveness works in small groups (i.e., how interconnected systems, practices, and traditions combine to create high-performing combat teams). One of the most overwhelming trends of combat effectiveness, though, is the importance of cohesion among small groups of soldiers. The strong bonds between soldiers allow them to fight and serve as the reason they fight. This finding—that soldiers fight for each other as their chief motivation—has been studied and validated all the way up to the recent operations in Iraq and Afghanistan. It is something so well-known that it is taken for granted by many and unknown to others. Numerous studies, especially after World War II, have presented the same conclusions about why soldiers fight.[10]

In *The American Soldier, Combat and Its Aftermath*, Samuel Stouffer and a committee of social scientists conducted a study of World War II combat infantrymen. During the researchers' questioning of soldiers on why they kept going during the war, they found that the soldiers' primary motivation for fighting were their strong group ties, that they "could not let the other men down."[11] In his book *Men Against Fire* army combat historian S. L. A. Marshall, also studying the motivations of World War II infantry soldiers, found that the reason soldiers could face the horrors of combat was because of "the presence or presumed presence of a comrade."[12] Their reasoning as to why they fight was because "they do not want to let their comrades down."[13] The reasoning behind combat motivation was also studied in German soldiers after World War II. Professors Edward Shils and Morris Janowitz interviewed German ground forces on why they continued to fight even up until Germany's defeat. They found that the soldiers' primary motivation was centered on interpersonal relationships within their primary group.[14] In military cohesion research, a primary group is usually a squad-to-platoon-size unit typified by cooperative, face-to-face relationships that develop over time.[15] During the Korean War, sociologist Roger Little found that the personal bonds between soldiers were the critical component of their survival in combat.[16] In the Vietnam War, sociologist Charles Moskos also interviewed soldiers, and in linking the soldiers' relationships to combat performance found that primary group cohesion served as a vital part in the unit's effectiveness.[17] In one of the most recent studies, Dr. Leonard Wong and a group of researchers from the U.S. Army War College conducted surveys of both American soldiers and Iraqi army prisoners at the beginning of the war in Iraq in 2003. They found that despite the changes in the world, as well as different generations and cultures, unit cohesion was still a primary combat motivation.[18] Across history the unchanging truth is that soldiers fight and die for each other more than any other reason.

Cohesion has been popularized by books as far back as the time of Socrates and Plato and glorified in contemporary movies such as the HBO mini-series *Band of Brothers*. It is intertwined with other factors of a unit's performance, such as motivation, leadership, and discipline in many ways but remains a vital key to the overall system. A poorly led cohesive unit would have fewer issues than a well-led unit with little cohesion.

The irony of cohesion is that there is no playbook. There is no army field manual that details how to build such a cohesive team that the soldiers are willing to die for each other. There are of course many things an army does to build cohesion. Conducting tough, realistic training and daily activities to create shared hardships and group identity are well-established practices. Team-building exercises are highly valued in the military, but some practices handed down over time have cohesive purposes that are not always understood, such as requiring military groups to eat together or sleep in large open bays during initial entry training. These are bond-forming experiences. As American society changes, so does the military. The challenge is identifying which transformations in society affect team building and the task of creating cohesion thereafter in the military.

Cohesion is commonly cited in two forms: task cohesion and social cohesion. Task cohesion is the members' shared commitment to the group's tasks, characterized by scholars as a "general orientation toward achieving the group's goals and objectives."[19] When task cohesion is present in a group, there is a prevailing belief that they will be able to successfully accomplish the collective and individual goals of the group and group members.[20]

Social cohesion is the almost mythical attribute people talk about in the "band of brothers" stories.[21] It refers to social bonds between group members that are bound by the group's working relationship. It is believed that the social bonds that exist between group members will manifest through emotional responses to other members of the group, such as feelings of liking and trust. When social cohesion is high in a group, members value the relationships and friendships that the group provides. This is where the answers to why soldiers fight have come from in the past. Soldiers are bonded to each other in very special ways, such as through hard training, living together, and especially through enduring stressful experiences filled with fear, adrenaline, and rawness. These bonds create moments in time and feelings that the soldiers share for the rest of their lives.

Over a twenty-five-year career, my experiences in the U.S. Army have led me to certain conclusions about leadership, team building, unit cohesion, and combat performance. From my early leadership experiences as a brand new lieutenant in Iraq to being a stay-at-home spouse to a deployed soldier, technology has changed the military and the combat environment and, with it, some of my ideas and conclusions about how soldiers face and live with war.

Though imperfect samples, my three Iraq experiences provide what social scientists call a natural experiment.[22] My two combat tours provide a different look at the everyday realities of combat, one of an invading force and the other fighting a protracted war. My time as a spouse to a deployed soldier provides a look at a side of war not as often connected to the daily fighting. These three experiences provide stark contrasts to how soldiers communicated with their different support groups both in and out of the war zone. What was interesting is that as soldiers continued to fight in Iraq and Afghanistan, the interconnectedness of society was evolving, but nobody paused to ask: What is the impact of the latter on the former? Are twenty-first-century communications altering the idea of a "band of brothers?" How will all this affect the future of war and our likelihood of victory going forward? And how will it affect soldiers in the long run?

2

Welcome to the Platoon (Primary Group Cohesion)

At the tail end of 2002, after completing OCS and the Infantry Basic Officer Leader Course, I arrived at my first duty station (an American base in northeast Italy) as a second lieutenant. Despite all that training and my eight years as an NCO, it would turn out that I still had much to learn. Case in point: the infamous gas mask run.

As a brand new platoon leader, I had the ingenious idea to run my platoon of forty soldiers around the small base wearing the gas masks given to us for use in the event of a chemical attack. The run was meant to quickly have the soldiers "suck together"—lingo meaning to suffer together. As a seasoned soldier, I knew that when soldiers survive difficult training as a group, they can achieve cohesive and lasting bonds. Shared hardships, whether created or endured through the nature of the mission, create those bonds. I had learned this early on in my career.

Regrettably my first attempt at applying this principle as a platoon leader failed to achieve that result. Here's why: running while wearing a gas mask is basically like wrapping your head in a very thick plastic bag, tying it tightly, and then poking one small hole in it as the breathing mechanism. Picture wearing a rubber Halloween mask sealed around the neck by a drawstring but looking more like a HAZMAT worker than a bank robber. Even without physical exertion, anyone will begin to sweat immediately. The small eyeholes that are covered by translucent plastic tend to fog up quickly. Now imagine trying to run while wearing the mask. Mucus starts flowing and, with nowhere to go, starts to fill your mask. God forbid you vomit, which some of the soldiers did, a few without first removing the gas mask. On top of all this, the unit was running in formation: in four aligned columns with me leading out front. Under normal circumstances, everyone would maintain the same speed and stay in step. However, these were not normal circumstances, which made the disintegration of the run even more apparent.

These unit runs are the tropes of military movies. They are symbolic of discipline, regimentation, and esprit de corps. The unit moves like a single organism and the body calls out cadence in one voice as the footfalls beat in steady rhythm. Unfortunately, when such a run goes disastrously wrong, it instead starts to resemble a crowd of protestors running from tear gas, which ironically might be why a person would want to wear a gas mask; it is symbolic of a breakdown in discipline and esprit. The formation became chaotic as individuals dropped out, gasping or vomiting and trying to catch their breath. Rather than hearing a proud cadence being sung, I heard coughing, complaining, frustration, and even anger.

My own feelings were of disappointment, not in my soldiers, but in myself. How could I have not expected this when the outcome was so obvious in hindsight? I was also momentarily gripped by indecision for how to handle this growing melee. I did not know whether to continue on or stop the run—admit my mistake and have everyone remove the now-hated gas masks or keep going. Neither seemed optimal. There was no right answer, no "school solution." My recent training had not addressed what to do when you've made a glaring mistake. I decided to continue the run and not show any visible signs of my internal struggle and anguish. I had made a decision and felt I had to stick with it and accept the consequences.

If I had fostered any unit cohesion, it was by unifying the platoon in their distrust of my judgment. I was not off to a great start, but I was determined to repair the damage I had done. Chalk it up as the first of many lessons learned.

This initial assignment as an officer was at Camp Ederle in Vicenza, Italy, about forty miles inland from Venice. I had been stationed here years before as an enlisted soldier. It was a comparatively small location, home to about nine thousand Americans—military and civilian. Despite its size, about two thousand yards from north to south, the base had all the normal support facilities: post exchange (department store), commissary (grocery store), health clinic, post office, bank, food court, gym, sports fields, movie theater, clubs, and recreational activities. In fact, the exchange is the largest American mall south of the Alps.

The city of Vicenza is a thriving, cultural metropolis of about a quarter million people, with many restaurants, clubs, museums, galleries, town squares, and palaces. The city of Vicenza and the Palladian Villas of the Veneto are a UNESCO World Heritage Site. Straddling the Bacchiglione River with a view of the nearby Alps, the weather is comfortable throughout the entire year. The surrounding area is mostly agricultural: farms and vineyards. It is unquestionably a beautiful setting and one of the most sought after assignments in the U.S. Army. Aside from the looming threat of war, life was grand.

I joined 2nd Platoon, Alpha Company, 1st Battalion of the 508th Infantry Regiment, 173rd Airborne Brigade only three months before we were to jump into combat in Iraq for the United States' invasion in March of 2003. As a platoon leader, I was responsible for forty infantrymen, ranging from the platoon sergeant, an NCO with over fourteen years of military experience, to privates only a month out of completing their basic training, advanced individual training, and airborne school.

The 508th Parachute Infantry Regiment has a rich history dating back to World War II. It played important roles in Operation Overlord (D-Day), Operation Market Garden, and the Battle of the Bulge. Nicknamed the "Red Devils," they also fought in Vietnam, Operation Urgent Fury (Grenada), and Operation Just Cause (Panama). At this time the First Battalion of the 508th was part of the 173rd Airborne Brigade, along with the Second Battalion of the 503rd Infantry and Battery D, 319th Airborne Field Artillery Regiment. The unit provides the Southern European Task Force (SETAF) with a rapidly deployable combat or peacekeeping element and are the U.S. European Command's (EUCOM) conventional airborne strategic response force. The soldiers in my platoon and I were proud to carry on the storied legacy of the Red Devils. This was my third time being assigned to this regiment, including once in Panama, and I consider myself to be a loyal Red Devil.

Besides my initial attempt at the special exercise session, I also had to cover standard details, such as inspecting and signing for all the equipment in my platoon. One quick, reliable indicator of a unit's discipline and readiness for war is how it takes care of its equipment. Soon after I arrived at the unit, I scheduled an equipment inspection. Each soldier laid out his individual gear—rucksack (backpack), helmet, tactical vest, body armor, first aid kit, sleeping bag, protective mask (the aforementioned gas mask), rain gear, canteens, entrenching tool (shovel), flashlight, and other sundry yet important items—as well as basic squad-issue items, such as radios, shovels, tents, and pickaxes. I went from soldier to soldier, checking for cleanliness and serviceability. Once the platoon passed inspection, the soldiers would be released for the day, so they were eager to complete the task. This led to them rushing the work and not ensuring that their equipment was in proper condition.

Unfortunately they utterly failed my inspection. There was dirt or rust on much of the gear, pieces were missing from some items, and protective masks were not packed correctly. So I informed them they had to clean everything again and that we would all be staying until it was done right. I watched as they argued with each other over who should have cleaned better, who should go to the supply sergeant for replacement parts, and who was responsible for the squad equipment, with no one accepting any blame.

After about twenty minutes with little being accomplished, I had them gather around and pointed out that their ability to work together is what translates into successful combat performance. If they could not team up on something as simple as an equipment inspection, they would not function effectively as a unit when under combat conditions. If we all wanted to come home safely from Iraq, we would have to first be able to go home at a decent hour after an equipment inspection. I reminded them of how they had all learned to combine forces in their field exercises and airborne training, which was much more grueling than this situation—an observation they nodded to in agreement. With this, the squad leaders and team leaders took a more active role in establishing a division of labor, and the soldiers took more initiative in helping each other out. The platoon passed the next inspection and seemed to have come together more as a unit, at least a little. Baby steps.

The first thing any new leader in an organization does is observe and assess. Based on my time as a soldier, sergeant, and officer, I had tacit knowledge of the indicators of a good platoon. Before I could explain what those indicators were, it was something I simply felt. It was really pattern recognition from almost ten years of experience. With experience you can quickly assess leadership, training levels, discipline, morale, and cohesion among soldiers. Evaluating these factors within your platoon is the first step to establishing a predictor of combat readiness.

Appraising cohesion is not easy. Its signs are not overt, but it is the most important attribute for a group of soldiers headed into battle. As previously mentioned, cohesion has been validated in multiple historical studies as the single justification for a soldier's motivation to fight.[1] Social scientists and historians have long pointed to the crucial role of what they called the primary group cohesion theory when explaining combat effectiveness.[2] The primary group is the small number of soldiers who constantly deal with one another on a face-to-face basis. The size is determined by the number of soldiers who will live and fight together as a team and by the number of men the individual soldier can know and depend on in a combat environment. To the extent that the soldiers composing a primary group materially and psychologically aid one another, particularly in achieving a common goal, that group can be called unified. From this cohesiveness comes the effective support and compulsion that keeps soldiers at their assigned task.[3] When trying to evaluate cohesion in a unit, you have to look all the way down into the primary groups, possibly as low as a team of four soldiers in terms of how they communicate with each other, as well as their body language and teamwork. But even observing those things will give you only a hint. Cohesion mostly manifests on the battlefield. In my case I would have to wait to see how cohesive my soldiers were.

When I arrived at the unit, the soldiers were done with all of their major training events. We were currently staying in the local area, not leaving the city of Vicenza, in anticipation of the war everyone knew was likely. I would be taking a platoon of soldiers into combat who were trained by someone else, had bonded in training, and knew each other well. That is actually typical for officers, and it did not affect the unit's readiness. Unlike more classical team-building development models, such as Bruce Tuckman's forming, storming, norming, and performing model, military units are not made up of strangers but instead are a group of people with vastly different levels of familiarity.[4] Some have been working together for years while one or two new soldiers will be added to the team on an ongoing basis. This manpower model creates its own complexity but usually works well when a new person joins a functioning team and steps into a known position, role, and set of institutional group norms. It is the army way.

My initial assessment of 2nd Platoon told me that the previous and current leaders had done a good job in developing, practicing, and maintaining all the systems that make up a military unit, especially the easily observable components of an effective team, such as discipline, standards, clear lines of authority, and tactics. There is always room for improvement, but I thought the unit was healthy, resilient, and ready. It was like watching a professional football team at practice. Everything looked and felt right. I just needed to focus on my job and role as the leader of the overall team.

By the time I arrived at the unit, I learned that most of the major training was complete for the year and had been conducted at training sites in Germany, where all the large training bases in Europe are located. When U.S. soldiers in Italy want to conduct anything above squad-level training, they usually have to fly or take a bus to those posts in Germany. Vicenza to Hohenfels, Germany, for example, is about four hundred miles, or an eight-hour bus drive each way. Thus, a platoon leader would not plan such a trip for just his forty troops. Exercises at those training areas are typically planned at the brigade level. Because the U.S. Army is either training for war or at war, training needed to continue even within the small base of Caserma Ederle. The high school football field on the base is probably one of the most used fields in all of Italy because the army units use it daily to train on tactics, such as reacting to ambushes or practicing squad-movement techniques.

After the debacle of the gas mask run, I was able to redeem myself with two local training events that proved to be very positive and helped reinforce the platoon's acceptance of me and the unit cohesion overall: the shoot house and a communication exercise.

One resource that was available on post was what we called the shoot house. It was a special building used to train for urban combat. The building was insulated with ballistic walls so units could even fire live rounds inside. Movable human-size silhouettes could be relocated as enemy targets or innocent civilian "do-not-shoot" targets. The building also contained furniture for further realism and complication. I liked to attach balloons to the enemy and do-not-shoot targets to enhance the experience. The popping balloons were not exactly realistic, but they were fun. I reserved the shoot house for my platoon so we could conduct squad enter-and-clear-a-room training.

The latter exercise goes all the way back to the attempted rescue of the Israeli Olympians during the Munich Olympics in 1972. After that failed raid, western governments developed specialized counter-terrorist units, such as the U.S. Army's Special Operations Forces, the British Special Air Service (SAS), the German *Grenzschutzgruppe* 9 (GSG 9, which is part of the federal police, rather than the military, for constitutional reasons), and others. These units developed and perfected tactics to conduct raids in high-risk close quarters (inside buildings, airplanes, or ships) to perform rescue missions or to kill terrorists.[5] The tactics provide soldiers the ability to enter a building full of the enemy and take them by surprise with such violence that the soldiers are likely to survive but the enemy is not, all while not killing hostages or other non-combatants inside small spaces.

The close quarters battle drills perfected by those special units were passed on to the rest of the army and are used frequently by infantry units, as are the enter-and-clear-a-room battle drill and others.

This was my time to shine. I was highly trained in the enter-and-clear-a room battle drill as I had executed the drill hundreds of times as an enlisted soldier and trained many other soldiers in the tactic when I was an NCO. Now as a platoon leader, I would be responsible for judging, providing feedback, and retraining the squad leaders, if needed. If I showed my competence, I would earn some much-needed respect early in my leadership assignment. I looked forward to that.

The enter-and-clear-a-room battle drill basically involves four soldiers standing very close together (stacked) against the wall outside the entrance to a room with their weapons ready to fire. If required, one of the soldiers breaches the door with an explosive charge, shotgun blast, or foot kick. The first soldier enters the room and moves to the left or right, depending on which way the door opens. The second soldier moves in the opposite direction of the first soldier. The third moves in the opposite direction of the second soldier and the fourth moves in the opposite direction of the third until each soldier is in the room. Soldiers are at most risk when passing through the doorway (or any other breach point), so they must move quickly and off to the side. During the entire movement, the soldiers have their weapons ready to engage the enemy, and each focuses his attention on his assigned area within the room.

For a well-trained team of four soldiers, these events—entering the room, shooting the bad guys and not the good guys—take seconds. Once the team clears the room, they move to the next room in the building or allow a second team to pass through the safe room and leapfrog, repeating the drill through however many rooms are in the house or building.

Not only is the enter-and-clear-a room battle drill a highly specialized military tactic but it is also a micro example of combat. It shows what it takes to be an effective team in battle and includes many of the mental requirements soldiers need to overcome fear in combat. For an individual soldier, it could be overwhelmingly scary to enter a closed room. But as a team, it is a rehearsed drill, a drill they learn to trust to keep them safe and that will lead to their success. Despite what is often seen on television, the soldiers move almost instantaneously to the sides to get out of the central "fatal funnel," which is straight in from the doorway. Any enemy force inside, if not caught by surprise, can just point a weapon toward the door and fire, no aiming required. For the soldiers it is like entering the mouth of a dragon, not knowing when the burst of fire is about to come. It is a very intimate small-group experience. Each of the four soldiers must rely on the other soldiers, working meticulously in unison and keying off each other. When lining up they are so close they are touching. They must trust that each soldier will do his part—it is the only way the drill works. All soldiers know that no one ever goes into a room alone. They can only survive by working together; they need each other as much in that moment as at any other time in battle.

Soldiers really enjoy this training. It is fun, fast-paced, and creates an adrenaline rush. When done correctly the exercise demonstrates mastery of tactical skills for both individuals and the team. Soldiers come out of it sweating, breathing hard, and smelling like recently fired rounds. (People often incorrectly refer to the smell as cordite, but cordite has not been used as a propellant since World War II. Modern ammunition contains nitroglycerin.) Because this is one of the few times we use live rounds in training, other than when we are on a firing range, there is a rare sense of real-life danger. It truly feels like being a soldier.

We spent a full day going through the shoot house over and over. I followed behind the squads on each iteration and gave them feedback afterward. I periodically relocated the silhouettes and rearranged the furniture. Sometimes one squad would clear the entire building, whereas at other times they would go through it in pairs of squads. It had been a few months since the platoon had done this type of training, so they were a little rusty. Several of the soldiers had joined the platoon since the last shoot house training, as I had, so they had not trained in this tactic for an even longer period and definitely had not trained in it with their squad. There were plenty of opportunities for me to give corrections. Just as I had anticipated, all went well and the soldiers really soaked up the instruction I gave them. They could tell by the things I said, how I demonstrated the tactics, and through my confidence that I was highly competent, at least on this subject. I came across as highly proficient and a true authority. They asked me questions, trusting my answers. Just as they felt like real soldiers from this training, I felt like a real platoon leader. The gas mask run was forgotten. We had experienced another shared hardship, in a sense. This instance was more mental than the gas mask run; it created the pressure to succeed at the training. But even more than the gas mask run, it bonded us as a unit.

The second training that reinforced my standing within the platoon did not actually involve most of the platoon: It was a radio communication exercise. It might surprise people that much of warfare is about talking, passing messages back and forth. Army doctrine defines basic infantry capabilities as *shoot, move,* and *communicate.* The ability to quickly exchange information is vital to surviving and winning battles. Conciseness is an essential element of effective battlefield communication. The ability to pass orders and information in a short amount of time can make the difference between life and death, hence, the military's fascination with acronyms. One nitpick that military people have when watching movies and TV shows about war is improper radio-telephone procedures and incorrect use of "prowords" or procedure words. No one in the military would ever say, "okay, got it" over the radio. There is both science and art to military communication. The science is the language and procedures, such as how to talk properly on a military radio. The art is understanding a leader or soldier's intended message. At times military leaders need to be able to give a verbal order and have it be carried out without soldiers thinking or hesitating— the "attack that hill" moment. Other times they need to differentiate a distressed voice from a merely anxious voice. It is very important that small military teams know each other well enough to understand the many nuisances of a person's voice, especially when the words are spoken remotely, such as through a radio, where all the nonverbal aspects of speech are lost. That is why communication exercises (COMMEXS) are so important and why the use of the radio and the practice of passing messages is incorporated into unit training as often as practical.

The COMMEX we were doing was part of our preparation for war, even though it took place weeks before we ever got the notice that our deployment to Iraq was imminent. I went with the other platoon leaders in our battalion and our radiotelephone operators (RTOS) into a building that was divided into small rooms, each containing a computer screen and a radio. We were given a long operations order (mission briefing) about jumping into a drop zone (DZ) in an unnamed country. We received our platoons' subordinate missions. Mine was for the platoon to assemble at the edge of the DZ and move to a designated location and establish a vehicle-blocking position. After receiving these orders, we went back to our small rooms and started the simulated operations, beginning with the platoon dropping from the aircrafts and assembling. I had to call in all the radio calls that I would be making on the mission. "I have 80 percent of my platoon assembled, have met minimum movement requirements, leaving White 7 in the assembly area to collect stragglers, moving to blocking position at this time." We were practicing the art of communication. I would learn in the actual event and throughout the deployment how important the art of communication becomes. Recognizing the sound of an angry leader conveys a very different message than that of a frightened leader. A calm voice means one thing, a stressed voice means another thing, and a voice losing composure means a third thing. By becoming familiar with the voices in the company in different situations during peacetime, we would understand each other better in wartime. This training exercise spanned several hours and contained a variety of scenarios simulating the many combat situations we might encounter. I was surprised at how real it felt and how it genuinely evoked emotions that I might feel and express in an actual combat environment. This training also went well. It increased my confidence as a leader while also teaching me new lessons. Because RTOs from throughout the battalion were with us, the enlisted men in the battalion quickly heard who had done well and who had lost composure and endangered his peers. As far as I could tell, I was among the former.

To say there is strong task cohesion for an airborne infantry platoon ordered to jump into enemy territory in the middle of the night is an understatement. With memories of 9/11 fresh in all our minds, and after years of preparing, we were ready for war, at least as ready as we could be without having ever experienced actual combat. You could say a peacetime army training for war is like a professional football team training year-round but never getting a chance to play a game. Of course all of us were scared of the unknown, but we were anxious to finally get to play a game. This shared confidence in our abilities and desire to fight was vital to our eventual performance.

One area in which I had a severe lack of confidence involved our vehicles. I had no practical knowledge of them before laying eyes on my fleet of eight military-grade trucks. Every position in the army is basically on-the-job training. Unlike most civilian careers, where job postings state a required number of years of experience doing a specific type of work, the army routinely inserts its employees into jobs for which they have no related experience or knowledge. They are expected to learn the jobs immediately—to hit the ground running. This is especially true for officers. When I arrived as a brand new platoon leader, I had major apprehensions about my duties regarding my platoon's vehicles. Sure I had been through the required infantry platoon leader training and had the benefit of a considerable amount of enlisted time, but I never had experience in a motorized platoon within an airborne unit. I had been light infantry my whole career, meaning on foot without automotive transportation or using vehicles for fire support.

But really, this was something the 173rd was making up as they went along. About a year before my arrival the unit developed the concept of motorized infantry, securing the vehicles and heavy weapons and experimenting during training. The normally slow-moving airborne infantry soldiers may fall out of the sky quickly, but once on the ground they moved like all the grunts from generations past. The vehicles allowed the airborne infantry to move swiftly around the battlefield and carry the heavy weapons they never had before, significantly upping the firepower they could bring to a fight.

While everyone in the army is engaged in some degree of on-the-job training, it is also an organization where one can learn from others. Leaders above, such as the company commander or senior lieutenant who is the executive officer ideally have been in your position. What saved me was the ready assistance 1LT David Bernstein provided me. David was also a motorized platoon leader but in another company. He had been in the unit for about eight months longer than I had, which to lieutenants is a lifetime. I was in the motor pool one day trying to find some equipment we needed to put more weapon mounts in the bed of our vehicles, and there was David. I was not sure if he could tell how nervous I was about all I did not know, but he was immediately warm and helpful, and generously shared all that he had learned so far: how his platoon had mounted their weapons, how they fought with the vehicles, how they organized their squads. I asked him every question I could think of. David really set me at ease, mainly with his amazing attitude of possibilities, tireless encouragement, and promises to share whatever he learned. He assured me that no one else in the brigade knew anything in this area either, that it was all constantly emerging and evolving. He also gave me all kinds of tips about what he had decided to do with his platoon leader vehicle. He was my lifesaver, my guardian angel. I would not see David again after the jump into Iraq, but during the tour I felt better knowing he was out there doing the same things I was.

In March of 2003 it was no secret to anyone that the United States was about to go to war with Iraq. It was all over the news. In Italy we heard and watched reports of units moving into position in places like Kuwait. We only waited for the word to go. In truth we did not know if our small airborne brigade of only two battalions would

Welcome to the Platoon

even be sent. The war in Afghanistan had been going on for over a year, and we had not been a part of that conflict, although the unit would deploy there a few years later. Rumors were rampant on our little post. We were put on short notice; that is, we were on call with the requirement to be able to be back at our headquarters and ready to launch within two hours of telephonic notification. We were told that once we got the call, we were to immediately come in. We were also told that once we came in, we probably would not see our families again until we returned from the combat zone. Looking back I honestly do not remember if we were on short notice for a couple weeks or a couple months. It just felt like a constant state of existence, of being on alert, with no beginning or end. Well, finally, there was an end—we got the call and were ordered to the headquarters.

During the waiting period, the brigade command allowed us more time with our families than usual, so I was at home when the call finally came in the middle of the day. "Sir, it's time" was the extent of the call, or at least all that I needed to hear. I told my wife Sara that the time had come and I had to go. Despite knowing this would happen and anticipating it for months, it still came as a surprise. Maybe we had secretly not believed we would really have to face this moment.

Unlike every subsequent deployment, we were given almost no notice this first time. We had loaded all of our vehicles and things to go to war, but that was weeks earlier. We did not know the day, week, month, or even if we would be one of the units to actually be sent. Then suddenly the moment we had been waiting for had arrived.

Sara and I had no children and had been married less than two years. I had been a soldier for almost ten years and, therefore, identified more as a soldier than a husband. That may seem odd, maybe even cold or heartless, but I had trained my whole adult life for this moment, to jump into combat and fight an enemy. Like many soldiers, I had hoped to be sent to war and would have been disappointed if I was not part of the fight, even though I would never dream of sharing that with my wife. She would understand it intellectually but probably would not accept it emotionally. Neither one of us wanted to have that conversation. I carried a picture of her in my helmet because I thought I loved her and would miss her. It was important to me as an infantry officer to be wearing that helmet in the war. So with these mixed feelings, my good-bye was stoic. Sara was also stoic, maybe mirroring my demeanor. The short notice made the good-bye very quick. I knew I had to get to headquarters as soon as possible.

Carrying photos of our loved ones as we go off to war suggests how we are influenced by movies and TV shows we watched as kids and even as adults. Our entertainment influences how we think about war and can even alter our experiences in war. We often act and react in a manner defined by what we have seen on-screen or in books; in war, as in sports, television shapes our relationships, school, work, parenting, and many other aspects of life. It may not be the smartest way to train our behavior, but it is an unconscious response to what we watch. I am sure we put photos in our helmets in part because we saw it in movies. It is what soldiers at war do, right? (This was still true in 2003, but by 2008 I saw no photos in helmets or few in living quarters. No one printed photos anymore by then.) The helmet is the universal symbol of being a soldier, from ancient Greece to today. In 2016 when I helped found the Modern War Institute at West Point, we almost made the helmet the symbol of the institute but eventually picked a logo representing the letters of the organization. It was close though and that is just another indication of the helmet's symbolic significance. So carrying a photo in my helmet gave the gesture deeper significance, connecting me to countless soldiers who had preceded me. In that way it was as much in line with my identity as a soldier as it was with my definition of a husband.

For the invasion in 2003 we also did not know how long we would be deployed. Would it be like Desert Storm, which was really the last major war we had as a reference, being that it was also fought against the Iraqi army? Desert Storm fighting lasted forty-three days, including the aerial campaign. I knew I would miss my wife, but in that moment she knew who I was. I knew what I had to do.

Maybe in my mind I wanted her to say, "Come back with your shield or on it," (a quote said to the Spartan king by his wife in the movie *300*, meaning the king should fight honorably with his shield and sword in hand or die in battle heroically and be carried home on his shield) but it was nothing like that. It was good-bye. She may not have been an ancient Spartan wife, but she held it together and so did I. Looking back, it was more transactional than anything else. I left her in the kitchen with one last hug and kiss. I got into my vehicle, watched the house in the rearview mirror, and drove to our headquarters to transition from husband to platoon leader of a combat formation being called into battle.

Because we lived off post in an Italian neighborhood, I was the lone soldier heading off to war. Almost all the officers and senior enlisted troops lived off post, scattered throughout the area. Therefore, many of us shared this moment of a separate, individual departure. On larger installations with plenty of on-post housing, the experience was likely very different. Families left behind could look up and down the street to see others in the same situation and immediately talk to other families experiencing the same moment.

For other soldiers in my platoon, their own good-byes may have differed from mine in small or large ways. Regardless, everyone who was accompanied by their family on this assignment or who had found a loved one in Italy made some variation of a good-bye that day. Some were as dry-eyed and efficient as mine. Others were tearful and protracted. Some left home more willingly, others were deeply reluctant. Neither was necessarily a measure of their love for their families, nor of their eagerness for battle. We are all just different people who handle major life events in our own way, sometimes without thought as to how it should be done. Once at war, we might share those moments with each other and, thereby, find mutual reassurance that we handled it fine after all, or maybe we did not. In any case the sharing would strengthen the friendships that would help us return to our families. The same would be true of our wives or girlfriends in Vicenza who were likewise bonding and helping each other survive the war.

While very different from the gas mask run, the equipment inspection, or the shoot house, our personal good-byes at home away from the unit were just as much collective hardships that contributed to the bonds within the unit and, therefore, improved our combat performance. These farewells marked the moment we were removed from our personal family to join fellow soldiers—a different family—to go to war.

3

Jump Right into It (Shared Combat Experiences)

After saying good-bye to our families on March 23, 2003, my unit was secluded on base in a large hanger. The next few days typified one of the most oft-repeated expressions in military life: "hurry up and wait." Following a two-hour deadline to report to headquarters, we were herded like cattle into the hanger, ready to immediately deploy to war, even if "immediately" meant days later. We would wait in that state of readiness and immediacy for as long as required by the army. Eventually we would either be given the green light to board our aircraft and go into battle, or we would be told that our deployment was postponed indefinitely and we should return home. Uncertainty is a soldier's constant companion.

Another aspect of the unpredictability of war was not knowing by whom or where these decisions were being made. At the platoon and company level we did not know if the brigade staff was examining options for our deployment, if CENTCOM in Tampa, Florida, was exploring alternatives, or if the deliberation was going on at the Pentagon. Any information that trickled down to us from the battalion level was of questionable reliability because it was likely far removed from the source. Even more frustrating, at least for me as a leader, was that we had no power, no authority, no input into the strategy, no voice. We were simply in receive mode. We were cattle being staged or moved around. That was the nature of the military and we all understood this, even when it was very frustrating. So we waited.

In the big scheme of things, our wait was not so long, just a couple days; only the first twelve hours were spent in the hangar. The

173rd Airborne Brigade finally got the order to move out. In the middle of the night, we loaded onto buses and were driven two hours from Camp Ederle to Aviano Air Base, which is about ninety-five miles northeast of Vicenza, Italy. We had an escort of Italian police, most likely to prevent any antiwar protests from stopping or interrupting our convoy. I gave the idea of protestors little thought but I knew they existed. The possible protests might also have been the reason for us traveling in the middle of the night. For that matter, it could also have been a factor in our delay in leaving Vicenza. In any case, we did not have any trouble on the way. If there were protestors, none of us noticed because most of us were asleep, in transition to the next phase of our journey.

Aviano is a NATO base run by the Italian military, but for all practical purposes it is home to the U.S. Air Force's 31st Fighter Wing. This is the air force's only fighter wing south of the Alps. All our aviation support for parachute training was provided out of Aviano, so we were very familiar with the base. It was not much larger than the length of the runway, well under two miles, but compared to Camp Ederle, it was the big city.

When we got to Aviano that night, approaching early morning, we all stared out the windows in amazement as we saw fifteen C-17 Globemaster airplanes lined up on the airfield. Almost no one, including me, had ever seen a C-17, let alone ever jumped out of one. They are humongous, and at first site they reminded me more of gigantic gray metallic whales than any airplanes I would ride into combat. Our training had almost always been conducted with the much smaller C-130 Hercules based in Ramstein, Germany. A few of us had jumped out of a C-141 Starlifter in the past during other assignments, but almost no one had jumped from a C-17. The size of the C-17s continued to amaze me as I stared at them throughout the day. They have a length of 174 feet, a wingspan of 170 feet, and a height of 55 feet—five and a half stories tall! The C-17s are about one and a half times the size of our usual C-130s. Each can carry 102 paratroopers, fully loaded with parachutes and gear. They're big enough to carry 85 tons of cargo, even an M1 Abrams tank. Their cruising speed is 520 MPH and their range is 2,780 miles. Also, C-17s have jet engines, whereas C-130s are propeller driven. At the time, there were no C-17s stationed in Europe, so these must have arrived from stateside. All of this was a very clear sign to us that we were in the big leagues now and that the U.S. military was putting its full weight behind us. The combat jump the army was organizing would be the largest since the jump into Panama in 1989. Actually the U.S. Army has only been using paratroopers in combat since 1942. Of course World War II images of paratroopers being dropped over Belgium and France are etched in the minds of most Americans, but since then there have only been a handful of combat jumps.[1] We were about to make history.

The buses dropped us at an open field where someone had roped off an area for us to begin what we call rigging up: getting a parachute, pairing up with a buddy to put on the parachute, getting inspected by a jumpmaster, and then getting on the planes; however, this was no normal setup. Usually we had smaller groups of one hundred to two hundred soldiers. This group would be about a thousand soldiers all lined up in long rows as far as the eye could see. We also needed equipment we had never practiced jumping with: live ammunition. Soldiers in the army train with either blank (not live) ammunition or no ammunition at all 99 percent of the time. This first instance of being issued a full supply of live bullets, hand grenades, mines, and other supplies was going to be a completely new feeling for most of us.

Someone had also set up giant speakers all across the field that were pumping out very loud, motivating rock music, such as Guns N' Roses's "Welcome To The Jungle" or AC/DC's "Hells Bells." It was all surreal to say the least.

We were subjected to war speeches from the brigade commander, battalion commander, company commander, and first sergeant. I would like to say these speeches were all inspiring, but since I cannot remember a single word or phrase any of them said, I guess they were not inspiring enough.

We were given all kinds of things that we had never encountered before, from special treats to unusual but still mundane items. This included food items, like Sunkist drinks, Snickers bars, granola grain bars, bottled water, etc., and new military equipment such as Fastex 9mm holsters, basic issue item accessories for our night vision goggles, and so on. Over the course of the day, we conducted pre-jump refreshers and rehearsed actions on the aircraft as we did before every jump. The army emphasizes continual practice to reinforce muscle memory and instinctual reactions. It is a risk-mitigation and lifesaving policy.

There seemed to be an assortment of other services and units going in with us—air force, special forces, 10th Mountain Division, possibly 1st Armor Division, reporters, combat photographers—it was hard to keep track. There were at least ten satellite communications (SATCOM) antennas up and running alongside our equipment. At one point I sat down next to a group of really big, secretive-looking guys. They looked like they came from one of the enigmatic Special Operations Forces (SOF). They had name tapes that were Velcro, which at this time of the war was a feature of uniforms that allowed individuals with jobs like those in the special forces to remove their name tapes before a secretive mission—a strong indication they were not average soldiers. These were all reminders that what we were about to do was a big deal, the *real* deal.

We were given index cards with our duty positions written on them; mine read "platoon leader." The cards listed the exact number of bullets, grenades, flares, and other equipment we would be assigned. We got in line where the ammunition supply point (ASP) had set up shop, handed in our cards, and received our ammunition whether we wanted it or not. There was plenty I did not want. I did not want most of my bullets to be tracers, which they were. Tracers are special bullets that glow when they exit your weapon at night. They leave your weapon looking like a deadly bottle rocket or shooting star. They are meant to help you see where your rounds are impacting. For a leader they help mark targets for where the soldiers should shoot, such as "See my tracers? Shoot there!" But they also showed the enemy where the rounds were coming from.

They burn rapidly as well, which causes your gun barrel to heat up quickly. Beyond the tracers, I also did not want the extra weight of five flares and a mortar round, but no one asked or cared what I did or did not want. We all were going to carry things we did not want to on this mission. It was part of the shared hardship.

Immediately after putting the bullets in our rifle magazines and the other items into our backpacks, we realized how much all of this equipment weighed. Every soldier's rucksack weighed over 100 pounds. That is no exaggeration: sometimes 100 pounds, 125 pounds, or even 130 pounds, and that was just equipment, not including how much the soldier or his parachute weighed. We were all weighed on the airfield to confirm the overall weight of each soldier. This mattered to the aircrew, not that there was any chance we would exceed the aircrafts' capacity. We were weighed twice: once with gear, once without. I am sure there is a good reason why, but I could not tell you what it was. It is not like we would be going anywhere without our gear. Maybe it was because we would not be wearing our rucksacks most of the time on the aircraft—they would be stacked together in one big heavy pile in the middle of the aircraft until we were close to where we would jump out. It is amazing that if you pack a backpack with just a basic load of ammunition; three meals-ready-to-eat (MREs); two quarts of water; two pairs of socks; a T-shirt; a few grenades; a few flares; some nuclear, chemical, biological protective clothing; a collapsible shovel; and maybe a mortar round or two per soldier, you get over one hundred pounds of gear pretty easily. Plus, the parachute weighs about thirty pounds. Despite being the biggest, baddest, most advanced military in the world, little has changed in history. Infantry foot soldiers must carry very heavy loads of equipment on their backs just to get to the battle.

Later news reports would describe the weight soldiers had to carry on the battlefield. In extreme cases, the loads were up to two hundred pounds. That might sound superhuman to civilians. To us it was insane, but we had to do it without question. On the bright side, we would never lack for any equipment, weapons, or ammunition that we might need in a fight. Movement in battle is also important and I was not sure how well we would be able to do that loaded down as we were. I was very glad my platoon had vehicles to get us from place to place once we got to the ground.

After finishing our rigging up, we took all the gear off again. This is not as ridiculous as it may sound. It was important that we got everything organized for departure first. By the time that was completed, it was time to eat. We left our gear and parachutes lined up where we had been, with soldiers guarding it, took our weapons with us, and were bused to a "chow" hall on base. There we walked in and saw something none of us had ever seen in the military, nor would we ever see again. The entire dining hall was full of food and included dozens of giant carts overflowing with full-size lobsters, huge T-bone steaks, corn on the cob, baked potatoes the size of a fist, and a wide variety of desserts, like giant pieces of chocolate cake—it was all you could eat. This was not the military we knew! It took only about three seconds for everyone to close their dropped jaws and relate what they were seeing to the famous scene in the HBO miniseries *Band of Brothers*, where the paratroopers are served ice cream before the big jump on D-Day. "They *never* serve us ice cream. . . . This is a death meal. That's it, it's a death meal." Death meal or not, we ate like we were starving, and we loved it. If it was going to be our last meal, we were going to enjoy every last bite. It was not our last meal. Those who were able slept the night on cots in an airplane hangar and woke to more "ice cream" treatment. They brought us breakfast that was again historic—more than we needed of biscuits, sausages, bacon, eggs, hash browns, orange juice, and more. We did not even have to get bused to the chow hall this time. They delivered it to us. Again this was something that never happened unless we were in the field on a training exercise.

Once our "death breakfast" had filled our bellies, we returned to the airfield, finished getting our gear sorted, and put it on again. The mood was different. We knew that the next time we unstrapped from the gear, our parachutes would have deployed in the sky over Iraq, and we would have landed in the combat zone. This was getting very real.

Donning an army parachute is a two-person process. Each jumper pairs up with a "buddy." The buddy lifts the parachute and sets it on the back of the other jumper. The two of them ensure shoulder, chest, and leg straps are properly positioned, fastened, and not twisted. The reserve parachute is then attached across the jumper's belly. Once the first jumper is all chuted up, the roles are reversed and the buddy dons all of his equipment with assistance from the first jumper. During the flight, the jumper's rucksack would next be clipped to the harness, under the reserve, hanging down in front of the jumper's legs. Finally the weapon case holding an M4 rifle would be clipped to the left side of the harness.

Each platoon has two or three jumpmasters who conduct the final equipment check, called a JMPI or jumpmaster personnel inspection. There are 107 points of inspection (from chest and leg straps to every spot a piece of the parachute harness snaps together) on each paratrooper that are done in about one and a half to two minutes, excluding the rucksack and weapons case. This inspection maximizes the soldier's probability of a proper parachute deployment, comfortable and safe descent, and landing alive. No one ever complains about enduring the JMPI. Luckily I was a jumpmaster, so I had the perk that I got to wait until the very last second to put on my gear with a buddy, only after I had already finished inspecting my share of the jumpers. Rank and jumpmaster status have their privileges.

At this point, mobility is reduced to almost nothing. Even switching from standing to sitting and vice versa is very difficult. Eventually everyone decides that we will not be going anywhere immediately and, despite the effort, decides it is okay to sit until directed to board. The thought of being in the aircraft and not having to move for a while was a very inviting concept. Sitting down on the tarmac may not seem like a big deal if you have not experienced being loaded down with all that weight, but being able to sit down and not be very uncomfortable was a big deal. The best method for getting seated is to pair up with a buddy and lean back-to-back with our chutes against each other. Otherwise it would be a stomach workout to not fall onto our backs, like unhappy turtles.

While we were waiting, a two-star general stopped by to check on us and to say a few inspiring words as he chatted amiably with the troops. One thing he said that spread like wildfire was that this mission would absolutely be quick—ninety days maximum. Everyone was elated by this news. It was not clear if this was just the general's personal opinion or a firm directive from further up the chain of command. Regardless, we were all brightened by the prospect of a near-term return home. I did wonder how anyone could know for sure how long a war would last. At this point the war in Afghanistan had been going for over a year. On the other hand, the first Gulf War lasted only about six weeks. A weighted average of those two data points made ninety days seem pretty believable. Plus, a general had promised us. Later our families learned from CNN that all troops in Iraq had been extended to twelve months. That is not how the message should be communicated. So much for the general's promises.

Soon we had to struggle back to our feet, plod like overburdened Sherpas to the rear of the massive planes, step up onto the lowered ramps, stumble into the cargo bay, and each plop in turn down into our respective seats. As we boarded the monster-size planes, most people were silent. There were four rows of seats running front to rear, two along the side walls facing in and two down the center, back-to-back, facing the sides. Our rucksacks were piled into the space to the rear of us, strapped to the floor. It would be about a four-to-five-hour flight from our base in Italy to our drop site in Iraq.

Because I was a jumpmaster and the highest-ranking guy at the back of the chalk (group of paratroopers exiting an aircraft together), I was given a headset for the flight so that I could take instructions from the aircrew. At two hours out, I got the news that it was time to distribute our heavy rucksacks (or rucks, as we called them) and clip them onto our parachute harnesses. Unfortunately I was one of the first to have my ruck put on since I was one of the last to board, and my ruck was, therefore, one of the first to be handed out. Another shared hardship.

Twenty minutes out, the plane started a violent descent into Iraq airspace. We had been flying at a higher altitude so as not to be within range of missile fire from the ground. For the jump, we dropped to below one thousand feet, not very high in terms of parachute jumps, to minimize our descent time under the parachutes and our exposure to enemy fire.

At ten minutes out, the jumpmasters shouted the warning, "Ten minutes," and everyone shouted it back as the butterflies in our stomachs tried to fly out. At six minutes, we received the command to "Stand up." We stood up and faced the rear. Upon hearing the command, "Hook up," we then clipped our static lines into the anchor line above us that ran the length of the aircraft. This was followed by commands to check the static lines and check our equipment one last time. The air force crewmen opened the doors on both sides of the plane, letting the cold air rush in—or maybe the cold feeling came from inside me. Then the jumpmasters were allowed to take their positions in the doors. The last two shouts were, "One minute!" and "Thirty seconds!" That meant it was time for our sphincters to pucker. My mind rapidly reviewed the technique for safely exiting the aircraft, and my body reviewed the muscle memory of the action. This was one time I absolutely had to execute the technique correctly. In between those thoughts, I reminded myself of what had to be done tactically once I was on the ground. I had a lot on my mind, as everyone else must have too. Many of them also must have been thinking of their wives and kids—not a distraction I had, although maybe some of them found those thoughts to be inspiring, more motivation to return home safely.

As the number one jumper on my side of the aircraft, I had the questionable pleasure of standing by the then open door as we approached the DZ. I had to stand there and watch the jumpmaster do his checks: meticulously planting his boots on the inside of the doorframe, then stomping his foot on a small walkway that gets dropped out the door, then firmly gripping the inside of the door. He leaned out into the void, the wind blasting him as he looked ahead trying to spot the DZ. No biggie, right? There are not a lot of jobs that require you to lean out of a flying cargo jet. If his grip slipped and he tumbled out early, he would be lost and alone somewhere in a war zone. Because of my experience serving as the jumpmaster on other flights, I knew what he was going through, but my own mind was racing in so many directions, plus there was the pain of trying to stand even for five minutes with that weight hanging off me awkwardly. It was very painful! It might seem odd, but my mind and body wanted *out* of that aircraft. A parachute weighs thirty pounds on your back but does not weigh anything when it is floating above you. The checks the jumpmaster was doing "had to" be done several times before we actually got to the DZ. Considering the sophisticated navigation equipment the pilots had at their disposal, the checks were likely an archaic holdover, but who was I to question the ritual?

The time finally arrived. On March 26, 2003, at approximately 1945 hours Zulu time, 12:45 a.m. local time, the green light came on, the jumpmaster yelled, "Go!" and hit me on my backside. My training kicked in. No hesitation is authorized, and I instinctively stepped out the door. My feet landed briefly on the ledge outside of the door and then my body, hitting the gusting wind, was sucked out into the air. There are two exit doors on the C-17, so on the opposite side of me there was another jumpmaster and line of anxious paratroopers waiting to exit the aircraft. One second after I was slapped, my counterpart experienced the same. This created a staggered exit of the jumpers while both sides dumped their cargo of anxious paratroopers. The staggered exit of bodies is an amazing act of coordination and science that with a naked eye looks like a constant stream of projectiles. Paratroopers almost always use the exit doors on the side of an aircraft instead of the rear ramp because the exit doors allow for more soldiers to get out quickly. That is the ultimate goal of a combat jump: get as many soldiers out of the aircraft and safely on the ground ready to fight as quickly as possible.

When I exited the aircraft, the sounds were overwhelming due to the engine noise and turbulence. We were required to wear earplugs because it was so loud. In addition to the sound, the jet blast of the massive C-17 pummeled me and sent my body tumbling through the night sky, violently throwing me about. Once my chute opened and the plane was a distance away, there was dead silence. I immediately took out my earplugs, letting them fall into the black void below me. Still I heard not a single sound. There was no feeling of descent, just a sensation of hanging in midair. I was alone with my thoughts—not all good thoughts. I wondered how fast I was falling and when the brutal impact of the ground would come, an impact I had felt in more than forty training jumps. For tactical reasons, we jumped on a moonless night. While this meant the enemy could not see us, it also meant we could not see below us as we fell rapidly toward the ground. I had a twist in my risers, the straps connecting my harness to the parachute, that kept the parachute from opening as broadly as it should. Theoretically this causes a faster descent and harder landing, but I was on the ground quickly so it did not concern me for long. The landing was surprisingly soft after all. As we were taught, I kept my feet together and rolled when I touched down, distributing the impact over five points of contact: balls of my feet, calf, thigh, buttocks, and "pull-up muscle" (the latissimus dorsi, or the muscle below the shoulder, on the side of the back). Oh, who am I kidding? I landed in a heap and miraculously was uninjured.

It took less than a minute for 954 soldiers of the 1st Battalion 508th Infantry, 2nd Battalion 503rd Infantry, and the 173rd Headquarters staff to exit the fifteen C-17s and another minute or so to hit the ground. We did not have time to ponder the historical significance of the event. We were American soldiers just dropped into a combat zone and had things that needed to be done.

I worked quickly in silence to collect up my parachute, putting it in a kit bag with the reserve chute and empty weapon case——having removed my M4—and leaving the bag in place. This was another sign of combat because in training jumps soldiers must carry those cumbersome parachute bags to a central collection point. Within minutes I had the bag filled, my weapon in hand, and my ruck onto my back. That may sound like a quick process, but it always felt like it took longer that it should, even more so when time was of the essence. Having just done a combat jump, though, I was pumped with adrenaline as I headed to where I thought the linkup point should be. In the silence, there was no way of calculating time, and I feared I was going too slowly. I really had no temporal sense. But I said, "Screw it," and pushed onward. In the darkness, I could not see other soldiers and certainly did not want to be a straggler. Even when I was able to put on my night vision goggles, I could not see anyone else. Crap, where was everybody? We must have been more spread out than I would have guessed. The darkness, terrain, and silence completely hid us from each other.

As I have since told everyone about the jump, I was surprised to learn that northern Iraq is more akin to the mountainous, cold, rainy, and vibrant green foliage of Washington State than the image we all hold in our mind of barren sand dunes abundant with camels. Here the mud was pervasive and invasive. The location chosen for our combat jump was a large rice-farm field, which makes sense because airborne drop operations require a big piece of open terrain without obstacles. As luck would have it, it had rained every day of the week before the day we jumped in. The ground was a mud bog. Moving through the mire carrying that extreme weight was the hardest physical thing I have ever done in my life. I fell frequently trying to take a step in the mud. I would fall down and be crushed by the weight of my ruck that followed every slip. It took every muscle fiber of my body to get up when I fell, and I fell a lot. It was as if I was in a mortal fight with the ground. Every step I took, the mud grabbed my boot like a vice and held it as I used every ounce of my physical power to pull that foot up. I was also trying to protect my equipment from the mud. I needed to be able to actually fight at any moment, but I felt I was being eaten alive by the mud, covering every part of my body and equipment, even my night vision goggles and my rifle! Mud on or in any of those vital pieces of gear could render me ineffective in battle, the last thing a leader wants to be. A soldier without a working rifle as well as the inability to see the enemy is useless. I could not allow myself to be useless, but the mud had other ideas. I wanted to cry in desperation. It was taking what felt like hours to move just a few feet and I needed to move over a quarter mile to get to our platoon's predesignated linkup spot. An immense amount of fear started to build up in me. Not fear of an enemy force that might be out there but an enormous fear of failing—that I was not going to make it to my linkup site in the required time. I knew that we had a short amount of time to meet up and then the unit would move out as long as they had a certain number of people, with or without me. I was minutes into my first important responsibility as a platoon leader and I was going to fail. I was going to fail to do my job. I was going to fail to even show up to do my part for the team, to lead them. It did not help my spiraling thoughts of failure that I was alone, in the dark silence.

Then I saw another soldier. Thank God! In training we are required to find someone else or a few others to move with off the DZ. I approached the shadowy figure and whispered, "Who is this?" He responded, "Private First Class Butler, Alpha Company." Praise the Lord I thought. Butler was not only from my company—he was one of my guys, a member of my platoon. I had an overwhelming feeling of relief. It really did not matter who it was, but someone from my platoon was a plus. Nevertheless, I was no longer alone. It did not help me fight the mud monster, but I mentally needed that soldier. Together, Butler and I made it to the assembly area.

The terrain was so hard to traverse that when we tried to move to a dryer location the morning after the jump, the lactic acid had already set into all of my muscles—in my thighs, calves, arms, forearms, hell, even my hands. I could barely move. I ended up spending twenty-five years in the military, endured some very hard workouts, literally exercised all day, completed thirty-mile foot marches, competed in the Best Ranger contest (like the Olympics of the military), but I have never again strained myself or been that sore from physical activity before or after that night and morning after struggling with that muddy morass.

Unfortunately not all the soldiers were physically or mentally capable of moving the weight they carried through the challenging terrain. Some just quit in place and laid in the mud until the next morning when the sun came up and they could see where dry land was. Others did worse—they laid there complaining of injuries until other soldiers came to drag them out. The next morning we each knew we would be weighed in the eyes of the other soldiers, and we would judge others in return. This was day one of assessing the value each individual contributed to our new group—our new family. This happens in training, but this was real life, real combat. The stakes were so much higher. I did not understand those who were willing to accept negative judgment from their fellow soldiers. Everything I had witnessed about peer pressure since middle and high school told me that we should all be trying our damnedest to win the respect of our peers. With the number of soldiers stuck, it proved how difficult those muddy rice fields were.

One of my soldiers physically could not bring himself to move when we were ordered to relocate from the linkup site to another position. He was apparently in so much despair about his inability to carry his gear that he decided that death was preferable to making his body do anything. Two sergeants in my platoon hovered over him yelling at him to get up. He pleaded with them to just leave him. The sergeants again yelled at him that this was not training and lying in the mud was not an option. My soldier opted for a different solution and attempted to commit suicide. He suddenly jammed the barrel of his rifle into his mouth and was about to pull the trigger. Luckily he was quickly tackled by the sergeants, who yanked the rifle away from him. Looking back, we all knew his rifle probably would not have fired anyway because it looked like he had stuck the barrel in a pile of feces while trying to hold himself upright in the mud. This soldier had completely disregarded a core value of a soldier—that we have to keep our weapons functional in order to fight. This was only hours into the war, before we had even encountered the enemy. We took his weapons away, called higher headquarters, put him on a vehicle, and never saw him again. Suicide or even talk of suicide is no laughing matter. I hope he got the help he needed, but I was also relieved that he was removed from my platoon so quickly.

Once we got everyone in motion, we executed our first mission of establishing one of the blocking position that formed a perimeter around the Bashur Airfield, which was adjacent to the DZ. American Special Forces and Kurdish allies had already been operating in the area before our jump, so we encountered no Iraqi opposition. We accomplished our first mission without firing a shot. The airfield consisted of a 6,700-foot runway in the middle of a grassy field. There were no buildings or facilities of any kind. Still, American forces would find it useful for inserting our follow-on equipment and personnel.

Within a couple days, having secured the meager landing strip, more C-17s finished delivering our trucks and other vehicles onto the airfield, freeing us to move south from Bashur. Tanks and armored Bradley Fighting Vehicles (BFVs) arrived in the days following our departure. Among the vehicles that were flown in were those specifically for my platoon's transportation. We were the motorized platoon of Alpha Company, which meant we were the only platoon in the company that traveled exclusively by vehicles instead of only on foot. For long movements, the other platoons were moved in large five-ton cargo trucks. My platoon's vehicles were equipped with weapons to include MK19 grenade launchers and M2 .50 caliber machine guns, both too heavy to be man-portable over any distance. So the platoon had eight high mobility multipurpose wheeled vehicles—HMMWVs or "Humvees." This is the military vehicle that spawned the civilian Hummer, or at least the H1 version. My vehicle was the up-armored M1114 variant, the only one in the platoon that featured an armored passenger area protected by hardened steel and bullet-resistant glass. The other vehicles were basically open-air pickup trucks with wood slats as the cargo rails. The grenade launcher was mounted in the roof turret of the three vehicles that carried them, while our M2 .50 caliber and M240 7.62mm machine guns were mounted on pedestals of the open-back vehicles.

On April 2 we moved about twenty miles southwest to a spot outside the Kurdish city of Irbil. Irbil is the capital of the Kurdish areas of northern Iraq. We established a position in an open field and set up in a defensive posture while we awaited further instructions. I positioned seven of the vehicles facing outward from our location to defend against any threats, with my vehicle in the center, forming a large patrol base. Within that perimeter, soldiers who were not on watch could take the opportunity to clean weapons, eat, clean up, and do other equipment and personal maintenance. This gave all of the soldiers a little time to acclimate to the fact that they were in a war. We had been in country for a week without enemy contact. We knew it would not last forever and there was the ever-present possibility of being attacked. So we kept our guard up. Every day without a casualty was a good day.

On April 8 we received orders to attack an Iraqi divisional head-quarters about fifteen miles outside of Irbil. This mission was the real reason why we did the jump. Our unit was meant to occupy these northern positioned heavy forces so that they would not get any bright ideas and try to head south toward Baghdad, where the main effort was bringing the entire weight of the American and Coalition military down on Saddam Hussein's forces protecting the capital. Operation Northern Delay forced the Iraqi Army to maintain approximately six divisions in the area to protect its northern flank rather than reinforce units facing the good guys, who were attacking Baghdad from the south.[2] On this night our battalion's mission was to escort our brigade artillery up to a position from which they could fire on the enemy's divisional headquarters. My company was the lead company, my platoon the lead platoon, and my vehicle the lead vehicle. I was reminded of the lyrics from Nena's "99 Red Balloons": "This is what we've waited for, this is it boys, this is war." This was what I had been anticipating, even looking forward to. It was my chance to lead men into battle, the very thing I had been training for throughout my military career. Yet this excitement was tempered by the pressure I felt to perform up to the highest expectations, as well as the responsibilities for the lives of the men under my leadership. The next few days would demonstrate how well I carried that burden.

We were to move forward in a convoy of vehicles. As we waited to leave, our company commander, a captain, came to check on things. While there, he asked one of my soldiers, PVT Smith, who was sitting in the back of the vehicle keeping to himself quietly looking down, if he was scared. I thought it was a weird question. Smith replied that he was scared; that really surprised me. I did not have any fear of the enemy. I had confidence in the platoon. I had confidence in their training, our weapons, and our superiority over the enemy. My fear was failing the rest of the soldiers as their leader. As in similar situations before, what caused me stress was whether I would live up to the standards of a good leader for my men. I knew from having been a young enlisted man that they were constantly observing me, judging me. Second lieutenants were probably judged more critically than any other rank, as they were the newest officers. How someone performed as a platoon leader likely set the pattern for the rest of their military career. I wanted that judgment from my platoon to be positive. I wanted to pass their test—not just for me but primarily for them. I also knew that they too wanted to end up with a positive assessment of me. They wanted me to pass their test. They deserved a good leader and I wanted to be that for them. So even if I did not feel the same type of fear as PVT Smith, I had to take note of his comment, and I did.

We started our movement to the objective. Along the way we had to stop and meet some special forces personnel who had been watching the Iraqi positions. At that stop my second in command in the platoon, SFC Stanford, came up to my vehicle and asked, "Are we going to be here long?"

I replied, "I'm not sure."

And he said, "I have to take a dump."

I said "Dude! Right now?"

He did not see the problem with it and countered, "Yes! I'll be right over there."

Again I found this odd. But what I later found even odder was that Stanford would do this every time we were about to go on big missions, where enemy contact was likely. I did not think about it until much later, but this was clearly his body responding to fear in its own way. Each of us probably had some physiological response to deadly fear. His was just more awkward and inconvenient.

Fear, or the psychological and physiological rollercoaster of responding to the stress of combat, does very different things to people. A well-documented response to fear or extreme stress is actually the opposite of what Stanford experienced. When a person experiences fear or stress, their body's sympathetic nervous systems orchestrates the "fight or flight" response. It manages the expenditure of energy in the body preparing to either fight or take flight, i.e., run away. Digestion is inhibited, epinephrine (also known as adrenaline) and norepinephrine are secreted, the bronchial tubes in the lungs are dilated, heart vessels also dilate, and muscles tense.[3] As most people know, adrenaline speeds the heart, increases blood pressure, and focuses vision; this is how the body prepares itself to fight or run. Being able to overcome fear or the stress of combat is a complex phenomenon. It is a very personal and often different experience as PVT Smith and SFC Stanford displayed. The individual soldier's mind perceives each event as a threat to existence, a need to fight or flee. But the military has figured out that training and repetition in drills, exposure to simulated combat stress conditions, and a deep personal cohesion to fellow soldiers all significantly contribute to override the otherwise normal human response. Somehow that had not worked as well for Stanford. Maybe he needed more training or repetition. He was eating the same diet as the rest of us, so it was probably more psychosomatic than physical.

We drove our vehicles under the concealment of night right up to the enemy's front door, a four-way intersection about two hundred meters from their frontline. We drove with our lights off, using night vision goggles. Try to imagine driving with no light and using only the green glow seen through goggles, with a narrow field of view and terrible depth perception. It is no easy task. It is a bitch really. We had trained on this task back in Europe, but this was an even more unfamiliar environment and terrain. The drivers pulled it off, though. Once we were at our destination, I had the platoon spread out in a line facing the enemy position, finding whatever natural cover and defilade was available. My vehicle was in the middle of the formation—right in the middle of the road actually. As the vehicles arrived in their spots, the squad members dismounted and either manned the crew-served weapons or took up individual fighting positions. Again this was their training paying off.

I had already given the orders to the MK19 gunners that they could open fire with the grenades as soon as we got into position. We had predesignated areas where enemy forward observers and mortar locations were, information provided by the special forces team, so the grenadiers needed to engage those targets first. We fired the first shot of the 173rd's war in Iraq.

The Iraqis immediately returned fire with their machine guns and mortars. But they did not really know where we were, so we saw the tracers from their heavy machine guns literally firing in circles, not a recommended method. We responded with grenade launchers, .50 caliber machine guns, and artillery from the battery we had escorted forward. At this point, adrenaline coursed through my veins as I directed my platoon's tactics via radio. I remember the first "crack" I heard that night. I had been told stories of what a round of ammunition passing by sounds like. When a bullet passes close to you it makes a distinctive "crack" that serves as a warning. If a bullet is not that close, you do not hear the crack but maybe a zip. I still was not scared. I knew that if I did my job, everyone else would be doing their job. Being a part of the group was empowering.

After about ten minutes in the intersection, we started to receive enemy mortar fire. Mortar rounds make a very loud and explosive boom on impact. We could not hear the smaller explosion the rounds make when launching from their mortar tubes, but it is really hard to miss the bigger one on the receiving end. I was surprised that there was no incoming whistle, like you hear in war movies, but maybe that occurs only with larger rounds, like artillery. In any case, I never want to find out. These were smaller 60mm and 82mm rounds.

Just after rounds started to impact around our position, I saw the battalion CSM by one of our vehicles. He must have been trying to check on the troops. His arrival surprised the crew, despite the good illumination provided by the moon that night. I knew we were about to start our pullout because I had gotten the call to get ready to move. I was able to speak to him as he kneeled behind one of the truck tires. After hearing one of the booms, he asked me, "What is that?"

I responded, "Those are incoming enemy mortar rounds."

Without hesitation, he said, "Oh, okay, see you later," and quickly went back to where he had come from. I chuckled and returned my focus to the men.

None of us had ever been on the receiving end of mortars. In hindsight it was probably a poor decision to set up in a four-way intersection because that made a perfect target reference point for mortars. In other words, the Iraqis would have very likely already plotted the location of the intersection and determined the calculations for aiming their mortars at that exact spot. Shifting their fire to nearby targets would be much easier with such an established target reference point. Lesson learned. We got lucky and I would not make that mistake again.

Fortunately we had mortars too. I was reminded of that when I heard a radio message on the company net: "Enemy vehicle coming down the road." That certainly piqued my interest since I was sitting in the middle of the road. I told my gunner to get ready and strained my eyes looking through my night vision goggles trying to identify the vehicle. I did not see it. Then I was blinded by a flash of white, followed by the sound of a loud boom. I saw an explosion right in the road just at the edge of where I had been scanning seconds before. I flipped my goggles up and saw bright orange and red flames. Our 60mm mortar team had hit the truck while moving. That was an amazing feat of both technical skill and luck. It had to have been a one in a million shot.

One of the major reasons that the enemy mortars did not get a chance to land a lucky shot on us was the fact that from the moment we pulled into our position, my two MK19 gunners had begun firing on their known or suspected location. The MK19 fires 40mm grenades linked together by a massive belt. The rhythmic sound of the MK19 was the background to the symphony of battle sounds we were enduring. Whoop, whoop, whoop. The two gunners were not just firing at where they thought enemy mortars were: they were being directed by forward observers that our unit had set up on nearby hills. One of the gunners, SPC Bessette, fired over five hundred rounds of the MK19 at an enemy mortar position that was almost two kilometers away. That distance is just under the maximum range of the weapon. The cross talk and adjustments between Bessette and the observer team were beautiful. While making corrections, I saw him fixing malfunctions in the weapon, barely missing a beat in the fine adjustments. "Fifty meters more . . . adjust right twenty-five meters . . . you got them, keep it right there." The observers confirmed that Bessete's rounds killed the mortar team, and he was credited with the first confirmed kill for the brigade.

Both gunners fired almost all of their rounds, what we call going "black" on ammo, which you never want to do because it leaves you in a very vulnerable situation. Luckily, before they completely ran out, the battalion artillery finished firing, having destroyed the enemy headquarters position and causing the survivors to flee. We were ordered to get back into our vehicles and pull out, moving back to our assembly area outside of Irbil. We were 1–0 at the end of our first matchup with the enemy. We had competed in our first "pro game" and come away with a win. It was an exhilarating feeling.

Back at our assembly area, we again circled the vehicles. Those soldiers not on guard duty huddled in small groups and very naturally talked about what they had just experienced. Without knowing it, they were continuing a tradition of warriors across millennia. As they cleaned their weapons and sat under the stars, they traded stories about what they had done and what they had seen others do. They described the sound of bullets passing by, the sight of enemy tracers, the smell that accompanies gunfire. They talked about how they felt during the battle, at times calm and methodical, often completely fired up, and sometimes freaked out. This process of post-combat decompression is a well-documented but not forced event. On this night it happened, and it felt right. The men were reliving the hardship and overcoming fear. And they were laughing. Soldiers always find things to laugh about, even in the most difficult situations; it is one thing I've always loved about them. This night they found as many reasons for humor as they could suck out of the event. One of the moments they found most hilarious was when one of the soldiers leaped frantically out of the Humvee, startled by the .50 caliber machine gun's loud and powerful opening burst. It was almost as if he had never heard it fired before, although he certainly had many times. That gave his squad and all of us a laugh for weeks. I joined in the laughter and the decompression, and was slightly relieved that I had given them no reason to be laughing at me—make that very relieved.

The tough combat jump and first firefight showed me how the process of combat creates moments of shared hardships among soldiers. At this point of the war, few of us in the platoon knew each other very well; maybe I knew them least of all. Surviving those stressful situations bonded us to a moment in time. We survived the life-threatening combat episode due to the collective action of the group, not individuals. Each soldier played a role in the group's survival. Shared survival in battle will always be a unique and valuable bonding experience, as I found when things went well, like they had today, and even more so when things did not go well, as I knew would eventually happen.

4

Home Away from Home (Shared Living Hardships)

Once in Iraq, we followed the traditions of war, such as writing home. Letter writing from the frontlines has evolved over the past few centuries, from the days of General Washington's lucid prose to his wife, Martha, to the sentimental emails of a young captain today. My own experience at war is instructional. Starting almost on day one of the war after jumping into Iraq, I wrote letters to my wife in my small notebook. On some days, I might have only scribbled a few illegible lines. We did not have envelopes, but someone mentioned that you could tear off a piece of cardboard from an MRE box and send it as a pseudo postcard—no postage necessary for deployed troops. We all sent these. At the very least these makeshift postcards were a signal to friends and families that we were okay.

As you can imagine, some days were better than others for writing. If we were sitting in one spot with no imminent mission, there would be a lot more time to write and give thought to what we would write than on the days when we were relocating, patrolling, planning a mission, or engaged with the enemy. There might be days that were emotionally more suited to corresponding with family and friends: when we were upbeat and wanted to share our optimism and enthusiasm; when we were lonely and needed to feel a connection home; when we were feeling philosophical and needed to muse; or when we were dejected and had to reach out, even if the response would be a long time coming. These days were better than the days when our emotions, if expressed, might only cause worry, anxiety, and fear for our family. Most of us were cognizant of how important it was to not add to the stress of our loved ones.

They were already dealing with a constant level of dread that horrible news could come to the door at any time. They very likely imagined that our experience in war was much worse than it was in reality, so reassuring them that we were safe, comfortable, well fed, rested, and even enjoying ourselves occasionally was as much our mission as defeating the enemy.

To illustrate this empathy my soldiers felt for their families, as well as their characteristically persistent sense of humor, take a look at one MRE postcard sent on March 31, 2003, by a sergeant in my platoon that read:

> Hey Mom and Dad (and of course the rest of the family too.) Just writing to tell you that I'm all right. The jump into "Bashur" (about 150 km north of Baghdad) Iraq went fairly well. There is so much I could tell you about, that's happened in the first few days . . . but I'll just wait until I get home to tell you ☺ Mom, don't worry I'll be fine, I promise. My mind is in the right place. I have "mentally" stooped to "their" level, and then some. Just a few more prayers could always help though—Dad, everything you predicted (your OPORD) has come true. Thanks! The Kurds (KDP) are thrilled to have us. I need a favor—when you write me back, send me 2 or 3 envelopes w/a few sheets of paper so I can write home like a normal person. As Always, I love you guys very much and hope to hear from you soon. I'll write again when I get the chance. Love, Brian

Analysis of wartime letters home like Brian's from over 140 years of American warfare—spanning the Civil War, World War I, World War II, Korea, Vietnam, the Persian Gulf, Somalia, and the Bosnia conflicts—shows consistency in their structure.[1] The letters employ descriptions and narrations attempting to illuminate for their loved ones the soldiers' distant realities and the remoteness of the experience, both geographically and in the lives they were living. Part of this is an awareness of the time-delayed connection, as the soldier conveys the experience of war with his social and emotional support network back home. As I would encounter in a much later

31 MAR 03

HEY MOM AND DAD,
(AND OF COURSE THE REST
OF THE FAMILY TOO.)
JUST WRITING TO TELL YOU THAT
I'M ALL RIGHT. THE JUMP
INTO "BASHUR" IRAQ WENT
FAIRLY WELL. THERE IS SO
MUCH I COULD TELL YOU ABOUT,
THATS HAPPENED IN THE FIRST
FEW DAYS... — BUT I'LL JUST
WAIT UNTIL I GET HOME TO TELL
YOU ☺ MOM, DON'T WORRY I'LL BE
FINE — I PROMISE. MY MIND
IS IN THE RIGHT PLACE. I HAVE
"MENTALLY" STOOPED TO "THEIR"
LEVEL, AND THEN SOME. JUST A
FEW MORE PRAYERS COULD ALWAYS HELP
THOUGH — DAD, EVERYTHING YOU
PREDICTED (YOUR OPORD) HAS COME TRUE.
THANKS! THE KURDS (KDP) ARE
THRILLED TO HAVE US. I NEED A
FAVOR — WHEN YOU WRITE ME BACK,
SEND ME 2 OR 3 ENVELOPES w/ A
FEW SHEETS OF PAPER, SO I CAN
WRITE HOME LIKE A NORMAL PERSON.
AS ALWAYS, I LOVE YOU GUYS
VERY MUCH AND HOPE TO HEAR FROM
YOU SOON. I'll WRITE AGAIN WHEN I
GET THE CHANCE.

LOVE,
BRIAN

(AIRBORNE WINGS w/ COMBAT STAR,
SORRY — I TRIED...)

☑ BASHUR ☐ IRBIL ☐ KIRKUK ☐ BAGHDAD

(MYPAY)/ASK.COM

MOM, PLEASE SEND MY CURRENT LES w/ YOUR LETTER — THANKS!

(ABOUT 150 KM FROM BAGHDAD)
← NORTH!

2. Cardboard message from Sgt. Brian Horn to his mom. Courtesy of Brian Horn.

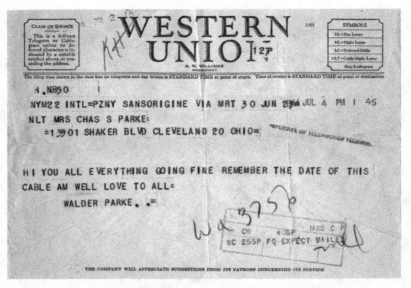

3. Telegram sent by a U.S. Air Force airman to his family during World War II.
Courtesy of the Ohio History Connection.

deployment, this time delay would essentially be erased through technology.

Here are additional examples from troops from different services, eras, and nationalities, which prove that these themes are not unique to a time, military branch, or country.

During World War II Charles Walder Parke, an air force navigator on a B-17 Flying Fortress, telegraphed his family in Cleveland with instructions to "remember the date of this cable." The date he was excited about was when he was promoted to 1LT.

Western Union Telegraph; Date Stamp: July 4, 1945
From: Sansorigine (French for "without origin" meaning not revealed for security)
To: Mrs Chas S Parke, 3901 Shaker Blvd, Cleveland Ohio
Message: Hi you all. Everything going fine. Remember the date of this cable. Am well. Love to all.

Another letter, this one from the Battle of the Bulge that occurred

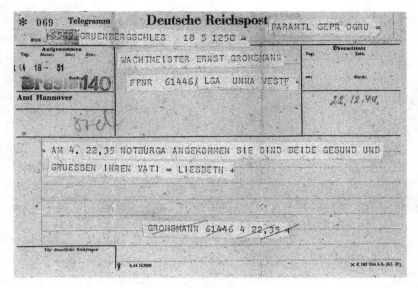

4. Telegram sent to a German soldier during World War II announcing the birth of his child. Courtesy of Marc Garlasco.

in World War II, announces the birth of a child to a German soldier weeks after it happened.

Luftwaffe postal system
From: Breslau (currently Wroclaw, Poland)
To: Master Sergeant Ernst Grossmann
Date: 22 December 1944
Message: On the 4th at 22.35 Notburga was born. She is both healthy and sends greetings to her father, Elizabeth

I wrote desperately to maintain a connection to my wife of only two years. Despite my attempts, there was a clear divide between what I was experiencing and what she was encountering at home. She endured a life without me there in Italy, far from her support network, in a foreign land that felt unfamiliar and sometimes unwelcoming. I was experiencing a whole new life, one that I had anticipated for a decade and was relishing. Of course I could not excitedly describe to her the exhilaration of combat leadership. My main responsibility was to my men, but I had a duty to my wife as well. I did not have to keep her physically alive, but her emotional survival and the survival of our marriage were very real onuses that were on my shoulders. We had not been taught about that in any army training.

So I did not write to Sara about the stress and fear. I did not detail the chaos of missions. Those were topics I discussed with the people on the ground with me because they were the only ones who could understand the context. I also did not want my wife to worry. The most I would tell her was "today was rough." Even that, I would later learn, was probably too much to share.

Mail call, when letters were delivered to our location, was always a bittersweet event. Mail calls traditionally have been a highlight of a soldier's time in combat.[2] Occasionally it was a low point, such as when someone received the dreaded "Dear John" letter, where a loved one breaks up with a soldier while he's in combat. Sometimes mail call would take place when the company 1SG arrived at the platoon location carrying mail, and at other times mail would come with our resupply of food and ammunition. However it came, it brought a sense of optimistic anticipation in each soldier. Knowing that someone cared enough to write a letter or send a care package of food, candy, and sundry items was enough to buoy the emotions of a deployed soldier for days. The letter might even include photos of smiling loved ones enjoying life back home. In the same way that our letters home were generally intended to reassure family that we were doing well, letters from home did the same for us.

It was about a month into the deployment when we started to receive letters. The first one I received was written by my wife on the day I left. I was filled with joy! That was the sweet part. But if we had a mail call and I did not receive a letter or box, I felt a small bit of sadness as it made me feel left out and forgotten. I knew this was not an entirely rational response. I could not expect Sara to write every day. Writing a letter takes time and, without me to share the workload at home, she had less time to herself. Also, postal transit was irregular. Two letters sent on the same day from the same loca-

Home Away from Home

tion could arrive a week apart. Even if Sara had written to me every day, there was a high likelihood that I would have frequent days that I would not get any mail. It was a letdown, a tiny gut punch. Trying to use logic when emotions were involved rarely worked.

Mail call was also about getting stuff, like candy, baby wipes, jerky, trail mix, or anything else we had or had not asked for and it was a surprise. One of my soldiers, PFC Jeremy Brammer, always received these massive boxes of food. He was a very popular guy because if we had an abundance—more than could be stuffed into our own allotted space in the vehicles we rode around on—then it was shared with our small group. Homemade desserts like cookies, brownies, even Rice Krispies treats were the best. If anyone got anything like that and was willing to share, he won the popularity contest. (Maybe that's where the term "brownie points" came from!) A favorite memory of mine includes a time when an elderly lady who I did not even know—she was someone a friend of mine had met—sent me home-cooked banana nut muffins. Oh my God, they were awesome! I definitely wish I had stayed in touch with her, even now.

I sent my mom frequent, short letters telling her I loved her, assuring her that all was well with me, maybe sharing a story about the different culture. For example, I described how the women and little girls hid when we were around. We never saw them on the street playing, working, doing household chores . . . nothing. This kind of thing was completely alien to my mother, something she could only experience through my letters. Those stories had the added benefit of not being about combat, giving her the skewed impression that my time in Iraq was more anthropological than martial.

In addition to personal mail, we also sometimes received mail addressed to "Any Soldier." These were often sent by schools or church groups, but anyone could send them. Usually they included personal, handwritten notes. When it came from a school, there might be dozens of notes, each of them very supportive, encouraging, and uplifting. The ones from kids were cute in their simplicity. In our unit, as in most, we tried to deliver these to soldiers who had not received much mail lately or who otherwise could use a boost. Sure they were not quite as nice as knowing that someone you knew was thinking specifically of you, but they helped morale a lot. Physical mail, something you can hold in your hand, is such a personal motivator, an emotional connection to another human, and it does not even have to come from a loved one. A Vietnam veteran remembering how a simple homemade letter made his day said, "To this day I have on my wall a picture sent to me in Vietnam drawn by a little child; it still means the world to me."[3] So if someone reading this book ever sent one of these letters or packages, you can take comfort in knowing that it really did reach a deployed service member and it was deeply appreciated. Some of the troops even sent thank you notes to the sender.

It was three months before we were able to make a call home. I should point out that based on Desert Storm lasting only forty-three days and the promise from the general at Aviano, we had originally hoped we would not still be in country at this time. Not being able to talk to our families for this long was far beyond what we had considered possible. On top of that, we were only able to make a phone call after standing in line for over an hour while visiting the big base at Kirkuk, where we had lived briefly during the opening weeks of the invasion before being pushed out into small villages. Once you made it through the line, you had to call an operator to connect you to the person you wanted to call. There was always a slight fear that the person you were dialing would not answer the phone. Who knew the time zone difference? They could be asleep when we called and often were. We could not predict what day/week/month let alone the time we were going to be able to call, so we gave it a shot any chance we had without bothering to calculate what time it was at their end. Fortunately most family members were glad to hear from us at any time, even at the expense of being rudely awaken because we were bad at math. I was so excited to finally hear my wife's voice. Phone calls were only allowed to be ten minutes, and the operator would interrupt your call to tell you that you had one minute left when you were near the end.

During my first call with Sara, I was angered that after the first few minutes she asked, "Why have some of the other guys been able to call their wives every day for the last month?"

Holding my tongue as best as I could, I explained, "Because I am living outside of the base, usually staying in spots for only a couple days or weeks. I am not like the people stationed at these big support installations who can mosey over to the phones on their lunch break."

She understood. Or at least I told myself she did. In retrospect, she probably knew the answer before she asked the question. She had received my postcards and letters and had talked with the other wives, so she was fairly aware of my platoon's situation. Her question was just an expression of her general frustration. She was powerless to change the completely undesirable circumstances she found herself in. It was only natural, if a little irrational, for her to take it out on me. I had to accept that it would be unfair of me, although maybe natural, to respond in kind. She did not deserve it, and it certainly would not help our marriage.

I tried to cut Sara some slack. I had left her in a foreign country with no ability to reach me to assist with the daily decisions with the home front. This had been the way of war for generations, probably as long as war had taken warriors to distant lands. We got married before 9/11. The only real war in our lifetimes had been the brief first Gulf War. Vietnam ended the year I was born. Small military deployments to places like Panama, Grenada, or Bosnia were all similarly short. We had had very little expectation of me going off to war for an extended period of time. And yet there we were. It was certainly harder on her in so many ways than it was on me. During future calls, I spent the time telling my wife how much I missed her and about all the things we would do when I got home. Again, I did not talk about what I was going through.

Ironically, letters and phone calls provided a much-needed source of news about the war. We knew next to nothing about how the war was progressing outside of our tiny sphere of awareness. In the Irbil location, our battalion mechanic, a warrant officer who was a prior enlisted SFC and had served in Desert Storm, had brought along a survival radio. He was able to tune in to "Voice of America" for news updates on the war. This was information we craved. It gave us the big picture and put our situation in context. Our battalion mechanic became a popular guy.

For almost the entire deployment, my unit lived in abandoned schools and government buildings. In the parts of the country where the war was being waged, from the south to Baghdad, the Kurdish north, and the west to Jordan, residents had fled major portions of the cities. We avoided commandeering private homes so as not to turn the populace against us, and moved instead into the public buildings. They provided us shelter but not much more. At least we were out of direct sunlight. We lived a mostly austere existence due to lack of power and working plumbing in these facilities. It was four weeks before we were able to take our first shower since jumping, and that was in a plywood box we built, with a bag of water that hung from a pole above us and was heated by the sun. Places like abandoned schools make great temporary bases since almost all of them in Iraq have large exterior walls, a gated entry point, and large buildings with rooftop access, giving good lines of sight around the compound. These were valuable military features but a sad reflection of what life in Iraq was like for the civilians, even before the war.

Staying cool was one of the main missions. June through September in Kirkuk had average high temperatures of over one hundred degrees Fahrenheit. The heat was constant and unforgiving. Monthly rainfall was barely measurable, and humidity was at zero percent all summer. Although it was a dry heat, that did not make it any better. We traveled to Iraqi ice factories, bought sodas from the local shops, and started organizing patrols where we would emplace guards so we could swim in the Tigris River. At one point the army literally ran out of water: that is right, ran out of water to provide to the soldiers. We were rationed to one water bottle a day but still required to patrol in one-hundred-degree weather.

I cannot express the sheer pleasure of getting into the Tigris. Although we had tried not to think of how filthy and grimy we had all become, it was hard to ignore. The simple act of letting the water wash away the dirt from my body and clothes was close to ecstasy. We could not quite get rid of the smell, but this was a good start. After swimming, we just laid in the sun as our clothes dried on us or were hung to dry. It was an incredible bonding experience. We were all sharing the extremes of living dirty and the relief that this small act gave us as individuals and as a group. We did not have laundry services until months later and that was only when we talked our Iraqi interpreter into taking our clothes home with him for his family to wash. We paid him, of course. The military did not figure out how to provide us laundry services until around our eighth month. War is stinky.

The Iraqi family laundry solution is a good illustration of how soldiers by their natures, especially the lower enlisted ranks, always find ways to improve their positions. They have a certain knack for it and tend to be the most creative and innovative people on the planet when it comes to making their lives more comfortable: I mean that with admiration and fondness.

The very first thing we did after ensuring we had security at a new site was to set things up to make our lives more tolerable. We tapped into low-hanging power lines to create sources for air-conditioning units we purchased at roadside markets. We found wood to make bathrooms, and if we were lucky made showers out of hanging water bags that were heated in the sun.

The important fact is that the improvements soldiers made were always oriented toward the group, not individual, conveniences. We developed innovative ways to make us all more comfortable. It would break social norms to focus energy on establishing comforts, such as personal air conditioning, that was not first provided to the larger group. As a leader, watching this mutual cooperation and collaboration was gratifying. It was a clear indicator of unit cohesion and, therefore, signaled the presence of one of the most important elements of effective combat performance.

Generally, soldiers ate their MREs at their positions or vehicles, either individually or taking turns as a team with their buddy, but once a day we all ate together. Food was brought to our location in insulated military containers called Mermites. Every member of the platoon filed through a serving line set up on the back of vehicles. It is military custom for the officer and senior NCO to eat last. If there was no food left when my turn came, I did not eat or I ate less. If there was plenty left, I might get a little more. Those were some of the pluses and minuses of leadership. This habit is something that many former officers cannot shake even decades later. The servers from company headquarters were usually good about having enough for everyone, even for the lieutenant. Everyone took their food back to the general platoon area and ate together.

It was during these casual meals without the pressure of being on guard against attack that I had real conversations with the members of my platoon. I talked to the four guys in my vehicle every day, all day, but this was the time I learned about how the rest of our small team felt about their months in the war zone, how they were handling the anxiety, or if they felt relatively little stress. We also yakked about fun things. We joked. We laughed. We broke down barriers without breaking down discipline. We were getting to know each other on an intimate level and bonding. This was a good time for the unit.

The large military airfield adjacent to the city of Kirkuk served at this time as the hub for most forces in the area. Kirkuk is the regional capital, about 150 miles north of Baghdad, and has a population of 850,000 people. The former Iraqi Air Force airbase was captured by coalition forces very early in the war and converted into a forward operating base (FOB, usually pronounced in one syllable) that enabled the United States to land large cargo planes and slowly flow troops, equipment, and "quality of life" items onto the facility. The buildup of the base started on day one, and given the resources of the U.S. military, progressed quickly. There was a general store, functioning swimming pool, Pizza Hut, and Burger King up and running within six months of our invasion. Talk about the American way.

We rarely visited Kirkuk from our more remote locations. Much like the frontline soldiers of World War I, World War II, Vietnam, and other wars, resentment of the comfort, safety, and luxuries of soldiers stationed in the rear is real. These soldiers are given colorful names like rear echelon motherf*ckers (REMFS) and Fobbits (from FOB). Despite the desires of frontline troops for the very comforts they mock, it is a point of extreme pride for the group to view themselves as tougher, harder, and more real than those who live in comfort in the rear. The suffering due to the living conditions was, in fact, another point of bonding. Ironically, to us anyway, its inhabitants named the base FOB Warrior. They probably did not find that as amusing as we did.

From a civilian perspective, it may seem crazy to think of a FOB as "the rear," but if thought of as a small city, approximately two square miles, the vast majority of military personnel assigned to a FOB never go out the gate. They remain in the relative safety of the FOB for their entire tour, eat at Pizza Hut and Burger King on a daily basis, and even go dancing on disco night at the Morale, Welfare, and Recreation (MRW) building. They sleep in containerized housing (picture a modified shipping container) and work at their computers in air-conditioned offices. Given their lack of interaction with anyone locally, I often wondered why many of those administrative and logistical jobs could not just be done from bases in the United States or Europe.

Surprisingly, or maybe not, many FOB personnel feel that the grass is greener—or the mud is browner—on the other side of the wire (how military personnel usually describe the walls, barriers, razor wire, or simply lines surrounding a base and establishing safe versus not safe areas). Anecdotally, a significant percentage of FOB soldiers would like to spend time off base, in more of a direct combat role. Maybe this is due to imposter syndrome, and I do not say that in a harsh or critical way at all. Many service members did not enlist to spend a year downrange doing PowerPoint. They wanted to return home safely with war stories about how they contributed to the U.S. accomplishments, how they were courageous, how they were warriors. They wanted to do what they were trained to do, not what their siblings with MBAs were doing in their corporate careers. Add to that, their FOB desk job might not be very interesting. According to a 2007 Pentagon study, "Boring and repetitive work was a main concern for 39 percent of soldiers and 33 percent of Marines."[4] Of course that includes infantrymen too.

There are risks for these troops. Some pull convoy or perimeter security duty, either by volunteering or being "voluntold." Further, the FOBs were sporadically attacked by Iraqi ground forces employing small arms direct fire. These attacks were typically repelled with comparative efficiency by the units providing base perimeter security. In most of these cases, friendly casualties were low or nonexistent. Far more often, the threat was from rocket or mortar fire from miles off base. Those attacks happened with regularity and caused casualties that were just as serious and deadly as any firefight that my platoon was engaged in. Despite our mocking, fobbits earn their combat pay, just like the rest of us.

All troops, whether out in the boonies or within the confines of the FOB, have a psychological need to feel safe. They need to be pulled back to what they view as safety in order to decompress. When soldiers—even in a FOB—live under the constant threat of rocket or mortar attack, the feeling of never being safe takes a mental toll. This has been shown in studies of wars from World War I, to Vietnam, up to today.[5] Even without being directly exposed to firefights, soldiers under constant threat of injury or stressful conditions can be greatly impacted by combat stress. Similarly there are even examples of troops who developed PTSD from hearing radio transmissions from their friends in battle even though they were listening from the security of an operations center on the FOB. So while we sort of joke about fobbits, they are still our fellow war fighters, and we recognize that they too make sacrifices.

Having said that, those of us who visited the FOB infrequently found there was valid reason to resent the cozier lives of our brothers and sisters in arms. On one visit to Kirkuk, several of us stood in line for Burger King with near-drooling anticipation of the deliciousness to come. We were covered in dirt from not showering or having a clean set of clothes in weeks, and smelled like homeless people. We were mostly oblivious to our odor and noticed only the smell of the Whoppers and fries. The people in line who were stationed on the FOB were complaining about the wait, possibly also aggravated by having to endure our scent and appearance. This struck us as absurd. Was a slow line at Burger King their version of "war is hell?" We felt immense anger at these REMFs, with their clean uniforms and soapy fragrance. We also felt a corresponding sense of proud elitism for being more warrior-like than they were. Our group was stronger than the REMFs—dirtier maybe but tenacious. Thank you, fobbits, for reminding us of that. By the way, Burger King was worth the wait. So were the showers.

While we were adapting to the unique and unpleasant living conditions, we were also still fighting while in a combat zone, patrolling everyday not really knowing what to expect but very aware we were in a war. Although we won our first battle and experienced lulls in hostile encounters, we never thought what would come next would be far more difficult. After the quick fall of the Iraqi Army, we really did not have a mission ahead of us.

We were experiencing the in-between time after defeating Saddam Hussein and before the U.S. government decided what it would do regarding the famous "Phase IV" operations (a military term meaning the post-conflict stability phase of a major operation to include transitioning all responsibilities to local authorities). This was before an insurgent force had mobilized (making this a part of pre-counterinsurgency operations) and before the U.S. government committed to help build a new Iraq, recognized now as "nation-building." Initially we mostly drove around Kirkuk attempting to stop looters and respond to people in the neighborhoods about violence in particular, even finding decapitated bodies. Disgruntled Shiites returned to houses from which they had been exiled and did so in vengeful ways. They had been forced out by the Saddam regime and its Sunni minority, which repopulated many cities, all to the advantage of Sunnis. We did not even have interpreters during this time.

This is not to say we drove around aimlessly. The military would never allow us to say that. We used colorful language like "presence patrols" or later, "intelligence gathering patrols." In reality we just drove around. It was during one of these presence patrols that an ambush occurred. It was a complex trap from concealed positions on both sides of the road, directed at the rear of our convoy.

On this patrol, I had my entire platoon: eight trucks, plus the company commander in his HMMWV in the middle of the patrol. My vehicle was in the front of the convoy; usually the leader is in the middle of a formation, but on missions like this where we did not have a set path, I liked to be in front of the convoy to make the decisions more easily regarding navigation. At this point our company had been pushed out of Kirkuk, into the hinterlands really. It was night and we were driving around the different villages just seeing what was going on. Were any people out? Was there any anti-American graffiti or pro-Baathist propaganda displayed?

We had driven through one village and then moved across a five hundred to six hundred meter rural area with farm fields on one side and woods on the other. We passed through the gap into the next village without much to report. A few old men came out to investigate the noise of our vehicles. Nothing looked out of place, so we decided to return to our temporary living spot at a chicken farm collocated with the battalion headquarters. We were passing back through that gap; as the lead vehicle I saw us approaching the next village. Next, over the radio I heard, "Contact, contact, contact." I yelled at my driver to stop and then heard large booms in the distance. Over the radio from the rear vehicles I heard, "They're firing mortars at us!" This was followed immediately by the correction, "No, it's RPGs." The enemy was using rocket-propelled grenades (RPGs) and heavy machine guns. We were surprised. We had never heard an RPG fired before. (By the way, it is a classic tactic to attack the rear of a convoy so that vehicles toward the front will be facing the wrong way and unable to help. That is what the enemy did.) My initial reaction was complete confusion.

At this point our training was supposed to kick in. The "contact, contact, contact" call was textbook, but the next call was supposed to be direction, distance, and description of the enemy, such as "3 o'clock, 100 meters, RPG and machine guns." That call did not come, so I was blind to what the hell was going on. It was a very frustrating feeling. I had screwed up. Leaders are always supposed to be in the middle so they can best see and manage the formation. I was useless at the front. I radioed back desperately trying to figure out what was going on. When I did not get an answer, I surprised myself and everyone in my vehicle, and without any thought of personal danger, I threw down the vehicle radio hand mic, opened my door, and with almost no feeling of my feet touching the ground, sprinted to the rear of the convoy, over one hundred meters. My radio-telephone operator (RTO) was especially surprised since his job was to stay as close to me as possible in case I needed to use the dismounted radio. He later said it seemed I was there in the vehicle one moment and gone the next.

The engagement was over very quickly. Only a few RPGs had been shot, followed by a little machine-gun fire. My soldiers returned fire and the attackers slinked away. When I got to the back, many of the soldiers had dismounted from the vehicles and started moving into the woods in the direction of enemy.

All firing had stopped, so I said to one of the .50 caliber gunners, "Return fire, damn it."

"Where?"

"Anywhere!"

Several minutes later there was more confusion on our end. Over the radio I heard, "Alpha 25 (one of the vehicles) has been hit. It's spewing liquids. We need to get it out of here." After a few minutes of investigation, I received the update, "Oh, it is just cans of fluid that were hit. Vehicle is fine."

When the dismounted troops returned from their pursuit of the insurgents, they found the enemy's firing point in the woods next to the road. There were four more rounds of RPGs and two belts of RPK 7.62 ammo ready to be fired. If the rear vehicles would not have responded so quickly, they might have been on the receiving end of those. I was proud of them. Most importantly, none of my soldiers were wounded in this fight. I am not sure how my thoughts of that night would have changed had someone been injured or killed.

The ambush had occurred only a few days after another difficult experience: the day the 173rd had its first fatality. An HMMWV had been hit by an RPG through the windshield. The windshield was made of ballistic glass that provided some protection against small arms but not an RPG. The glass seemed to have caused the detonation to happen on the exterior of the window, which may have saved the lives of the other soldiers in the vehicle, but the blast still continued into the face of a soldier. He raised his hand to protect his head, but that did no good. The soldier was immediately killed.

Because my platoon was the closest, we were called to pick up the body and take it to Kirkuk. This is still a very vivid memory for me because, although we did not know the casualty, the cloud of sadness of our brigade's first killed in action (KIA) was huge. As they loaded the body into our vehicle, one of the medics handed me the soldier's dog tags and asked, "Sir, what do I do with these?" That image of his outstretched hand and the dog tags of that KIA are burned in my mind forever. I had always seen dog tags as the ultimate symbol of my military service. They were the quintessential artifacts with which to identify a soldier. But from that night forward, dog tags would mean something else to me.

It is crazy how sometimes it is the small things that affect us the most. I was prepared to see enemy deaths. In basic training we had the refrain, "What makes the grass grow drill sergeant? Blood, blood, blood," which meant the blood of the enemy, and was clearly a small attempt at dehumanizing enemy death.

About a week after the ambush, another platoon in our company set up their own ambush in the same spot where we had been hit. I did not expect the enemy to be dumb enough to come back to the same spot, but sure enough three guys from the enemy came bebopping down the road and walked into a prepared ambush. The platoon tore them to shreds with all their fire power. My platoon vehicles were used to help scoop up enemy bodies and transport them. It was gruesome stuff but did not bother any of us a bit, at least as far as I could tell. In contrast, handling the dog tags of our own brigade's soldier hit me hard and still bothers me today. Weird. For the whole forty-five-minute drive to where we turned over the body of our fallen soldier, I thought about what to do with his dog tags and what to say to the medic. I ended up just repeating what the medic soldier had recently said to me. With an outstretched hand, I simply said, "I have these."

After my platoon was ambushed, our company decided to move into that area and establish a constant presence. We searched for a place big enough for our company and settled on a water treatment plant. Situated on the banks of the Tigris River, this would be our temporary home. The plant had only one building that was mostly unusable so we lived in, on, and beside our vehicles. These were the first moments in the deployment when we were able to establish a routine because it seemed that we would be there for a while.

The company was alone here, separated from our next higher unit. The battalion headquarters was a half hour away at the chicken processing plant. There was a lot of down time and all we had to do was talk with each other. It was during these times that I learned about my immediate small group.

It is said that war contains long periods of boredom punctuated by moments of sheer terror. Contrary to the well-known phenomenon of deep social bonds being formed when small primary groups of soldiers experience life or death in combat together, research suggests that strong bonds actually form through social cohesion, during the hours and hours of boredom that make up soldiering.[6] We definitely put in those hours. We ate together, slept near each other, and talked about everything from our hometowns to our bucket list for after the war.

We established a pattern of life at the water plant consisting of guard duty and patrols into the local village. When we were not on patrol, we were together. After patrols we would form into small groups and initially discuss what happened on the mission and then everything else in life. Most importantly for bonding as a team, we also often opened up about our families and friends in Italy or stateside. PVT Phipps was proud of his sister who just started college and said she inspired him to do the same when he got out of the army (and most of the soldiers intended to get out). SGT Malay worried about his father's third bout with cancer but bravely declared that Dad would beat it again. PFC Webster griped about how he was treated unfairly at the Ranger Indoctrination Program. SGT Enos confessed that he had difficulty supporting six kids, and the combat pay was helping a lot. SSG Foley was given a hard time by his squad because he did not want to get a dog that his girlfriend wanted to keep her company while he was away. He thought it signified too much of a commitment to her. "A ring is a commitment. A dog is just a walking crap machine," they teased. And so it went.

They would frequently turn to me with questions about my life and plans. It was a balancing act for me in terms of how much to share. On one hand you are the leader whose actions and orders the soldiers will follow even when their human instincts might advise them otherwise. You never know when the "attack that hill" moment will come and you need your soldiers to follow that order without hesitation. There is supposed to be a buffer between the officer and the men. You get to know them, you come to love them, but to be frank, you are not supposed to be their best friend. It makes being an officer a lonely position at times, but that distance is a necessary part of the job. Nonetheless, I came to know the soldiers in my vehicles fairly closely. We shared our stories, jokes, and struggles, all while maintaining the buffer. The same went for when I was in a larger group of my soldiers.

Make no mistake, troops can smell insincerity a mile away, so I had to be genuine. A conversation still had to be a two-way street, or I would get roadblocked in future conversations. I also had to keep in mind that we all wanted them to still view me with respect. I was not hiding anything that could lead the men to lose respect for me. I just wanted to remain somewhat of a role model for them. If I shared that my wife was miserable and angry at me, hypothetically, that might help build a bond but at the expense of a modicum of respect. How could I later give advice about their relationships if they saw my marriage as being dysfunctional? Not that it was yet, but all of us were facing challenges. I had to weigh how much of my life would be beneficial to share. A private did not have the same considerations to keep in mind.

Overall I found ways to be transparent with the men in a way that was mostly positive. I revealed how Sara and I handled the stress in a productive way, rather than sharing examples of how we fell short. If I mentioned any disagreements she and I had, it would be followed by how we were able to work them out. Sometimes the soldiers called me out good-naturedly on my sugarcoating. Occasionally they even had useful suggestions for me. I appreciated that they cared enough to want to help. I can honestly suggest one never disparage the intelligence of infantrymen; they will surprise you every time. Also never underestimate how much they are willing to help a fellow soldier, a fellow paratrooper, a fellow Red Devil.

The bonds that we developed from knowing someone as a person, rather than as a soldier with whom we bonded through a shared stressful situation were different. Both are critical. We fought to defend our friends, and friendships were being created in these moments of stress as well as during hours of boredom. The bonds created were irrelevant of rank and position. I was witnessing what Dr. Lenny Wong and others had validated in recent studies of why soldiers fight, that the hours and hours soldiers spent together out of battle was as key to their bonding as being in combat together.[7] Soldiers were becoming the type of friends Medal of Honor recipient Audie Murphy referenced in his famous justification for his suicidal charge of German positions, "because they were killing my friends."[8]

In this early part of the war we established a baseline of the 2003 system of communication and connection between us as soldiers in a unit, between the combat zone, and on the home front. I observed my own and my soldiers' connections with family, friends, and the outside world. We found ways individually and as a group to be somewhat comfortable in the midst of combat. Everything from eating, sleeping, hygiene, and recreation was done with the group in mind, or at least originally designed with that thought, and that contributed to our unit cohesion. Looking back, this time provided a picture of an ideal situation of bonding in combat, without connection with the outside world. We as soldiers got to know each other and became friends due to reliance on each other as companions and as a support network. Getting to know one another in this way is an important part of the bond (liking and trusting someone) that is needed in social cohesion.

5

I Can't Leave (Group Identity)

I never thought war would entail so much moving around, from the grassy fields in Irbil to all the different small villages. By the time we had reached our temporary home at the water treatment plant, we had already moved eleven, yes eleven, times in a matter of a few months.[1] Each move was a new adventure. The initial move and the first few places we called home were the most epic. After our one large operation near Irbil after our jump, our entire unit continued south, probably looking like a moving circus camp, with hundreds of soldiers packed into giant open-air cargo trucks with equipment strapped to any bar or panel that could hold weight.

We moved from Irbil into Kirkuk, arriving on April 11, 2003. The Iraqi military guarding the city had faded away just a day or so before as a much superior force of Peshmerga fighters accompanied by U.S. Special Forces teams advanced toward the city. Kirkuk had a population of over half a million in 2003 and has grown since then to about a million by 2020. It was in this area, which back in time, Alexander the Great decisively defeated the last king of the Persian Empire, Darius III, at the Battle of the Persian Gates in 330 BC. The city had been mostly spared from the destruction of combat operations as far as we could see, outside of a few craters that once served as checkpoints into the city.

Driving into Kirkuk, we went straight into a former Iraqi Air Force Base called K1 on the northwestern edge of the city. As soon as we parked our trucks, we were assigned positions to guard. My platoon got the front gate, which was fine, as that allowed us to witness and even talk briefly to a pack of paramilitary operators who were looking for one of the special forces teams that had entered the city before us. (We assumed they were paramilitary operators, based on the mix of males and females in the group along with the extremely advanced equipment they wore.) One of the critical components of being in the military is esprit de corps or, or in plain terms, a belief of value and pride in your organization. A key component of building that sense of self- and collective-worth is a belief that your group is better than other groups—not in a condescending way of course but as a healthy rivalry. In the military there is a well-established hierarchy of who is considered the best, the most lethal warriors. That hierarchy does not shame any other group, but in the mind of each soldier it does establish a place. At the top of the list are the different units within the U.S. Special Forces (Green Berets), Ranger Regiment, and other special organizations, while toward the bottom are regular U.S. Army infantry soldiers. As the 173rd Airborne Infantry, we considered ourselves in the middle. So when this group of paramilitary operators showed up, we were not star struck but respectful.

If we were not guarding something, we were exploring. This was the first real Iraqi place where we had an opportunity to investigate. Our previous stops were literally in open fields (usually of mud, dirt, and sand). Being on this post felt like a real "you-are-not-in-Kansas-anymore" moment. It gave us a feeling of landing on an alien planet. As the invasion force, we were cognizant that we were the first American soldiers to have been in these areas. We were the first Americans that many of the Iraqi citizens had ever seen other than on TV. Everything was new and very different. We explored the numerous bunkers littered around our assigned area. Each one was like a time capsule. Food had been left on heating stands, and clothes and equipment were hanging or laying on beds ready to be used. There were command bunkers with maps and fully operational radios. The Iraqi military had literally dropped everything and had walked or ran away.

The taking of war trophies is strictly illegal, but to be completely honest, much of the exploring we did was looking for cool things left behind by the fleeing Iraqi military. We found Iraqi flags, posters of Saddam Hussein, AK-47 knives, and military clothing. My platoon sergeant and I each found pristine Iraqi military helmets that we wrote on with all the names of our soldiers and later mailed home.

We were only at K1 for around thirty-six hours before we were told to pack up and move about four miles northwest to the city's main airfield, the Kirkuk Regional Air Base, that would later become a major operating base for all U.S. military forces in the area, and even later the spot of the Burger King incident. The move made immediate sense, as the air base was much larger and had a massive runway that would support the goliath U.S. Air Force cargo planes that would immediately start arriving to bring in all the necessary equipment, supplies, and people to convert an old rundown civilian airport into a little slice of U.S. military power.

Our initial mission after the fall of the Saddam Hussein regime was to prevent mass civil chaos. We patrolled the streets of Kirkuk on our "presence patrols." It was like we were saying, "The U.S. military is here." We were there for sure—driving around without interpreters, unable to talk to anyone, and having no clue what to look for other than if we saw someone doing something bad. That was our attempt to maintain order. At times it felt like we were just the outlaws riding into town in a western movie, causing the townspeople to barely escape inside until we left.

We were also sent on daily missions to establish and run water and propane cooking gas distribution sites. These usually turned into scary riots as we attempted to maintain orderly lines that would turn into flash mobs with us scrambling out of the area whether we were done handing out the goods or not. It was in part our fault. We would arrive in an area with the goods, try to set out wire to surround ourselves and the trucks with the supplies while gesturing to the civilians to form lines, enter at one point, and exit at another. But the civilians knew the supplies were limited and it was a first come, first serve situation. They refused to stay in lines, pushing people into the wire, forming into a mob, yelling at each other and eventually at us. We later got better at passing out materiel—more on-the-job training again—but it was always scary stuff.

As the post-conflict chaos increased due to the local police and other government agencies no longer bothering to go to work, my unit pushed out of the airfield and moved into an old Ba'ath head-quarters building in the city. One of the daily stops on our patrols was a concrete factory not far from our new home. Set a couple miles outside of the city, the factory covered about fifty acres and was very machinery intensive, like any concrete plant in America. It featured many multistory structures, pipes, conveyor belts, smoke-stacks, vertical storage tanks, and the remnants of large piles of sand, gravel, crushed rock, and cement. The ground between the build-ings was unpaved, just dirt etched with the tracks of large trucks. The place still smelled like a factory, although it was no longer oper-ational because of the war.

At this point in Iraq, looting was rampant. The Iraqi citizens were looting everything, and I mean everything. The real booty from the stores, banks, and office buildings was gone within hours of the Iraqi military and other security force walking off the job those first few days of April. Looters then transitioned to pillaging the buildings by stripping the copper wires, then all wires, pipes, and eventually the bricks. Clearly the immediate short-term need to feed their families took precedence over the long-term needs of having a functional society and economy after the hostilities. This set the stage for what happened at the concrete factory.

Large groups of Iraqis converged on the concrete factory each day with heavy-duty tools, donkey-pulled carts, and wheelbarrows. Like a band of hyenas taking apart a dead elephant, the factory was dismantled a little at a time. By the time we first saw the facility, it was already severely picked apart, with only the framing struc-tures left to be deconstructed. No machinery, electrical infrastruc-ture, plumbing, raw material, or supplies remained. A few cranes remained that were just too big to move, I guess.

Our task was pretty futile, like trying to save a sandcastle on the beach as the tide is rising. When we would show up, groups of ten to twenty looters would scatter in all directions. If we caught someone, we usually threatened jail, dumped their loot, and let them go. They would return to finish the job as soon as we left, but we had to at least try to restore order. It never got violent, nor was it meant to.

On one of the visits to the factory, our patrol entered as usual, and the routine group of looters immediately took off running. I was not with the platoon this time. Our platoon often had multiple patrols out at a time so we split who was with which element. This patrol consisted of the platoon sergeant with his vehicles and two other trucks with a dismount squad in the back. The platoon sergeant's HMMWV always consisted of our platoon medic and his driver. Our medic was SPC Cory McCarthy. Infantry platoons almost always include a platoon medic. These soldiers are not doctors. Nonetheless, they are highly trained. They are more like a combat emergency medical technician (EMT) than doctors. But we almost always refer to them as Doc.

The platoon medics serve not only as the emergency care for wounded soldiers, they also care for the health of the platoon members on a daily basis. The competence of each platoon medic varies, but in my experience they take great pride in caring for their platoon, and in turn, the platoon highly values them. These platoon medics also vary in their bedside manner. Doc McCarthy was no-nonsense. When we stopped during a foot march, Doc would come by and demand to see each person's feet, whether they wanted to show him or not. Rank did not matter. He'd say, "Let me see them, Sir," or "Take this pill [our weekly antimalarial meds we had to take in Iraq] now, Sir." Our love for Doc was a great example of that brotherly love that develops when you know someone cares about you and you care about them.

When the looters started running, the squad of nine men gave chase on foot. The Iraqis were not burdened down with gear, so they were getting away. Out of nowhere, one of the soldiers giving chase, SPC Ewell, took a knee, trained his rifle at one of the looters, and shot the looter in the back. The looter fell to the ground screaming. The squad stood motionless in shock over what had just happened. They just stood there staring at Ewell in disbelief. The dead silence was broken only by a scream of "medic!" as the sergeants in the squad jumped into action and began administering first aid to the now-wounded civilian. Luckily Doc McCarthy was there. He applied pressure dressings to the gunshot. He also let his emotions fly: "Why the f*ck did you do that you motherf*cker? Get the vehicle, NOW, you stupid sh*t. This dude is dying." The civilian was put into one of our vehicles and raced back to the main airfield in Kirkuk where our main aid station was set up.

Ewell's action was completely uncalled for, unjustified, and irrational. His squad members were not only shocked at what he did but they were also pissed. Ewell initially protested that he was fed up with the looters getting away every day, but that was not the point. This is not what we, as Americans, do. We are the good guys. We do not shoot unarmed civilians, especially those fleeing, who pose us no threat. Not only was it against the laws of armed conflict, this was against the values, norms, and ethics of being an American soldier, of being a part of our unit.

His squad leader brought Ewell to me and reported what had happened. By the time Ewell got to me, his story had changed. Now he said he was just firing a warning shot, something we were also not allowed to do. Then he said he thought he saw a weapon in the looter's hand and invoked the right to self-protection that we give all soldiers. I said, "Which is it, Ewell, were you firing a warning shot or did you see a weapon?" He settled on believing he saw a weapon.

In my officer leadership training, there were classes on war crimes, ethics, and military justice. I remembered, vividly, sitting through multiple classes just about the 1968 My Lai Massacre. On March 16, 1968, a group of American soldiers entered the village of My Lai, Vietnam, and brutally murdered over five hundred unarmed civilians, including women and children.[2] The My Lai Massacre was one of the most horrific and vulgar acts of violence committed against unarmed civilians in modern American history and now serves as one of the most in-your-face lessons on what it means to be in the profession of arms. It is used to teach the importance of the laws of war, code of conduct, ethics, and more. Despite that training, I never actually expected to be faced with the situation of one of my troops shooting an unarmed civilian. It was more of a theoretical, academic concept, especially in contrast to subjects like tactics, weapon training, and troop leadership. Yet here it was.

You might think that given everything I have said about unit cohesion and being willing to die for one's fellow soldiers, that the other soldiers present—Ewell's friends and squad mates—would circle the wagons in defense of him, regardless of his guilt or innocence. That is how these situations are portrayed in movies and TV shows. The few historical examples I knew of pointed toward soldiers standing behind their fellow team member who had committed the crime. Based on these limited data points, I expected the soldiers to cover for Ewell. To my surprise, from my first questions to the soldiers, I was relieved that they showed no thought of concocting a story to protect their battle buddy or of following Ewell's story that they viewed as preposterous. They made me proud with their integrity and values. During the official investigation of the event, I saw the shooter's entire squad turn their backs on him. They reported his action as something that was not accepted in "their" squad. Each of his fellow squad members told the investigating officer how abnormal Ewell's actions were to the group, how upset they were with him for his decision. They valued their primary group, their squad as a whole, over blind loyalty to an individual.

So cohesion not only bonds individual soldiers to each other, ideally to the point they are willing to fight and die for each other, but this unity also creates a group identity. Being a member of the group becomes something of significant value to the individual soldier. The group also establishes norms or rules to dictate proper behavior both on and off the battlefield. This establishment of group norms is a practice that has been seen during all wars, although the mores vary nation by nation due to underlying cultural differences. The norms shape the group construct of what is right and wrong. These rules are established by actions more than words. Research has validated it throughout history; the Duke of Wellington's soldiers in the Peninsular Campaign of the Napoleonic Wars formed mess groups that maintained small cadres and regimental norms.[3] Soldiers who showed cowardice on the battlefield were cast out of the mess group and faced starvation as they had to fend for themselves.

The establishment of group norms can be a double-edged sword, though. Ideally, group identity and norms are created in cohesive small groups that are in line with the moral, ethical, and legal guidelines for military forces in combat. But in worst-case scenarios, when other elements of the group's overall military system are missing, such as the command and disciplinary systems, harmful group norms can be established. A modern example of this is the squad of American soldiers from the 5th Stryker Brigade deployed to Afghanistan in 2010 that over months developed schemes to kill unarmed Afghan civilians. Under the support and guidance of their squad leader, SSG Calvin Gibbs, the squad used drugs, killed civilians, and even kept body parts of their victims as trophies.[4] This is an extreme case, of course, but a real example of what can happen if group norms that do not align with army values are allowed to exist.

SPC Ewell had broken his squad's norms of acceptable behavior. He had brought shame upon his squad and our platoon. His actions were disgraceful and illegal, and the other men were quick to prove he was alone in that disgrace. He had betrayed the unit by behaving without honor. He had, in fact, made it harder for us to work with the Iraqi populace and had made it more dangerous for all of us. While he did not face starvation, he did face punishment under the Uniform Code of Military Justice (UCMJ), the military justice system that punishes criminal offenses under military law. The UCMJ is another vital part of the overall military system running in the background of everyday combat life. Just like the criminal codes of any society, it guides individual actions, shapes values, and changes with the times.

Our chain of command wasted no time in responding to Ewell's actions. An investigation was started the same day. Every soldier who witnessed the event was interviewed. Even I was questioned. I was not there, but that did not matter. I was responsible. Had I allowed warning shots to happen on other patrols? Had I allowed a climate of not following the laws of war or other rules to be disobeyed? In the end, SPC Ewell was not punished. We were all shocked as we expected him to be taken away, thrown in prison, and never heard from again. I did not get to see the findings of the investigation or the investigating officer's recommendation to the chain of command. But with Ewell's final defense settling on his belief that he saw a weapon and for other reasons, the battalion commander had weighed the risk of what punishing a soldier for shooting at someone he thought was armed against punishing the soldier for unlawful actions. Punishing a soldier for shooting at someone he thought was armed could send a message to other soldiers who would then possibly be scared to shoot when faced with an armed enemy. On the other hand, any blatant violation of our rules of engagement had to be rapidly punished to deter others from doing wrong. It was clearly not an easy decision. It did not matter; from then on, Ewell's every move was scrutinized. He had demonstrated that under stress he could not be trusted.

Another aspect of soldiers' commitment to their unit involves their responses to getting injured. You might expect that an injury is a golden ticket to get out of the war zone and return to the safety of home. The exact opposite is true. History is full of stories of soldiers putting aside their personal injuries, refusing treatment so they could stay with or get back to their small group, their unit, their "family" in the war zone, including that of Special Forces CPT Robert "Chip" Eldridge, who was severely injured after his vehicle was hit by an antitank mine in Shkin, Afghanistan. Eldridge sustained an eye injury and extensive damage to both legs, including multiple fractures and a shattered ankle. A large piece of his leg bone was found on his vehicle's floor. Despite his life-threatening injuries, he refused treatment or painkillers from his team medic, who had been driving the vehicle, so that he could remain coherent while continuing to lead his unit. In the hospital, Eldridge's leg was amputated, yet he disregarded all his treatment plans and tripled his daily physical therapy regime, working out several hours a day so he could make it back to his unit in under six months rather than the doctor-directed twelve months.[5]

This phenomenon really was the most amazing thing to see in person. Every single one of my soldiers who were injured were only interested in staying with the platoon or getting fixed quickly to get back. I cannot tell you how many times I heard, "I am good, sir, really," or "I do not want to leave." I get it. I would have felt the same way in their shoes. As much as war is hell, leaving war before your buddies do is a far deeper level of Hades. This is a common story written in books and highlighted in movies. Men become so bonded with their fellow soldiers that they will escape from a hospital and make their way back to their units. I do not know if civilians can relate when they see these scenes in films, but it's a 100 percent accurate and honest depiction of a combat reality. I would see this in multiple situations.

Early in this deployment one of my soldiers received a message from the Red Cross that his grandmother had died. Families can contact soldiers quickly through the American Red Cross in case of personal emergency. The Red Cross then does all the work to go through the many levels of military bureaucracy to get the emergency message to that exact soldier. It is really an impressive system. The speed of the message can be as fast as less than a day. When my soldier received his Red Cross message all he wanted to do was to make a phone call home, not leave. His family may not have understood, but his battle buddies did. That was far more important. He could explain it to his family when the entire unit redeployed. In the meantime, to him, his unit needed him more.

On August 11, 2003, we struck our first improvised explosive device (IED). There were many more to come, but this was the first. We were escorting an Iraqi informant to a small village not far from our base to identify the house of a former high-ranking Ba'ath party member who was suspected of financing attacks on coalition forces.

We were in a five-vehicle convoy, with half my platoon and the company commander and his vehicle in the middle. As I mentioned before, most of the HMMWVs we drove during this time had open backs where soldiers sat, totally exposed. While crossing a bridge and large open rural area along our route, a 155mm artillery round buried next to the road was remotely command detonated. This means the bomb had a wire running out of it and we later determined someone had to be standing close by, pushing a button to initiate it. The bomb exploded no more than five meters from the rear vehicle. I happened to be looking in my passenger side view mirror and saw the explosion that engulfed our rear vehicle. I could not believe what I was seeing. It was like I was watching a movie without understanding what I was watching: I saw a large white explosion, then lots of red and orange. Time stopped and the colors were so vibrant that they were surreal. It is still etched in my mind many years later.

The rear vehicle had stopped in the road. I ordered the rest of the convoy to stop and I ran back to the vehicle to see who was hurt or dead. Gunners on top of the other vehicles were firing their machine guns at suspected enemy locations. I was proud of their immediate response, but realized this was the beginning of a faceless enemy. Unlike the earlier ambush, which was up close and personal, we knew this was a trap set by unseen enemies who did not stand to fight, meaning we could not fight back.

When I got to the vehicle that had been hit, I saw what I had feared. Shrapnel from the bomb had ripped through the back of the rear vehicle. The whole group had been rocked by the concussion, with three soldiers hit by the shrapnel. The most seriously injured was our medic, Doc McCarthy—the one soldier you especially do not want to lose in battle. The shrapnel had sheered the forward assist charging handle and most of the butt stock from his weapon. More significantly, a large piece of shrapnel had cut off his thumb, which hung by a sliver of skin. Blood was spewing steadily from his hand, but his calm tone was almost even more startling. Doc looked at me and said calmly, "I have arterial bleeding, you need to get me out of here immediately." From his medical experience, he knew he was in danger of losing blood too fast and could die if he did not get medical attention very soon.

There were two other people down in the back of the truck who had also been hit by the shrapnel. The gunner, SPC Keller, had taken it in the back, but luckily his plate of body armor had taken most of it, all but two slivers—one in his neck and another in the hip right below his belt line. If he had not been wearing his vest, he surely would have died. A rifleman, PFC Murphy, also caught a few pieces of shrapnel. He would need patching up but was in no immediate danger. Amazingly, Doc maintained his composure and coached other soldiers on applying a pressure dressing to his hand. I ran back to my vehicle as fast as I could and signaled for the convoy to drive forward out of the kill zone. Once clear, we stopped to establish security.

When we radioed for a medical helicopter extraction, what is called a 9-line medical evacuation (MEDEVAC) request, we were told that the ambulance exchange point was back in the direction we had come. We would have to drive back through the ambush area, not something any of us were really excited to do. I ran to the commanding officer's (CO) vehicle and gave him the minimal information: number and severity of casualties and the need to move back to the exchange point. He had been on the radio and was tracking everything and just said, "Roger, go."

We turned the convoy around, my vehicle again in the lead, and drove back across the bridge. Gunners were firing at both sides of the road as we went, and we drove fast, as fast as the HMMWVs could go. At almost the exact same point where the IED had exploded, BOOM! I saw another explosion in my side mirror. What the f*ck? Another IED? It was the CO's vehicle. This time it was not a bright flash like before but more of a dust cloud. I radioed, "CO's vehicle hit." We all slowed, but the CO came across the radio, "Keep driving, keep driving," so we sped on and quickly left the area. The CO's vehicle limped on, slowing us down a little, but we reached the ambulance exchange point in less than ten minutes.

We formed a security perimeter with our vehicles, putting the vehicle with all our casualties and the CO's HMMWVs in the middle. We could see the helicopter approaching; both Keller and Murphy

I Can't Leave

pleaded with me that they were okay and did not need to be evacuated. I had to order them to board the helicopter because their shrapnel would have to be dug out, and during this stage of combat operations in Iraq, such surgical procedures could only be conducted in a few places in all of Iraq. All three soldiers were actually evacuated either back to military hospitals in Germany or, in the case of Doc, to the United States. None of them were able to return before we ended our combat tour, but I am sure they tried.

After the ambulance helicopter flew off, I looked at the CO's vehicle. One of the tires was severely damaged, so they had needed to drive it on its shredded remains. Now that the wounded were safely on their way to care, I ordered our patrol to return to where we had been attacked to clear it and investigate what had happened. In the middle of the road were the remnants of the 155mm IED, with a wire leading over three hundred meters to the nearby woods—so the enemy had command detonated it from there. Fortunately the explosion was only a low-order detonation, that is, it did not go off as designed. Most of the 155mm round had stayed intact, really just splitting like a banana and only spraying some of its skin as shrapnel into Doc and the others. Had it adequately exploded, the damage to the soldiers sitting in the open vehicle would have been much, much worse. The second explosion was apparently caused by the CO's vehicle running over what remained of the 155mm round. We really got lucky that time.

Chance is what we call "Murphy" in the military, knowing it always plays into combat operations. That was definitely the case in another incident. One night we were running supplies to one of the other platoons and patrolling the main highway that got us there. Once we got to the other platoon and dropped off the supplies, one of vehicles would not start. I called headquarters and requested that the battalion mechanics be sent to assist—a normal procedure. I was told that I would have to drive back to our base to get them because there was no other patrol that could escort them to me. The mechanics in this case meant a single vehicle with a lot of tools and two highly motivated soldiers with amazing expertise, but they could not travel around by themselves. "Shit, this is going to be a long night," I thought.

I told my platoon what we needed to do, and we began to drive back to base to pick up the mechanics. About halfway back one of our vehicles got a flat tire. This is not easy to do with a HMMWV whose tires are made of thick tread and lined with a run-flat designed to make the tires keep rolling even if shot full of bullets. But we were driving our vehicles everyday, all day, so the tread eventually wore down and weakened. I told the guys in that vehicle to hurry up and change it. It was not long before they reported that not only was their tire jack not working, we did not have a working tire jack in any of the vehicles. It was at about this moment that I had an eerie feeling about what was happening. I have only gotten this feeling a few times in combat. I had that gut feeling that something was not right. I felt something like a subconscious warning to change course or that something bad was going to happen. There was nothing I could do about it, but it loomed over me like a dark cloud. I called back to headquarters and explained the situation. I was sure I would get an earful from the company commander once I got back.

The commander put together a patrol to bring the mechanics to me. It must have been 0100 hours by the time the mechanics had changed our flat and we were ready to move. At that point we needed to turn around on the highway to head back to where our other vehicle was broken down. We drove at night with no lights, using only our night vision goggles. The less the moon is out (providing ambient light), the less the night vision goggles help. This was an extra dark night, with no moon or stars. I remember my driver, SPC May, asking my gunner, PFC Butler, if it was clear. The gunner on top of the vehicle always had the best view. The last thing I remember was Butler's "Yeah, it's good." As we began our turn, BAM! Our HMMWV was T-boned by a civilian van that was driving on the highway at over sixty MPH with its headlights off. I have no idea why. We were slammed into on the driver's side.

The carnage was gruesome. Five Iraqis in the van dead, others severely wounded. SGT Wood, my forward observer, and May were on the driver's side and were really messed up—metal from the vehicle's sides went through their legs. I was knocked unconscious for a moment. When I woke up, my helmet and glasses were off, and all the debris from our vehicle and ammo cans were lying on top of me. Our interpreter in the seat behind me was silent. I did not know where the gunner was. Our entire heavy machine gun on the top of the vehicle was sheared off. By some crazy bit of luck, the gunner was okay, but he had been thrown out of the vehicle. The interpreter was also miraculously uninjured. If we had not been in the up-armored M114 and instead in one of the less protected M998s, we would have all been dead, although the Iraqis might have fared slightly better.

As my head cleared, I saw that other soldiers were trying to get May and Wood out of the vehicle. Others were radioing for an air MEDEVAC. I checked on May and all he wanted to talk about was that he was okay and did not want to be sent home; he did not want to leave the platoon. He had metal pieces of the HMMWV sticking out of his leg and who knew what kind of unseen injuries elsewhere. But his only concern was that he not be forced to leave the platoon, just like the soldiers involved in the IED attack before him. Interestingly, May was from a relatively wealthy family with a number of celebrity connections. His heart, though, was with his fellow soldiers, regardless of their backgrounds. These responses and other selfless acts continued to amaze me, no matter how many times I witnessed them. Loyalty to their friends and their platoon was stronger than their concern for their own well-being.

The next day, those of us who could walk were back out on patrol, despite one entire side of my body being covered in a nice purple bruise, from my shoulder to my calf. If we were not evacuated, we were still on the clock, and honestly, it's the only way we would have it.

When the battalion lost the first soldier I actually knew personally, it shook me pretty hard. It was my friend, 1LT David Bernstein, who had taught me about our vehicles when we were back in Vicenza. He and another soldier were killed in October 2003. It was October, so things in Iraq had somewhat slowed down, except for the IEDs, mortars into the outposts, and civil disturbances. Our battalion commander's convoy had been ambushed the previous month and he had taken a round to the leg that required him to be evacuated back to the United States. We had a new battalion commander, but other than that, the days went on as usual. Most days we patrolled, interacted with the community, returned to base, and repeated that routine the next day. It was pretty quiet and I was starting to feel a little comfortable. Yes we were still at war and the risk was always present, but we were doing okay and I was hoping we might get out of there without any more serious losses.

On October 18 we heard a call on the battalion command net of troops in contact. One of the platoons in the battalion was being ambushed and needed help badly. The radio traffic really picked up. The contact was easily twenty miles from us, out of our company sector, but just like almost everyone in the battalion, we were listening in. A few minutes later I was told by my company commander to move to the ambush site and be prepared to fight. My platoon was being tasked to support the battalion in any way we could, just get there. We rushed to the site. My company commander told me to switch my radios to another company's frequency and take commands from them as they were directing the response. That other commander instructed me to form a blocking position outside of the ambush site to prevent any enemy forces from escaping. We headed to that location as quickly as we could, but we did not realize that we had been called after the event. We did not know it yet, but by the time we got there, the massive firefight was over and the two soldiers had already been evacuated. At one point a convoy came from the direction of the attack. They stopped and I talked to the lieutenant who was with them. He told me that it was 1LT David Bernstein and that his convoy had been surprised. He then recounted the story, some more of which I learned later.

Bernstein, who was the Charlie Company executive officer, was traveling in the last of a three-vehicle convoy returning to post when the site came under rocket attack. His convoy was closest to the location from where the unit believed the rocket had originated.

He was directed to intercept the attackers. As they approached the location of the rocket launchers, they were attacked by machine-gun and RPG fire. The driver of Bernstein's HMMWV lost control and crashed into a berm, becoming separated from the other two vehicles. The gunner PFC John Hart was killed by enemy fire. The driver SPC Joshua Sams was thrown out of the vehicle and became trapped under the wheel when the vehicle stopped on top of him. Bernstein jumped out and returned fire at the attackers; he was hit in the upper thigh by a bullet, severing his femoral artery. He continued to crawl around to the driver's side of the vehicle and attempted five times to get to the vehicle's steering wheel and gas pedal to get the vehicle off of Sams. He was finally able to move the vehicle off Sams and then Bernstein pulled him out from underneath. With this final selfless act, Bernstein collapsed from loss of blood. By then the other two vehicles were able to return, and the enemy retreated. The other soldiers did what they could to stop the bleeding. A MEDEVAC helicopter was called in, but 1LT Bernstein never regained consciousness and was pronounced dead at the hospital.[6]

Bernstein received a posthumous Silver Star and was buried at West Point, his alma mater, with full military honors. At the funeral, his former platoon SFC Frank Lauer paid tribute to Bernstein in a eulogy, "Greater love hath no man than this, than a man who lays down his life for his friends.—John 15:13. . . . All infantry soldiers have Lieutenants, but how many of them are proud to say, 'That's my Platoon Leader'? I can tell you no matter what time of day, no matter how tired the platoon was from a twelve-mile road march, a pool PT session that was more like drowning PT, or from an all night mission in Iraq . . . the soldiers of 2nd Platoon Bravo Company were always proud when they said, 'That's my Platoon Leader.'"[7] In 2004 we dedicated a FOB to Bernstein—the former Iraqi Tuz Khurmatu Airbase that became home to several hundred 25th Infantry Division soldiers—and called it FOB Bernstein.

1LT Bernstein exemplified the band of brothers principle in real life as a leader so bonded to his men that he gave his life saving one of them. It truly shook me and my soldiers that we did not reach him in time to help. We lost a few people on that deployment. There were fortunately no KIAs in my platoon, although we had a lot of wounded soldiers: the three evacuated after that first IED, those injured in the car wreck, and another IED later, which was smaller so that no evacuation was needed. It was a painful time for all of us. I lost a good friend, and everyone in the platoon was emotionally impacted by the event. We lost other friends to their wounds too when they had to be evacuated and were not able to return as they so desperately wanted.

To me, one of the key elements in these stories is how the soldiers did not focus on their own injuries but rather on their fellow soldiers. Doc McCarthy continued to advise the others on first aid for himself and the other two injured troops until they reached the MEDEVAC helicopter. His actions clearly reduced injuries that could have turned life threatening for him and the others. Doc would ultimately lose his thumb entirely, but that was far better than it could have been. SPC May and SGT Wood wanted nothing more than to ignore their wounds and stay with their fellow soldiers, their friends. And 1LT David Bernstein valorously gave his life trying to save another soldier. Witnessing these acts of selfless service was a real-life experience of the band of brothers phenomenon. Without this, war becomes an individual experience rather than a group journey. Cohesion not only motivates soldiers to fight but creates a new self-identity for each soldier who is a group member. Each soldier views his self-worth in part as being a member of the group. They will accomplish great feats and provide acts of selfless service for the other members of the group, to continue to do their part in the group, and ultimately to remain in the cadre. The collective defines their identity. They value each other above all else.

6

A Different Army and a Different War

The U.S. Army of 2003 and the U.S. Army of 2008 were as different as night and day. In 2004 when the first units arrived to replace those of us who had invaded Iraq to take down the Saddam Hussein regime, the army had transitioned from an invading force into a counterinsurgent/nation-building force. By the end of 2006, the war in Iraq seemed lost. A major report showed that the new Iraqi government was failing and the country was on the verge of civil war.[1] At the beginning of 2007, President George W. Bush announced a controversial plan to increase the number of U.S. troops in Iraq by more than twenty thousand, an effort that became known as the "surge."[2] That year proved to be the deadliest year for U.S. forces since 2004. The surge required the army to not only send more troops to Iraq but to increase its numbers overall to support the rotation of troops to two war zones, maintaining over 20,000 troops in Afghanistan and over 130,000 deployed to Iraq.[3] In as early as 2006, the army started to miss its recruitment goals, attempting to recruit and in-process 80,000 soldiers but only able to get 70,000.[4]

In reaction, the army was forced to implement multiple policy changes to bring people into the army. These changes included providing waivers to enlist high school dropouts, felons, people who were overweight or had medical or mental health issues, and many others normally not qualified. The army also increased the length of combat deployments from twelve to fifteen months.

The army also had to implement a controversial military policy known as "stop-loss," or what many of us would later call the "back door draft." Stop-loss meant that tens of thousands of soldiers who had voluntarily enlisted in the army for two to six years were then forced to stay in the army and deploy to combat, usually for a second or third time, even after their contracted time was up. The army "stopped" any soldiers from getting out of the military because they could not recruit or keep the bare minimum number of soldiers they needed to fight the wars in Afghanistan and Iraq. The U.S. Army had broken what could be deemed a psychological agreement with the soldiers—a pact that they could enlist, do their time, and get out. The trust between those soldiers and the institution of the army was immediately broken. It is easy to imagine that a large group of soldiers forced to stay in the military and forced to redeploy—some for multiple years for the goal of nation-building—would struggle in achieving that goal. In other words, they struggled to build task or social cohesion over and over again. How do you believe in a mission or have a positive attitude about your job and fellow soldiers when you are forced to deploy to do a job against your will? The answer is as complex as how and why soldiers are willing to face the dangers of combat.

The U.S. government's difficulty in assembling a fully volunteer force dates back to 1973, when the United States eliminated the draft and transitioned to an all-volunteer system. The major assumption undergirding that move was a belief that Americans would volunteer for military service when national security was at risk. The drawn-out wars of Afghanistan and Iraq proved that assumption incorrect.[5] Even in the beginning of the transition from a draft military to a volunteer one, there were voices of concern. Crawford H. Greenewalt, a member of President Nixon's 1969 Commission on an All-Volunteer Armed Force, wrote to its chairman stating, "While there is a reasonable possibility that a peacetime armed force could be entirely voluntary, I am certain that an armed force involved in a major conflict could not be voluntary."[6]

Catering to an individual soldier's motivation to enlist, stay in, and serve in combat is not new, but the shift from a draft to an all-volunteer army forced the military to deal with the demands of retaining eligible, willing, and quality volunteers, and to making military life more appealing on a scale unlike any in the past. As I saw in 2008, there were reverberating effects from catering to individual motivations.

Much of the thinking about quality of life issues for individual soldiers evolved with the change to an all-volunteer army, where the soldiers' morale, welfare, and comfort factored into their desire to stay in the military. The Better Opportunities for Single Soldiers (BOSS) Program was established in 1989 with the mission of enhancing the morale and welfare of unmarried soldiers, increasing retention, and sustaining combat readiness. One of the wins for the program was converting barracks into single-person living spaces more akin to dorm rooms. Across the U.S. Army, soldiers now live in two-person suites that include doors to their individual rooms. They share only a common kitchen area. This consideration of individual space and personal freedom has become an important goal for military personnel.

These changes happened with little research into the effects they would have on unit performance in combat, and stem from the military's long history of often doing things without really knowing why. This issue of lodging is an example. In training, military billeting is always group style, in big open bays filled with bunk beds.

Research shows that proximity, or physical distance, directly affects the likelihood of establishing a connection with someone. Proximity is desirable for building cohesive teams.[7] People who live together or near each other are most likely to befriend or "click" with one another. It seems to make logical sense. The army may not have known about such research, but it had been shoving soldiers together for a long time. The term "barracks" brings to mind large rooms filled with soldiers in bunk beds stacked two high at very close proximity. Based on multiple factors, the army decided that individual spaces are best for soldiers.

Then came prolonged combat. When the Iraq War changed from a narrowly focused combat mission to a long-term nation-building project, the increase in the number of bases in Iraq started and never stopped. The military attempted to make soldiers as comfortable as possible by providing them with many of the luxuries they were used to at home. Because the American military has enormous resources, it was able to mobilize an enormous amount of personnel, equipment, and building supplies to create "homes away from home."

There are clearly positive benefits from increasing the quality of life for combat soldiers. Recent research conducted by Leonard Wong and Stephen Gerras, titled "CU @ the FOB: How the Forward Operating Base Is Changing the Life of Combat Soldiers," explores the advantages achieved by providing secure posts fully equipped with the modern luxuries of home. These large installations provide soldiers with an escape from the constant danger of combat, minimize the wearing effects of hunger and fatigue normally present in continuous combat operations, and reduce the isolation of combat.[8] These advantages have been shown to reduce the factors of psychological stress commonly found in forward-deployed combat soldiers during past wars.[9]

Yet fully equipped home-like bases also come with negative effects. Advancements in cellular service and access to the internet and social media brought something of a new "hyperconnection" for soldiers in combat. Soldiers can maintain daily contact with the family, friends, and communities back home. This new and unprecedented connectivity between soldiers and their loved ones has shifted the family from an abstract to a concrete concept in the minds of deployed soldiers.[10] Soldiers thus have a foot in the deployed world when outside the wire and a foot back home to deal with the problems, stresses, and worries of day-to-day family life when they return to their base. This creates a very real competition between family life and combat life for the soldier's time, commitment, loyalty, and energy.

Staying connected to family and friends, however, may make combat deployments easier on soldiers and their families, especially when living separated for extended periods. It allows soldiers to be a part of their families' daily lives. The days of sitting down to write letters to reflect on their experiences and frame their environment and feelings, with the added delay in information from the front to home, are gone. But staying linked with the outside world also means the soldier may not be as in tune with his combat community. These external connections provide soldiers with social support networks as opposed to the small group of fellow soldiers whose bonds are viewed by scholars and soldiers alike to be vital to effective combat performance. Soldiers now talk to each other less, especially about their shared experiences from the patrols and missions, and instead fill their hours of boredom with Facebook updates, real-time messaging, and phone calls home. Ultimately, because this level of connectivity has never been available before, there is very little research regarding its impact on social cohesion and combat performance. I saw this firsthand when I transitioned into this new world of combat, where the lines between war and home are almost always open.

In early 2007, 3rd Brigade, 4th Infantry Division based in Fort Carson, Colorado, was preparing for an Iraq deployment. For the previous four years, the brigade had been in repeated cycles of twelve to fifteen months in Iraq followed by twelve months out of Iraq, returning home and coming back to do it again. When the brigade then received an early deployment date to support the Iraq "surge," many leaders wondered what would happen if they were unable to reach their required troop strength. The 3rd Brigade was one of the last of the surge brigades sent to the Baghdad area under what was called the Baghdad Security Plan.

To reach 90 percent end strength, the brigade commander, COL John Hort, directed the deployment of many soldiers classified as "non-deployable" or not fit for duty (e.g., physical and mental health profiles, recent drug offenders, DUI cases, etc.). Soldiers felt there was a culture that "all must go." In a local newspaper article, "*Official: Troops OK in Noncombat Roles*," COL Hort justified taking more than seventy-nine soldiers with known medical issues by stating they would be assigned to desk jobs and that many would be returned home if it was determined that they could not receive the appropriate care while in theater.[11]

The unit was also undermanned in officers. Many of the company commanders were left in their posts well past the time they were supposed to have transitioned to other jobs. The army usually does not leave a captain in command for more than two years. Most of the commanders in the 4th Infantry Division served more than that. That is why I got the call in November of 2007.

At this time, I was serving in the Ranger Training Brigade as an instructor in the U.S. Army Ranger School at Fort Benning, Georgia. After returning from Iraq in February 2004 I had entered college in Italy. I became an officer through a degree completion program, which allows NCOs and soldiers serving in the army to apply to OCS without a fully completed bachelor's degree. Soldiers must complete OCS, serve their time as platoon leaders, and then return to college to finish their bachelor's degrees before moving on in their army careers. All officers must have a bachelor's degree before they can be promoted to captain. In February 2005 I completed my degree from the University of Maryland University College located on base at Caserma Ederle in Italy. I then moved to Fort Benning to attend the army's Infantry Captain's Career Course. While in the course I was promoted to captain and competed to be a ranger instructor (RI). Being an RI was a dream come true. The boy from small-town Richmond, Indiana, who had watched ranger videos in the recruiter station had not only served in the 75th Ranger Regiment and graduated from ranger school but was now CPT John Spencer, an RI helping the army train and graduate rangers.

I had served as an RI for nearly two years by November 2007 and was due to move to a new duty station in a few months. One day out of the blue, I received a phone call from my assignment officer asking, "Do you want company command in combat?" I did not hesitate to respond with, "Yes Sir!" since that is what an enthusiastic officer is supposed to answer with—and I meant it. My wife and I had divorced after I returned from Iraq in 2004. It seemed she *was not* into the military life of deployments. Oh, and there was an Italian guy she met while I was deployed that she *was* into. I was now a single infantry officer waiting to take company command. The only concern I had was that I was offered a mechanized infantry unit. That meant the unit was equipped with M2 Bradleys. The M2 BFV weighs 27.6 tons, has a three-man crew, and can carry six infantrymen in the cargo area. It is armed with a turret-mounted 25mm cannon, an anti-tank missile launcher, and a full suite of high tech onboard computers and optics for targeting, reconnaissance, and serving as the mobile protected firepower for infantry dismounts.[12] Put simply, they are very big, heavy, tracked infantry fighting vehicles that look like small tanks. I had only been in light, airborne, and ranger units. What did I know about Bradleys or mechanized infantry? I asked my assignment officer if I needed to attend the Bradley Leaders Course that most infantry officers heading to a mechanized unit attend. He simply said, "No, you'll pick it up when you get there." And there it was again, the army's on-the-job training mentality. My assignment officer also stated that I would need to leave immediately, drive to Fort Carson, Colorado, put my belongings in storage, and get on a plane for Iraq. And that is exactly what I did. In just over three months after the call with my assignment officer, I was sitting in Baghdad, Iraq, in February 2008 with no idea about what I was getting into.

The unit I would join, Alpha Company, 1st Battalion, 68th Armor, had arrived in Iraq in December 2007 with the 4th Infantry Division and was first sent to FOB Prosperity to either stand guard at the entry control points to the base or to escort resupply vehicles between American bases. The company was left to these missions even when the rest of the battalion was moved into the central Baghdad area to take over multiple vital neighborhoods in early February 2008. Alpha Company was known throughout the battalion to be poor performers. These impressions were mostly due to their company leadership, CPT Niddle and 1SGT Ramos. It also came from the company's performance at the National Training Center (NTC) in California before the deployment, where the training center cadre and battalion leadership noticed their poor performance. On the way to Iraq, one of the platoon leaders ran his M2 Bradley (which costs millions of dollars per vehicle) into the M2 Bradley in front of him while doing a training exercise in Kuwait. The soldiers knew their reputation and if they had any social cohesion, it was as the outcasts.

Located in the heart of Baghdad's Green Zone, FOB Prosperity was built around Al-Salam Palace, which was previously one of former Iraqi president Saddam Hussein's many homes. The grounds were about a half-mile across. The palace had two hundred rooms with approximately one million square feet of floor space. From the outside, it looked six stories tall but really had only three floors with high ceilings. The inside of the palace had marble floors, granite walls, and ceilings that had hundreds of thousands of hand-carved and hand-painted flowers. Unsurprisingly, it had been a beautifully ornate architectural masterpiece. Equally unsurprising, it was no longer as beautiful. Still, by army combat standards, it was like a Ritz hotel. By 2007 FOB Prosperity was a base full of the amenities of a small metro city in the United States. It had a shopping mall filled with American and Iraqi shops, including a Green Beans Coffee store, a mega gym that spanned an entire floor of the palace, a stocked fishing pond, swimming pools, tennis courts, and a dining facility that rotated cuisines on a daily basis and offered a 24-hour short-order (fast-food) line.

Most soldiers had their own rooms or shared with one other person. They also had fiber-optic internet access that not only gave them access to the internet 24/7 but also linked their Xbox gaming systems to their fellow soldiers in other buildings. They would play games like Call of Duty together in their off times. Most soldiers also had flat-screen TVs; one soldier even had someone mail him a forty-two-inch screen TV. It is ironic to me that soldiers living either alone or with one roommate would go online to connect with other soldiers just a few buildings away and in the same unit. I doubt a study of soldiers forming bonds through hours of time spent together, in the boredom of deployments, would show the same results when replaced with separate but connected online games.

Soldiers lived in their city away from home just as if they were not deployed. When it was time to conduct missions, the soldiers left their private spaces to organize as a unit and conduct missions, and then they would return back to their personal spaces. These living areas were not barracks but rather containerized housing unit (CHUS) that resemble mobile homes. These units were designed for two soldiers, but many in Alpha Company lived alone. If a soldier truly wanted, he could go on missions with his unit, return to his room after, and then go eat, workout, use the internet, and go to the movies or the pool by himself.

While at FOB Prosperity, Alpha Company was run like a stateside or garrison unit. The 1SG administered physical fitness and height/weight tests, conducted barracks inspections, and held formations. These activities are normally conducted in a garrison, not while in combat. The 1SG had never been deployed before, so it must have seemed like normal army training or business practice to him on the large FOB. In this garrison-style living situation, though, issues started to arise in the company, possibly due to complacency. Soldiers were caught drinking, missing formation, and violating other discipline standards. There was even an incident where a soldier, clearly inebriated, walked out of his living quarters, pointed his loaded rifle into the air, and fired it.

In March 2008, forces loyal to the Iraqi Shia cleric Muqtadā al-Ṣadr, known as Jaysh al-Mahdi, or JAM, began a series of violent attacks against U.S. and Iraqi security forces in Baghdad and other Shia dominated areas. These attacks were believed to be a response to the Iraqi government operations in the Shiite holy city of Basra. The most troubling attacks involved firing barrages of rockets from Sadr City toward targets in the main part of Baghdad, including the Green Zone, which housed Iraqi government offices and foreign embassies. Sadr City was a two-mile by two-mile square about eight miles northeast of FOB Prosperity in the northeast corner of the Baghdad, with an estimated population of two million—exclusively Shiite residents. The attacks also included a greater number of RPGS, IEDS, and machine-gun attacks against U.S. forces around Sadr City. My battalion happened to be operating in the immediate area and bore the brunt of many of these attacks. At this point in the war, Sadr City was known to be the most volatile area in all of Iraq. It was off limits to the U.S. military, based on a decision by the Iraqi prime minister after a single U.S. air strike killed an estimated forty-nine Iraqi civilians.[13]

Because of the increased attacks and reorganization of forces, Alpha Company was called out of FOB Prosperity in May 2008 and ordered to occupy an austere outpost known as Joint Security Station (JSS) Ur, less than a mile from Sadr City. By this point Alpha Company had already been cannibalized, meaning many of its soldiers had been given to other companies. One full platoon of forty soldiers was given to Delta Company. The company was also required to leave an element of about twelve soldiers at Prosperity to continue guarding gates. The rest of the battalion was stationed at Combat Outpost (COP) Callahan, where they had been since late February, off one of the main roads of Baghdad and about four miles south of Sadr City. JSS Ur was west of Sadr City and only about two miles away from COP Callahan through crowded city streets. One of the primary purposes of the JSS Ur location was to secure an AEROSTAT (helium balloon with a high-powered camera) that allowed American forces to see inside the no-go area of Sadr City. The small piece of land called JSS Ur was literally a giant sandbox that a previous unit had chosen and then surrounded with large (over eighteen feet tall) concrete barriers, forming a perimeter wall. Initially there were no structures within the JSS, and soldiers slept on their vehicles or in the limited shade provided by the vehicles and concrete walls. Eventually the army starting trucking in CHUs and putting seven to eight soldiers in each. JSS Ur and especially the giant balloon floating in the sky were an invitation to the enemy fighters inside Sadr City. The soldiers at JSS Ur were constantly attacked by mortar fire coming out of Sadr City. One time, when the balloon was brought down in the middle of the day for emergency maintenance, multiple RPGs were fired at it as it approached the ground. From then on, it was only brought down at night. Most of the mortar fire was extremely inaccurate, but the threat was real enough. After these continued attacks, more concrete walls were brought in to surround each of the CHUS within JSS Ur, which then created a maze of concrete walls with tiny openings throughout.

The size of the outpost required more than thirty soldiers at a time to be on guard duty in two-man concrete towers as well as the one gate into the JSS. Mainly because of this large guard force requirement, but also due to the number of soldiers taken from Alpha beforehand, CPT Niddle sought approval to make protecting themselves and the AEROSTAT the company's *only* mission. He wanted an exemption from sending patrols out to engage the local population immediately surrounding the JSS walls and the neighborhood beyond. This requirement was something all other companies in the battalion and theater really understood as a vital part of their own security while fighting a counterinsurgency. Nevertheless, approval was granted and the unit settled into a daily routine of stationary and roving guard duties, followed by sleep and then repeating it all again.

Soon after arriving at the outpost, the company leadership, with the encouragement of the battalion and brigade commanders, submitted requests for the comforts of their previous lifestyle on FOB Prosperity. They ordered a prefabricated Morale, Welfare, Recreation (MWR) trailer, fully equipped with computers, internet, and phones. They also ordered a mobile store that could bring cigarettes, candies, soda, and other luxuries on a weekly basis.

I was settling in at combat outpost (COP) Callahan. A massive four-story building, the COP was an old shopping mall that previous military units had turned into a post. It was not a real post, as it was only one building and a sand parking lot, but it could hold over four hundred soldiers and served as the headquarters for our battalion, which had taken it over from a battalion of the 82nd Airborne Division based at Fort Bragg, North Carolina, before I arrived. When I arrived at Callahan, I was informed that I would not, as I had been told, be taking a company any time soon. I had rushed to Iraq under the assumption that I would immediately be leading a company, but the company everyone was scrambling to fill, the one I was told to move to Colorado for, had been filled before my arrival. I had to wait for another opening.

From the day of my arrival, I was presented with daily reminders that Iraq of 2008 and the U.S. Army in Iraq in 2008 were nothing like the Iraq or army I knew from 2003. For example, immediately upon talking to one of the first persons I met in the tactical operations center, I knew he was not right. I did not know what was wrong with him at the time, but the outward symptoms included a major stutter and an extreme short-term memory deficiency. It was straight out of the movie *Memento* but worse. He would stop mid-sentence and just pause and then restart but from two minutes earlier, repeating the same thing he had just said. It was really scary. I eventually found out that he had been in tanks on four separate occasions when they were hit by an explosive force penetrator (EFP), a new vicious type of IED. A tank is the only vehicle I saw take an EFP strike and keep rolling. Inside the tank, though, the crew still takes the brunt of the hit. The soldier I met had severe traumatic brain injury (TBI). At that point, I did not know what TBI was, but I knew the guy I met was not okay. This was a new type of war on many levels.

I was assigned to the battalion staff as an assistant operations officer and had the additional duty of serving as the Iraqi Security Force liaison officer. Fancy words for the person responsible for tracking and paying the local militiamen, called Sons of Iraq, contracted by American units to guard individual neighborhoods. In hindsight, not immediately getting a company command was a godsend, despite all my frustration. I had not been to Iraq since 2003 and had not been in a leadership position since 2005. Sure I had been an instructor at the army's prestigious ranger school, but I was just being foolish to think I deserved to jump straight into command. Being assigned to the staff allowed me to take a crash course on combat in Iraq. I was able to travel with the battalion commander to many of his meetings, including visits to all the current commanders to watch how they were running their companies, and able to spend hours in the battalion command post being mentored by the battalion operations officer, MAJ Rob MacMillan. I tried to soak up as much information as I could from Major MacMillan, the battalion commander, the other company commanders, and anyone else as appropriate to prepare for my day, my turn at bat.

I settled into life at COP Callahan. It was definitely not the life of Iraq in 2003. Despite its remoteness, COP Callahan had a small mess hall that served hot food twice a day, shower trailers for an allotted one shower a day, and a small room with weights and mats for exercising. There were two small rooms where the unit allowed local Iraqi men to sell local treats, Iraqi cell phones, bootleg DVDs, and many other goods. There was also a 24-hour internet café with a handful or so of computers. All our work computers had email, but the café allowed Facebook, Skype, and other types of social media programs not authorized on government computers. My days, weeks, and months turned into predictable episodes. I emailed friends and family on a daily basis and called home occasionally. I also tried to make as many friends as I could in the battalion headquarters. As a company commander, I knew that the more people I knew in headquarters, the better off I would be when I was out leading a small outpost. The Explosive Ordnance Disposal (EOD, think civilian bomb squad) platoon leader especially caught my attention. For one, she was beautiful. She was only a first lieutenant and I was a captain, but I still tried to get to know her. She was having little to do with that. She and one of her soldiers were the only two females in the entire building with over three hundred male soldiers. She was very aware of and defensive about perceptions of what people thought if she talked to someone too long or smiled too big. Still that did not stop me from dropping by her desk in the command center whenever we were both there. I'd start with, "Yo EOD, what's up?" Later, my daily emails included ones to her.

I was connected with the outside world more than I'd ever imagined possible in war. I would often go to the computer bank at the end of the day and log on to Facebook just to see who was online. I split any spare time I had with studying, exercising, and communicating with friends, both back home and within COP Callahan, mainly bugging 1LT Emily Shockley, the steadily more receptive EOD officer. I studied what I thought I needed to know to be a company commander—reading doctrine, thinking through what the commanders I visited were doing, staying aware of the situation in the battalion area of operations. Despite all this, I had no clue what was in store for me.

When Alpha Company moved to the austere environment of JSS Ur, the soldiers were able to maintain their connections with phones, email, and social media mainly (a few had personal cell phones bought at local Iraqi markets) through the convenience of the MWR trailer that was so important to the leaders who visited the soldiers.

On July 1, 2008, MAJ Jon Gossart, the battalion executive officer, walked up to my desk at COP Callahan and said, "You want command? You'll get Alpha at the beginning of August. Get over there and start your inventories," and walked off. His brevity was clearly a byproduct of my complaining (professionally, of course) to him that I had been in Iraq for five months and still had not been given a company. My opening came when CPT Niddle continued to not perform well, or at all, as a combat commander. In only a few weeks of being at JSS Ur, Niddle and Alpha Company had already had multiple incidents. The battalion and brigade commanders were visiting them weekly and at times daily. Trust me when I say that if the brigade commander is visiting your small company-minus outpost weekly, there is something wrong. Both the brigade and battalion commanders gave Niddle orders to improve the conditions and security of the JSS. They would visit, give orders, wait a few days, return and find nothing had been done. After that lack of change continued, despite their very frank advice, they targeted Niddle for the earliest replacement possible. And there I was. I packed my few things and caught a ride to JSS Ur the next morning.

When I stepped out of the HUMVEE at JSS Ur for the first time, all I could see was brown. It was like I was in a movie without color. Everything was covered in brown from the sand-dirt—not quite sand, not quite dirt. The concrete walls were covered in it, the vehicles were covered in it, and even the soldiers I saw were covered in it from head to toe. I was not in Kansas anymore, Toto.

I asked to be taken to the company command post. I was hoping to meet CPT Niddle there, but I found the company executive officer (XO), 1LT Slate, instead. We exchanged introductions and I asked for Niddle. "He's asleep, Sir," Slate said.

"Asleep? It's 10:30 in the morning." I retorted. He then informed me that the commander, the 1SG, and the executive officer had divided up the day into eight-hour shifts, each man covering the duties of commanding the company. Niddle had the night shift, from midnight to eight o'clock in the morning. (Soldiers later told me that during his shift he just watched movies on his computer). This blew my mind; I can tell you that it is not normal for a commander to share his responsibilities in combat. Sure all commanders need to sleep, but these guys had created shift work of commanding and leading the company on a day-to-day basis. Not a good sign.

After 1LT Slate told me that Niddle could not be woken unless there was a major emergency or someone higher ranking was asking for him, he told me that he, Slate, had created a schedule for me to start my equipment inspections. It is a standard procedure for the incoming company commander to arrive at the company a month early to start inventorying all, and I mean ALL, the equipment in the company. It is much more formal and legally binding than when I was platoon leader. The inventories must be completed within thirty days because the change of command between two captains is usually scheduled at the end of that time. On that day, the incoming commander will have signed for the equipment, especially for a mechanized infantry company with fourteen Bradleys. With each Bradley costing over $3 million we are talking over $40 million dollars worth of equipment. The next day I started my inventories, wondering if I would meet Niddle; I actually never did.

Just as when I was taking over a platoon in 2003, the inventories gave me a great opportunity to meet the soldiers and assess the unit. Each day I had a set time to meet a small group of soldiers who would set out their weapons, vehicles, communication equipment, and other items for my inspection. The inspections were mostly by platoons or squads so that the platoon leaders, platoon sergeants, or squad leaders could organize the soldiers into the inspection drill, almost like a military ceremony. The equipment would be meticulously laid out. The soldiers would stand next to their equipment, and on command, each would hold up a piece of equipment and then call out the serial numbers that are etched in every single piece of equipment the military owns. And I mean EVERY piece of equipment, from vehicles to tiny weapon brushes. Once the numbers were called, a supply sergeant and I would cross that number off our massive list.

Immediately upon observing and interacting with the soldiers in Alpha Company, I felt something was wrong. There were clear signs of a lack of leadership, no standards, and discipline issues. These are easily remedied factors. But these soldiers interacted with each other differently, or at least in a manner I had never seen in my fifteen years in the army. I had never before heard a soldier say "F*ck you, Staff Sergeant," and I was uneasy with their teamwork, how they talked to each other, how they received and followed orders. I spent a lot of time over the first few days in the JSS's command post observing. Sometimes I would just sit in the command post in awe. At one point, I decided I needed to start writing down the things I would have to address: care of equipment, standards, respecting NCOs, and more. My list grew every day.

Another very shocking observation I made while sitting in the command post was that these soldiers were not battle tracking: One of the few jobs of a command post is to track where people are going, where they have been, and what is going on in their sector at that time. It is pretty simple stuff. Patrols call in when they leave a base, state how many vehicles, people, etc., they are taking with them, and where they are going. They then make frequent radio calls telling the command post where they are, when they stop, and what they are going to do at that stop. That way the command post always knows where all patrols are in the sector. Police do it, and the military in combat definitely does it. But Alpha Company's patrols just left the wire and came back a few hours later. They did not submit any status cards or patrol reports when they returned. I also knew from talking to the leaders and soldiers during my inspection small talk that they did not even have a task and purpose, i.e., a reason for going out or a plan of what to do once they were out there. The entire company was on the same eight-hour rotation of security, patrol, and rest. My list of concerns continued to grow and surprisingly (when I later looked back) started to look like John Lynn's systems of what was needed for an effective combat unit, despite the fact that I had not heard of him or his research at that point.[14] All of these systems were either not present or flashing red. I knew to my core that what was going on in Alpha Company was bad, very bad.

On one of my slow inspection days, Ramos decided to walk me around the JSS. All he talked about were police calls, what the military calls a group of soldiers ordered to walk around and pick up trash—tidiness. He showed me with pride that he had shut off the one shower trailer because he had found a used razor left in a sink. He showed me with a smile how he had formed the headquarters platoon soldiers into a work detail doing menial work all day because they were not patrolling. They served food to the other soldiers, did most of the picking up of trash, and made sure the showers were kept clean. I could tell when I talked to this group that they clearly had very low morale and felt they had no purpose, except one of the headquarters soldiers. I saw him standing with a familiar long metal stick stuck into a burning steel drum. I immediately knew what he was doing. He was burning sh*t. Alpha Company had built five wooden latrines, each equipped with doors at the bottom where 55-gallon drums that had been sawed in half were placed to catch body waste. These half drums would be removed, filled with diesel fuel, burned, and then put back. This is historically viewed as the worst task that could be assigned in a war. All soldiers hated the "burning sh*t" detail, and it was often used as a punishment job. I approached this solider, curious about what he had done to pull the infamous sh*t burning duty.

"Hello, soldier."

He looked at the rank on my helmet and snapped to attention with his shit stick. With one of the biggest smiles I've ever seen, he said, "Gooooood morning, Sir."

I asked my question: "Soldier, what did you do wrong?"

He looked puzzled, asking, "What do you mean, Sir?"

I rephrased my question, "How did you get this detail?"

He replied with a laugh, "Oh no, Sir, I asked for this job. I love it. People leave me alone, it's easy work and I do not have to go . . . out there." He paused and pointed to the concrete walls of the JSS, "You know, out there."

I was so confused but also amused by his happiness. I just said, "Carry on, soldier." I'd have to look into that later.

There were clearly residual problems in the company because of the current leadership, but I've seen many units with poor leaders that were still strong groups. This group lacked a collective climate. I started to pay closer attention to the soldiers, noting the way they spoke to each other and interacted as a team. Watching them lay out their equipment and do their inspections was like watching a sports team workout or do a practice game. The way the lower enlisted talked to their NCOs was not right. Members of the same rank in the small groups communicated with each other in a more transactional way. I saw fewer of the brotherly friendships I had seen in my previous units. Positive and open communication is a sign of cohesion in a small group. Verbal interaction in war is vital. A cohesive team knows the inflection of each other's voices. They know when a person is in distress versus just under normal pressure.

I also saw negative leaders in this unit. Leadership can be both formal and informal, and positive and negative. Formal or official leadership is like a military chain of command, where rank and duty position denote to whom others should and must listen. Informal or unofficial leadership is when people in the team have the ability to influence the actions and establish norms for the other team members. This might be seen in groups that are all the same position, at the same level. It is peer leadership. In Alpha Company, I saw younger soldiers with influence over their peers; these men were the "f*ck this" types, and they were corrupting others. Usually this can be stamped out with directive leadership correcting those behaviors.

In Alpha Company, I even saw senior NCOs negatively influencing others. One troubled me the most: SSG Delgado. He was a squad leader in 1st Platoon, but had influence even outside his squad and platoon. He was a mountain of a man, weighing over two hundred fifty pounds and standing an easy six foot three. He had a presence that could not be forgotten or overlooked. He wore his clothes and equipment in a manner not as prescribed by regulation and he had longer hair and sideburns than the other soldiers. He spoke differently, in a nonmilitary manner, but when he gave orders, the soldiers followed. I could tell he was a bad influence. He was a seasoned veteran with over three years deployed in Iraq. Soldiers respected him and I could see in their eyes that they were modeling his behavior, such as answering superiors in an informal way. They would respond with, "Yeah," rather than "Yes, Sergeant." Or they refused to do things that they considered "not important."

There are many forms of power used by leaders or present in organizations like the military. There is expert, coercive, legitimate, reward, and referent power.[15] The army relies heavily on legitimate and coercive power. Context matters of course. The military practices all forms of power. Delgado clearly had referent power in his squad and throughout the platoon. Referent power relies on strong interpersonal relationship skills. It allows influence over followers because of the followers' admiration, respect, or identification with the leader. The junior soldiers respected Delgado and desired to be like him. That was something I would have to change if this squad, platoon, and company were going to improve. I would have to change either Delgado's behavior or the span of his influence. Neither would be easy. I put it on the list.

Lastly I saw that the platoon leader of 3rd Platoon, a second lieutenant, had zero influence over his men. Interestingly it was the same lieutenant who had wrecked his M2 Bradley in Kuwait. He would tell sergeants what to do and they would barely stop to listen. When I spoke to him one-on-one, he blamed the state of the platoon on the treatment of the company as the black sheep, which resulted in the soldiers not caring. He was full of excuses. Maybe some of his issues were valid, but real leaders identify issues and make plans to resolve and overcome them, not provide them as excuses to superiors. I actually met with all the platoon leaders in the company during any time they had that aligned with openings on my never-ending inspection schedule. I was not in charge yet, so I could not order them to meet with me, but they understood the deal. The disappointment I felt in 3rd Platoon's leader was balanced with meeting 1st Platoon's leader, 2LT Mike Kane. I could tell he was beat down by Alpha Company's situation and schedule, but he was still focused on his role as the platoon's leader. He recognized his challenges, even the issues with some of his men, but he did not complain to me. He talked about the issues, but also described ways he had tried to deal with them. Much of leadership under stress is about attitude, and Kane was doing exactly what he needed to do—keeping a positive attitude. He had also just recently arrived in Iraq and had been in Alpha Company for only a month.

I knew my job would be to coach and mentor these young officers, and these early talks allowed me to do critical first steps in leadership: listen and assess. This was also the first time I had heard the term "stop-loss." I think I was aware of the policy before but had not thought about it until hearing two soldiers joke, "Oh, you thought you were done? What are they going to do to me if I don't follow orders, send me to the worst place in Iraq? Stop-loss baby!" I also started to meet soldiers who were non-deployable, meaning at some point a medical doctor, disciplinary action, or army regulation had deemed them to have not met the minimum standards that big army had set, which allowed a soldier to deploy to combat. One soldier had a medical prohibition (the military terminology is "profile") from wearing a helmet or body armor. I later found out this was the case for my happy sh*t-stirring soldier. It was not only his happy volunteerism and apprehension of going outside the base that kept him where he was: he had a medical profile preventing him from wearing body armor because he had crushed his back in a car accident over a year before. Why a soldier who was medically prohibited from wearing body armor was in Iraq was beyond me.

I also casually queried the lieutenants about going out on patrols with no actual mission. I would ask, "So, what are you doing when you go on patrol?"

2LT Kane at least was trying. He said, "Sir, without any guidance or orders from CPT Niddle, I'm trying to make it like a ranger school patrol. I give the platoon areas of interest and we work security halt drills anytime we stop."

The leader of the 3rd Platoon replied, "Well, we are supposed to drive around." I pushed back, "What do you mean drive around?" I'd get a dumb look and a disheartened, "Sir, I understand what you are asking, but we're the black sheep, we know it, we're told to just drive around the JSS. No one wants us doing real stuff out there."

This was the "Bad News Bears" team of an army unit. The weight of "fixing" this company started to set in deeply. My list was getting huge. As young officers, we imagine taking command of a squared away unit where the stress is learning how to command. Not a simple job but predictable. Just keep everything working smoothly and you'll have a successful command, you think. Taking over a screwed-up company that is missing some of the most basic elements or systems of a working unit is never considered. Everyone can imagine and prepare for known and unknown challenges but this was different. In a positive view, which I really tried to take during this time, when you take over a stellar unit, the only way to go is down, or maybe you stay the same. When you take over a unit like Alpha Company, there's a lot of opportunity to make noticeable improvements.

As I continued the inspections, my to-do list of things I needed to address when I took the company at the end of the month continued to grow. They needed to establish standard operating procedures for going on patrols, issuing plans and orders, inspecting the men, weapons, and vehicles before going outside the wire, addressing cleanliness of the soldiers, focusing on discipline, directing how the soldiers would address their sergeants and lieutenants, knowing the reason they were going on patrol, and cleaning their weapons after patrols—all basic military stuff.

A major problem with platoons going outside the wire to simply drive around is that it is 100 percent reactive. The concept then was that they would drive around until attacked. In that way, they could identify an enemy to fight. In 2008, though, there were very few incidents of armed forces attacking us. It was the time of the IED, so these patrols would never encounter an enemy to fight. They would only be the targets of IED attacks, making it a one-way battle. There was nothing to be gained, only a lot to be lost.

One of the reasons that cohesion is such a vital piece of the systems of an effective fighting unit is that it allows humans to override their internal fight-or-flight responses. It allows soldiers to overcome fear and move to destroy the bad guys who are trying to kill them. The soldier needs to trust that the person to his right or left will be there to help him. The other soldier is there to go through the experience with him. It is human nature that the soldier needs to feel he is not alone, that someone else is there and going through the same events. The soldier also needs to feel essential. That is why scholars warn people to be careful about imagining future wars or investing in technologies that involve a single soldier in an Iron Man type suit fighting mostly by himself.[16] The military system works because the soldier knows the other soldiers need him to do his job and vice versa for both to survive. The psychological requirements for soldiering in combat is well documented and time-tested.[17]

However, in Iraq in 2008, the U.S. military was fighting a very different type of war. The firefights that we had experienced in 2003 mostly stopped within weeks and the mission turned into a nation-building operation. Soldiers were fighting against insurgents who were using guerilla and terrorist tactics to strike the U.S. military, anyone working with or for the new Iraqi security force, and in many cases, civilians. The use of IEDs was one of the primary types of attacks conducted by the insurgents.

The IEDs of 2008 were much deadlier than those of 2003: the

A Different Army

enemy had evolved. Gone were the IEDs made of 155mm artillery or 60mm mortar shells. In 2008 most IEDs were EFPS made of machined copper that when ignited formed a molten lava slug that could penetrate multiple inches of armor and had advanced activating mechanisms, such as infrared sensors.[18] Soldiers rarely found an IED with their naked eye unless they were part of a route clearance team with special equipment and training. Except for those soldiers in one of our tanks, an IED was going to cause serious damage and death. All IEDs are a faceless enemy. There are no adversaries the soldier can fight back against, and there is no preparation for an IED attack either. It really is just a deadly grim game of chance. Each patrol outside the wire was a roll of the dice. It does not matter how trained the soldiers are when they know that nothing they or their teammates do will affect their likelihood of surviving an IED. Cohesion is needed to fight, but you do not fight IEDs.

In 2008 soldiers were hit by IEDs every week, sometimes everyday. Some caused casualties, some did not. As soon I entered Iraq, IEDs were a part of my daily thoughts. Every time I got in a vehicle and reached for the door handle, I experienced the same sinking feeling in my gut, wondering, was this the day? For much of the ride I felt like I was waiting for a punch to the face while my hands were tied behind my back.[19] My heart rate spiked and I felt nauseous when I saw spots on the road that looked like they could hold an IED or where one had exploded in the past. The feeling was very similar to the fight-or-flight response, but there was no one to fight and no way to escape. It is a feeling of complete helplessness. In response the body doesn't release fight hormones like adrenaline; instead the stress causes it to produce increased levels of cortisol, a neurochemical that elevates blood sugar and aids in metabolism but is also linked to anxiety and depression.[20] Every drive was a game of Russian roulette, and there was little I could do to improve the odds. So not only was I entering a fight for the health of Alpha Company, but each time I got into a vehicle I was in a personal fight of survival.

In late 2007 another faceless enemy also appeared on the battlefield: the improvised rocket-assisted munition (IRAM). These were specially constructed weapons designed to destroy the bases that soldiers viewed as their safe havens. As soon as American soldiers appeared in Iraq and set up posts, those places were the targets of attacks by mortars and rockets. This allowed an enemy that did not want to fight Americans head-on to shoot at them from a distance, with low risk to themselves. There was a great variety to the types of mortar and rocket attacks on American bases. Most of the larger military bases set up cement shelters every few hundred meters so that when the attacks happened, which was frequently, they could sound an alarm and people could dive into the bunkers for relative safety. But IRAMS were something never seen before. They were massive sets of four to ten trashcan-type launchers that would propel propane tanks refilled with one hundred to two hundred pounds of explosives, scrap metal, and ball bearings. Large vehicles disguised as dump trucks or transfer trucks would pull up right outside the wall of a combat outpost and set off their payload. The "flying IEDs" would sail over the compound walls and explode upon landing in the interior of the base. Their range was only up to about 150 meters, but the IRAMS were so powerful they received the name "FOB destroyers." Much like IEDs, these weapons were nearly impossible to detect. Soldiers in guard towers or at the front gate would never be able to tell the difference between normal civilian traffic and a massive bomb except for that split second when the truck stopped next to base. By that time it was usually too late.

All soldiers experience combat stress in battle, but not all soldiers engage in what is commonly thought of as battle, fighting the bad guys. Even those whose job is close combat may rarely get the chance to fight. In Iraq that old saying about war involving long periods of boredom punctuated by moments of terror was very true. However, in 2008 all of us, even those not in combat arms jobs, faced moments of terror, often on a daily basis. Although an infantryman's training helps to manage the stress of a firefight, there is no training for waiting to be blown up by a roadside bomb.

While theories of how and why humans endure combat are centered on cohesion and the love of their primary group, there is also a well-documented effect of what happens when soldiers feel like they are helpless against attacks. Some soldiers cannot handle the psychological impacts of such helplessness and can no longer function. This response was called "soldier's heart" in the Civil War, "shell-shock" in World War I, "battle fatigue" in World War II, "operational exhaustion" in the Korean War, and "post-traumatic stress disorder" after Vietnam.[21] The impact of war on soldiers varies from person to person, but cohesion, feelings of a group and a shared experience, and the power to have a fighting chance are usually listed as factors that enable some soldiers to endure the worst of conditions. What I witnessed when I returned to Iraq in 2008 was a reduced effect of many of those factors. Sometimes the weakening was an unintended consequence of efforts to improve morale and retention. When I took command of Alpha Company, it was up to me to reverse the declining level of reliance among soldiers, which was no easy task.

7

Get the Internet Back Up!

On July 6, 2008, I left the soldiers at JSS Ur to go inspect the platoon of Alpha Company that had been given to Delta Company to guard another small site, JSS Sha'ab, and to work with local Iraqi police to run a small emergency response center for the area. JSS Sha'ab was just a short distance from JSS Ur, also on the northwest side of Sadr City. This platoon, 2nd Platoon, was different from what I had seen so far of the rest of the company. The platoon sergeant, SFC Patrick Donovan, ran a tight ship. His squad leaders were demanding of the soldiers. Donovan and the squad and team leaders had made sure all the equipment was laid out correctly, and the soldiers spoke to the NCOs with respect and discipline. I heard soldiers joking with each other on the side, as friends. This was a tight team. It felt like the army I had known my entire career up to that point.

There were other positive signs—the equipment was all accounted for and well maintained, the soldiers' uniforms and grooming were not just in accordance with army standards but beyond what was required. The bearing of each member of the platoon showed pride and confidence. They looked me in the eye when they spoke to me, and they gave complete and spirited answers to my questions. They wanted to make a good impression on me, and I sensed that it was so their platoon would look good, that it was not only for themselves individually. The squad and team leaders knew their men, their backgrounds, and the current situation. Morale was high, especially in contrast to the rest of the company. Records indicated that 2nd Platoon had the highest retention and reenlistment in the company, possibly in the battalion. By any measure, 2nd Platoon was exceeding army standards.

The one negative aspect about the group was that the platoon leader was weak and basically remained silent during my entire visit. Despite the selection standards that go into all commissioning channels—training and education through OCS, Reserve Officer Training Corps (ROTC), or the U.S. Military Academy at West Point—some of the lieutenants would prove to be less capable leaders than we hoped for. This platoon leader was one of those. Although he had been around for more than half a year, I attributed the strength of the unit to the platoon sergeant, not the platoon leader. The sergeant was a model NCO. My guess is that, like any good platoon sergeant, Donovan had been doing his best to teach this lieutenant to be a stronger leader, to reach his potential. I also attempted to assist in grooming him over the next several months, but sometimes there is only so much you can do with what you have been given. Sometimes a person's potential is not as high as many of his peers.

While I was thinking about the failings of the platoon leader, I was also struggling to disguise my own self-perceived shortcomings. I was fairly consumed by imposter syndrome, specifically and very much like 2003, with respect to the vehicles. I was confident in my leadership knowledge, tactical abilities, and organizational skills. It was mostly the part related to vehicles and vehicular warfare that felt like a disproportionately large piece of the job. Maybe it was just my uncertainty that was consuming me. As I have mentioned, despite my year as a motorized platoon leader, I had only been in light infantry units until now. Even with all I had learned about motorized infantry from 1LT David Bernstein and my own experiences, I was still in unfamiliar territory. My assignment manager's light spirit about me learning when I got on site and my inability to attend the Bradley Leaders Course was playing out as badly as I had imagined. I had tried to use my time on staff to study the Bradleys and mechanized infantry tactics, but studying something like that just does not scratch the surface compared to experience. In fact, my first ride in a Bradley was when Alpha Company took me from JSS Ur to JSS Sha'ab to do these inspections, inspections that I felt woefully unprepared to conduct. I could not let the soldiers know I had never been in a Bradley before! I had to pretend to know what I was talking about and speak with enough authority and confidence, albeit false confidence, to be convincing. I admittedly hoped that the lieutenant, rather than Donovan, would have assisted in the inspection as it might have made the experience less intimidating.

I had similar insecurities when 1LT Otis Ingram later joined Alpha Company as my new executive officer, replacing the one I had inherited from my predecessor. Ingram was so good at his job that it gave me a bit of an inferiority complex. I had no doubt that he could run the company better than I did, and he actually did while I went on leave for two weeks. He ran everything smoothly and without incident. He was "The Man." I never had to worry about anything in the company after Ingram arrived. He backstopped me so well that I never had to doubt if something would go wrong in my absence. He knew what had to be done at any moment and made the company look good. Ingram modestly insisted that he was not all that I thought he was, but I witnessed that he was. He frequently told me that I could correct or question him or give him critical feedback, but I honestly never found anything he did that required critique. He was that good, which sometimes made me feel bad about myself. I might be overstating my lesser standing in the comparison, but there were days I felt that way, in retrospect anyway.

A day after visiting 2nd Platoon at JSS Sha'ab I went to inspect a small element, a squad-plus of a dozen soldiers from Alpha Company who had been left behind at FOB Prosperity to continue guarding one of the entrances. I was greeted there by SSG Fincher, a squad leader. Like Donovan, Fincher was a solid leader. He was doing everything right and the squad's equipment was accounted for and well maintained. This again was a relief after some of the discouraging indications I had observed at JSS Ur. I got mixed feelings from some of his men, though; a few had that "I don't-give-a-damn" attitude. I could tell Fincher had to use a more assertive, direct lead-

Get the Internet Back Up!

ership style (think drill sergeant to a private), rather than what we call a participative style, where the leader seeks the input of the subordinate before making decisions. These soldiers would have to be watched closely. Still, I was happy to have an ally, a positive role model and leader in Fincher and would be happy to be his ally in return. It was good to know that despite the negative and unprofessional things I was observing in Alpha Company, I had steadfast and professional leaders like Donovan and Fincher, who could be used as guides to put the company back on track.

One instance stands out regarding the lack of professionalism in Alpha Company. It occurred when a patrol left their interpreter behind on Route Grizzlies (one of the main roads around JSS Ur). First Platoon was providing security for the construction of a defensive wall along the route. Once that platoon was in its position to protect the engineers who were building the wall, the platoon leader spotted a man approaching who was dressed in U.S. Army clothing and wearing a mask but was clearly not a U.S. soldier since he was without the rest of the U.S. military uniform—a rifle, helmet, body armor, uniform patches, gloves, sunglasses, etc. The platoon leader drew his weapon on him and ordered him to stop. He almost pulled the trigger when he spotted a 9mm handgun on the Iraqi man's hip, thinking he was a member of JAM trying to get close to the wall-building operation. The man, an Iraqi, started screaming the platoon leader's name, pleading with him not to shoot—he was the interpreter for the 3rd Platoon. That platoon had departed the area, forgetting the interpreter after positioning him on the far side of the wall. Personnel accountability is an absolute must in the military, especially in a combat zone. Forgetting someone, losing track of anyone, is unforgivable. To make matters worse, this was the second incident in less than a month of the same platoon leaving someone behind. The first time, 3rd Platoon accidentally left one of their men, a U.S. soldier, unaccounted for when departing a position about a mile and a half from JSS Ur. To be clear, this does *not* happen in the military. The soldier had to run after the vehicles and fired his weapon in the air to get his platoon mates to notice him. That episode could have easily ended in disaster for that soldier and become a major international news fiasco. CPT Niddle and 1SG Ramos waved off both incidents and took no action to prevent it from happening again, obviously. It was quite the opposite: they berated the platoon leader who reported these incidents to them as a fink and a "Blue Falcon," military slang for a backstabber.

It was no shock to me or anyone in the company, or even in the brigade, that things went even more downhill for the company at JSS Ur while I was still preparing to assume command. On July 7, less than a week after I had started my inventories and while I was still at FOB Prosperity with Fincher, two Alpha Company soldiers who were believed to have been getting high by huffing compressed air were in their living quarters at JSS Ur playing a game of "trust" with a 9mm handgun. SPC "B" placed his Beretta M9 handgun to the neck of PFC "R," thinking if he pressed the muzzle hard enough into his buddy, the weapon would not discharge. This may seem like a crazy thought, but it is a function of the weapon. While cleaning the handgun, many soldiers discover that when you press the barrel of the weapon into something firm, like the palm of your hand, the slide is pressed to the rear and the hammer will not fall when you pull the trigger. The insanity of this is that these two soldiers were attempting the feat with a fully loaded weapon. So of course the weapon fired when they pressed the barrel into a nonsolid surface, in this case the neck of the other soldier, causing a gaping wound and immense damage as the bullet passed through R's neck and out his chest, paralyzing him below the waist for the rest of his life. Clearly there were many known and unknown factors that led to that trigger being pulled, but I felt strongly that it was a direct result of poor leadership and lack of discipline. In a unit with just average military discipline, the chance of something like this happening is close to zero. Soldiers know that weapons are not toys. Compressed air, which is used to clean equipment such as computer keyboards, was explicitly ordered to be a controlled item kept behind lock and key, never in a personal living space. Getting high in any manner is not allowed in the military and is never a factor of consideration for troops with any sort of discipline and cohesion. Soldiers should fear repercussions from their peers and NCOS, as well as from their platoon leaders and company commander. They should also want to remain mission-capable because their battle buddies depend on them. This incident was a *huge* red flag. Even so, it was not the end of the problems that Alpha Company would have before I took command.

Less than twenty-four hours later, the unit hit rock bottom. At around 1300 hours on July 8, a large semitruck, topped by aluminum soda cans to give it an appearance of those cans being the cargo, pulled up outside the walls of JSS Ur. The driver pressed a sophisticated detonator and unleashed hell on earth. The truck had been rigged as an improvised rocket-assisted munition (IRAM). This IRAM consisted of nine large metal canister bombs, empty propane tanks that were each filled with 150 to 200 pounds of explosives, scrap metal, and ball bearings. They were loaded onto a semi-tractor trailer modified with rails that allowed the bombs to be lobbed over the outpost's high concrete walls. Seven of the rockets landed inside the walls of the JSS. The first immediate danger was to a group of soldiers huddled around a Bradley, where there were PX items such as cigarettes, soap, and shampoo being sold. The soldiers were completely exposed. Most other troops who were not on guard duty in the towers or out of the JSS on patrol were in their CHUS on their rest rotation, many of whom were sleeping. There was nothing to stop a bomb from crashing into the top of the thinly lined metal CHUS, but the large concrete vertical barriers surrounding each structure provided a lot of protection from nearby ground-level blasts. Upon snapping awake, some of the soldiers were able to get into their armored Bradleys not only for protection but also to be ready to respond to the attack if the commander issued any orders, which he did not. Other soldiers remained in their CHUS, hugging the floor. There was very little the men could do other than get as low as possible. One NCO, SGT Sanchez, jumped into the front of a large cargo truck. The truck took the brunt of multiple explosions, smashing all the glass and turning the vehicle on its side. Sanchez was not physically injured, but the concussions and trauma of the experience deeply scarred him for years to come.

Once the rockets stopped exploding, many people started to come out of hiding, hoping to receive orders to attack something. But the lull in the explosions was short-lived. The IRAM truck caught fire after five rockets had left the truck. The fire then ignited the two remaining rockets that had failed to launch, causing them to explode. The soldiers were in shock. The explosives were more powerful than anything anyone had ever experienced.

Miraculously, there were no fatalities, but the physical carnage and psychological trauma of this attack ran deep. Damage to the buildings, vehicles, and equipment was extensive. Generators were hit and spewed dense, black smoke. Some ammunition could be heard cooking off from the fires. Trucks were destroyed, leaving only their charred skeletons. The bombs that hit the ground left craters ten feet across and a few feet deep. The T-walls, which were six-ton steel-reinforced concrete blast walls around the JSS, had holes the size of basketballs, and many were thrown to their sides like they were dominos simply tipped over. The explosions knocked out the electricity and with it, any hope of air conditioning, showers, and the internet. Air conditioning was crucial, with high temperatures averaging one hundred degrees and often spiking far higher; now there was no escape from the heat. Even the Iraqi people had swamp coolers (devices similar to air conditioners that cool air through the evaporation of water) in their houses and minimized moving around in the peak heat of the day.

The number of soldiers who suffered concussions from the bombs was widespread and harrowing. Weeks after the attack, one of the sergeants who suffered a concussion went to the medic complaining of headaches. It was determined that he had hundreds of fractures in his jaw. He was evacuated back to the United States and within weeks lost all of his teeth.

The insurgent group responsible for the attack, Kata'ib Hezbollah (an Iranian-sponsored, anti-American Shiite militia), had their own film crew recording the attack so they could use it for propaganda purposes. Additionally the video showed images of the downed AEROSTAT surveillance camera, the primary mission of the JSS and a searing symbol of victory burned into the minds of anti-American forces. This was truly adding insult to injury to the greatest degree possible.

There was one ironic "hero" or at least standout who emerged from this debacle, adding further disgrace to the unit. As implied, the worst of the three Alpha Company platoons was 3rd Platoon. The platoon had a platoon leader, but the platoon sergeant, SGT First Class Brown, was the overbearing face and personality of the unit. This platoon was clearly the low tide mark of the company. Immediate visual indications of the lack of discipline in this platoon revealed that many of the soldiers simply did not comply with policies on the wearing of uniforms. They did not wear the camouflaged outer shirt with their armored vests, just the tan undershirt. They did not wear gloves or eye protection, which is required for safety. Oddest of all, they had sewn patches onto their uniforms that were unrelated to our unit, which they had probably bought from local markets or civilian sources, something I had not seen anywhere else in the military. They had committed the most egregious cases of negligence, almost leaving behind one of their soldiers, (as described earlier). A few days later, the incident with the two soldiers huffing air occurred, also members of this platoon.

Just as serious was that 3rd Platoon was rumored to have been lax in making positive identification (PID) of enemy combatants before engagements; PID is the requirement to establish a reasonable certainty that the proposed target is a legitimate military target. They were also known to have shot dogs and other animals. They even joked about firing on civilians who may have been noncombatants. In one such story that occurred in a restricted area just outside Sadr City, where they should not have been in the first place, they pulled up to the very line that demarked the zone where American soldiers were banned from entering, and rotated their Bradleys in a tight circle, making a very loud and distinguishable sound. They were essentially thumbing their noses at enemy fighters who may have been nearby across the line in Sadr City. These American soldiers were looking for a fight. On one of these fishing expeditions, the enemy obliged and fired RPG rockets at the patrol from inside a building. The 3rd Platoon took the opportunity to fire wildly into that building and others until they were out of ammunition. This allowed Brown to report a mighty encounter with the enemy. It also allowed the inept company leadership to put Brown and many of the other soldiers from the patrol in for valorous awards. Brown's shenanigans were not only illegal, the wild firing into Sadr City also increased the possibility of causing civilian injuries and raised the already high tension with the local population in the immediate area of the JSS. SGT First Class Brown and his squad leaders were awarded Bronze Stars with the "V" device (denoting "valor") for their actions.

Brown was a con man and somehow came out of that time smelling like a rose, becoming Niddle and Ramos's favorite, both of whom praised him in front of other soldiers. This kind of misplaced public encouragement served to undermine attempts by the better leaders and soldiers in the company to instill proper military behavior. Each one of 3rd Platoon's actions were reportable and worthy of investigation. I did not become aware of them until over a decade later while doing the interviews for this book. But the stories only validate the bad gut feelings I had while interacting with the platoon on day one of arriving at JSS Ur. When the better platoon leaders or platoon sergeants tried to report any 3rd Platoon infractions to the previous company or higher-level leadership, they were ignored, scolded, and even threatened.

When the IRAM attackers were moving into position along the walls of the JSS, Brown and members of 3rd Platoon were supposed to be patrolling the perimeter of JSS Ur, watching for potential attacks. Instead they had been directed by the company XO to escort the mobile post exchange (PX, or store) to JSS Ur. It was 3rd Platoon's vehicles that were open and serving as the PX when the attack occurred. While I doubt Brown's presence would have prevented the attack, the lessened security could have been a contributing factor, emboldening the attackers. Instead, Brown's vehicle threw the PX supplies to the ground and buttoned up. Once all the bombs had fallen, Brown, without orders, took off in his Bradley and headed outside the gate. His Bradley drove straight over the AEROSTAT, which at this time was just an expensive flattened balloon on the ground. The tracks from the vehicle got entangled in the balloon and strings, immediately immobilizing the Bradley. You cannot make this stuff up. After dismounting and cutting much of the balloon up, Brown was able to get his vehicle free and raced out the gate. When he reached the IRAM truck, which was a burning hulk of metal at this point, he opened fire on it with his Bradley's 25mm cannon. Again this reckless firing put more civilians in danger with no rational military objective. For this pointless action well after the attack was over, Brown received another Bronze Star with the "V" device. It was total nonsense—demoralizing to soldiers who acted properly and encouraging continued or increased malfeasance.

Another irony is that the huffing tragedy may have prevented the IRAM attack from being much worse, or the idea was at least floated by some of the soldiers possibly trying to reason away the horrible forty-eight hours they endured. Because of the shooting incident, Ramos imposed mass punishment on the company by forcing everyone to wear their body armor vests and helmets whenever they were not in their CHUs. Before this the soldiers only needed this heightened level of personal protective gear when outside the walls of the JSS. In the intense July heat, all of that equipment was very uncomfortable, so most soldiers just stayed in their CHUs, which were air conditioned, rather than in the chow hall, the MWR CHU, or out in the open. Compared to the days before this punishment, far more people might have been in more exposed locations and would have been killed or injured. In war, chance is always present. "Murphy" had returned, this time to help us a little bit. It is horrible to say one tragedy may have reduced the impact of another. More likely it was another attempt to rationalize away all the core problems of Alpha Company.

I received a text from 1LT Shockley: "Have you heard what happened at Ur? You better call the TOC." I had an Iraqi cell phone for calling my local Iraqi security force counterparts. I also used it to text Emily (just under the level of being annoying, or slightly above it). At the time, I was at the major FOB in the area, Camp Taji, where I had hitched a ride trying to get myself from FOB Prosperity back to JSS Ur. Evidently Alpha Company had driven me to FOB Prosperity without even asking or reporting it to anyone else. No surprise there. Once the battalion commander found out that I was at FOB Prosperity, he had some choice words for Alpha Company, who had not only traveled without notifying battalion headquarters but had also passed through multiple units' areas of operation without coordinating passage with them—an unsafe lapse in procedure. Again this was something very routine and required of all combat units. The battalion commander told Alpha Company in no uncertain terms that they could not launch a patrol to get me home. I was on my own.

After calling the battalion to see what was going on with Alpha Company, I was given orders to get on the first convoy I could find and get to battalion headquarters. I got on a resupply convoy that was leaving at 2300 hours. On arriving at battalion headquarters, I went directly to the battalion commander's office. He informed me that I would be taking command of Alpha Company immediately, only a few days after starting inventories. Normally a few weeks were allowed for a command transition to take care of all administrative accountability. The IRAM attack had been the last straw of many blatant deficiencies in the company commander's competency as an officer, let alone the commander of a unit in combat. The decision to relieve CPT Niddle of his command had probably been made after the huffing shooting incident. After the IRAM, the brigade commander, a full bird colonel, had driven to JSS Ur, told Niddle to get into his vehicle and drove him away! His command had ended as shamefully as it had been performed. I was the guy who would have to clean up his mess.

The battalion commander's only real instructions to me were

to "fix it." Fix it? All of it? He said Alpha Company needed a strict hand. He also gave me the ability to fire or remove every person in the company except the 1SG. "Dismantle entire platoons if you need to," he told me. The 1SG was one of the problems that I wished I could remove, but I was stuck with him. Maybe I could bring him in line and get him to understand my leadership style.

Near midnight on July 8, I was dropped off at JSS Ur by a logistical convoy, and as my boots hit the ground I immediately took command. The old commander was long gone (later reassigned to a staff position at brigade headquarters). I unceremoniously assumed wartime command of a mechanized infantry company, just what I had wanted, but not in this way or under these circumstances. When in command, take command.

When I stepped off the vehicle at JSS Ur, it was pitch black and deadly silent. Normally there would have been a glow of light or sounds of activity from the CHUs, vehicles, and other normal sounds of a combat outpost. The electricity and activity, however, had been stamped out by the IRAM. There was an overwhelming smell of burned structures and diesel fuel. With the JSS main generators destroyed by the IRAM, there was no light anywhere. I had not been issued night vision goggles yet. I stumbled my way to where I knew the company command post had been. I could feel the distinct poof of "moon dust" with every step of my boot. Moon dust is what happens to sand when it is repeatedly driven over and churned by mechanized vehicles like tanks and Bradleys. When you step into moon dust it is like stepping into a giant pile of baby powder. Many soldiers imagine it is what walking on the moon feels like. I made it to where the command post had been. There was a soldier manning a vehicle that had been pulled up to the command post CHU to serve as the power source and radio communication.

I told the radio operator to assemble all of the NCOs in the company so I could talk to them. Really I ended up talking *at* them. I wanted to first give them a clear message and we could have a conversation later. I told them we would start with a clean slate, that the past was the past, and I would not incorporate it into anything that Alpha Company would become. They needed to lose and stamp out any negative attitudes about squads, platoons, and the company. Today was day one, like 0100 hours in the morning. I also said there would be no gray areas regarding standards. I was not making new standards, but we would follow military standards, customs, and courtesies. We would do things the way we all knew they were supposed to be done. It would be black and white, right or wrong, not gray. Who knows if I said the right things that night. I guess we would find out in the very near future.

On the night of the attack, one of the second lieutenants called home on his personal cell phone, like many other Alpha Company soldiers, despite the fact that most of the outpost was destroyed. He called his wife assuming that she would have found out what happened from other wives because of the near-instant access to the battlefront that new connections provided to the outside world. She had not heard, so the two of them discussed the trauma. "It was hell on earth," he told her. He confided that he and his soldiers felt extremely demoralized, like no one in the battalion even knew they were out there at JSS Ur, getting their asses blown sky-high. He lamented that they had no direction, no leadership, and were just doing the best they could. This was the environment I was taking over, the one I hoped to significantly change.

I did not sleep the first night. By the time I had finished my talk with the NCOs it was already approaching the morning, and I did not have a place to sleep even if I wanted to as all of the buildings had been demolished or severely damaged. On the second night, one of the soldiers voluntarily offered to let me sleep for two hours on his mattress on the floor in one of the few CHUs that was at least still standing, while he was on guard duty. I will always remember that small act of thoughtfulness.

Very quickly the morale impact of the attack became clear. In the days after the attack, two SFCs received mysterious Red Cross messages from home requiring their immediate departure from Iraq. A staff sergeant, a sergeant, a corporal, and a specialist requested to see behavioral health specialists back at Camp Taji and did not return from their visit. Soon after the IRAM attack, another of the sergeants "accidently" slammed his hand in a vehicle door breaking his fingers. He appeared relieved that he needed to be evacuated. He later even sent some of the soldiers in his platoon an email, "Later, bitches." I was not sorry to see him go. Negative attitudes, feelings of not wanting to be a part of the team, pessimism, and fear are highly contagious. The rest of the company did not need any of these additional stressors.

After a big enemy attack like what had occurred, the military will sometimes send behavioral health specialists to question soldiers about how they were feeling, how they were dealing with what happened, and to provide one-on-one counseling. I saw that as a good thing as the military was taking mental health very seriously. Anyone who stated having problems at these screenings was sent back to Camp Taji for further counseling. The team of specialists hit the ground shortly after I had already sent the first batch of soldiers back to Camp Taji for evaluation. Unfortunately many more soldiers in the company reported they could not take it anymore. This could have been caused by the traumatic stress of the IRAM, preexisting mental issues compounded by the event, both, or neither. The decision about the soldiers' fate was out of my hands. But I felt these soldiers did not have the overwhelming desire to stick with their friends as I thought they should. Nor did I see that they exhibited any visible regret about abandoning their fellow soldiers. This was a huge contrast to the attitude I had witnessed during my first tour in Iraq. These soldiers did not display that bond with their fellow soldiers that was the norm in 2003. Some seemed to be looking for any way out of the unit rather than doing everything they could to remain with their team or come back as quickly as they could. They were finding any excuse to abandon their friends for the safety of the FOB or a departure from Iraq. As a final sign of such a broken team spirit, Ramos was scheduled to go on two weeks of leave (vacation) two days after the IRAM attack. Without hesitation or thought of shifting his dates, he left. Boom, gone! That left me to reconstruct the unit, literally from the ashes like a Phoenix, without the company's senior NCO. He did not even consider rescheduling his leave to look after his men after the IRAM attack. When the troops might have needed reassurance and encouragement from his leadership, he was gone.

That a soldier can take leave during their combat tour is probably surprising to civilians; it's not only allowed but required for soldiers whose deployment will last over twelve months. Even when a unit was understrength, as most were, there were people from the unit out on leave. The army recognized that it was psychologically important to give combat troops a chance to take a break, to decompress. This was similar to soldiers in the Vietnam War taking rest and relaxation trips to Thailand or other destinations. During the wars in Iraq and Afghanistan, the soldiers almost always returned to their homes and families during these leaves. The army cannot keep soldiers under the mental strain of constant alertness, always knowing that they can be attacked at any time; in the recent counterinsurgency wars, living among the local populations has meant that the threat of being attacked is always present. In other wars, such as World War II, entire units would be pulled back to safe areas where their minds could rest. Again this was a practice with cohesive qualities as it kept a group together for rest rather than sending individuals off to decompress alone. That is not the case any longer. Soldiers in units doing fifteen-month tours, like Alpha Company, were under threat of attack from IEDs during every vehicle ride, and during every minute of their time inside their small bases from mortars, rockets, or other devious faceless enemies, such as IRAMS.

Personally I'm not sure if the mid-tour leave was completely beneficial. When I finally had the chance to take my leave in October after being in Iraq for about nine months, I really needed the break mentally, physically, and emotionally. I hated leaving my company, but I was leaving them in the very competent hands of my executive officer, 1LT Ingram. My worst day of the tour, in many ways, was my return from the leave back to Iraq because my mind and body had become relaxed, as they were supposed to. When all the

Get the Internet Back Up!

stresses of day-to-day combat and command came rushing back to me, it was tough, almost devastating.

The brigade commander, COL Hort, visited me shortly after the IRAM attack. He was not condescending or overbearing about solving all the company's problems overnight. He only made two direct commands: One, make sure the soldiers were wearing gloves and eye protection (like either of those would shield them from a bombing). The second order was to "Get the internet back up." The internet? That was the farthest thing from my mind, but it showed me what our current leadership felt soldiers needed: the ability to talk to their family and friends. How odd. I was more interested in preventing another IRAM attack, more injuries, or even deaths. Protecting my soldiers while increasing our combat effectiveness was higher on my list of priorities than email capability. Motivating the company so more soldiers would not find excuses to leave the combat zone was more important than Facebook. Adequately dealing with the very real mental and physical injuries from the IRAM attack was more crucial than allowing my soldiers to play video games. Addressing the long list I had compiled of what was wrong with this unit was more vital than posting selfies. Still I had to follow orders like all soldiers. I would learn to work within this new combat environment, even with what I felt was the misplaced prioritization of getting the internet back up. I would have to find the right balance. Otherwise I might end up as ineffective as my predecessor, although if I just showed up to work every day, odds were high that I would be more effective regardless of my intentions and past observations.

8

Conditions for Social Cohesion to Form

Before taking command of Alpha Company, I had sixteen years of military experience preparing me to be the leader of an effective combat team. Military teams can be as small as those in a nine-member squad or as large as 140-member companies. Sociological research has shown that there is a maximum number to the size of group that can truly know each other intimately, establish social coalitions, create bonds, and establish governing norms.[1] The magic number of a naturally bonded group of humans is 150,[2] which happens to be the upper end of an infantry company. A group above this number can of course be a team but not one that relies primarily on social networks, information flow, and intimate relationships. A leader of up to 150 people can know each person in the group individually and lead them based on those personal relationships. Larger groups cannot be led as effectively as smaller groups, so a division cannot be commanded with the same practices as that of a company; however, a division can become a system of effective companies; the leadership and management styles as well as the practices are foundational and just a bit different when on a larger scale.

Whether I knew it or not, I was trained in the very systems John Lynn describes in his analysis of true unit combat effectiveness, as detailed in the introduction. I had trained, practiced, and experienced every aspect of soldier and team interest, motivation, and especially the military system.[3] I am not unique in this claim. Almost everyone at my rank had been through the officer training I had received. What was distinctive about my background was that I had spent almost a decade in the enlisted ranks, giving me more time being a part of teams as well as in a large number of leadership roles. While officers assuming company command typically have had only one or two platoon leadership jobs, I had had team leader, squad leader, and platoon sergeant positions in addition to platoon leadership. I had also gone through the NCO professional development courses, and I had been an instructor at the U.S. Army Ranger School, the world's premier small-unit training organization. None of this meant that I was automatically going to be any better at leading a company than my predecessor, as experience does not always equate with knowledge or wisdom. For some individuals, years of experience may have created and reinforced bad habits or taught the wrong lessons based on false interpretations of those experiences. Regardless, I knew I had a sound footing as I started the job. While most of the troops had only recently met me for the first time, they were all probably aware of my background. Having served in the enlisted ranks for eight years and having been an RI would give me a leg up, maybe two. The combat jump wings on my uniform also brought me some respect. Sometimes being prior enlisted helps in being given the benefit of the doubt from the soldiers. On the other hand, it can hurt when disgruntled soldiers or subordinate leaders may think, "This guy thinks he knows it all." I was aware of that possibility and would do my part to avoid giving such an impression. I knew that those advantages would only serve me for a few days. The more important judgments would be formed when the soldiers witnessed my actual performance as a commander, which was in my control for the most part.

The ultimate crime of Alpha Company's former leadership pair was not that they were poor leaders, although they were, but that they were absent leaders. They erected a barrier between themselves and the troops and stayed firmly behind that barrier. They allowed most of the systems of an effective military unit to go on autopilot, which led to decay. Much like William Golding's *Lord of the Flies*, a new form of power, different ways of doing things, and different systems were created in the absence of leadership.[4] These new and different ways were less desirable and ultimately more perilous for the men in the unit.

I had to replace that new form of power with traditional, present military leadership. I had to bring us back to the proven, effective military systems for the good of the troops under my command. Most of the soldiers welcomed the reestablishment of the military systems they remembered from their training and former assignments. When they had enlisted, it was with the expectations of those systems. As much as some of them may have outwardly enjoyed the lax, Wild West environment under the former leaders, even the more rogue mannered among the soldiers embraced the return of structure. Similar to a parent or coach who imposes rules and discipline and are loved more by their children or athletes for that strictness, a military leader who enforces military standards is followed more readily by soldiers who are accustomed to such standards. There was no reason to be a dictator, but I followed regulations and expected the Alpha Company soldiers to do the same. Almost all of them were happy to do so. The discipline, standards, tactics, operations, traditions, and administration were all elements of the effective teams I had been a member of in my military upbringing. Normally I addressed those elements fairly easily with time and supporters. I was also trained in how to foster cohesion and teamwork using a wide variety of methods.

I do not mean to oversimplify the challenge. The conversion to a fully functioning unit would not happen automatically. How do you build a team or group in combat that not only had very little existing social or task cohesion but also lacked many of the systems that make military teams work? How would this work in a world where soldiers are more connected to their outside social networks than to each other? How did they cope with the stresses of combat through Facebook posts and phone calls to people who were not there with them? What do you do without social cohesion in the military? Could you build cohesion in a team with so many of the other systems of an effective military unit missing? Could this be accomplished while the team was conducting combat missions? I

Conditions for Social Cohesion

can only relate this experience to trying to build a plane while in flight or cleaning and reassembling a weapon while in a firefight.

I made a mental plan to focus on task cohesion and group identity, while also slowly working on getting all the other necessary elements of the military system, such as discipline, tactics, and communication up and running. To this end I gave orders to get soldiers back out on missions, but this time I made sure the soldiers—every last one of them from private to lieutenant—knew the reason they were going outside the wire or standing guard in a guard tower. They would know what we were supposed to achieve while out and what to look for when on guard. I told the lieutenants: "I want every single soldier to know why they are on a mission and what exactly they are trying to accomplish," and to focus on "task and purpose. Say it back to me."

We use task and purpose in the military to develop mission statements. These statements are supposed to be issued for every action a unit takes, every time it makes a movement, goes outside the wire, or starts a guard shift. Everything a team does should have a purpose. Before the big attack, Alpha Company patrols were going out to just drive around jss Ur. Most of the soldiers on the patrols only knew that they were going to get into their vehicles, drive around for a few hours, pull security when they stopped, and then go back to the base. Just the simple step of ensuring that every soldier was aware of an actual mission brought a noticeable improvement in morale. When the platoon leaders gathered the men together and issued an operations order, assigning subunit tasks, the subtle reaction from the soldiers could be observed in their expressions, posture, questions, and the energy in their movement. They had a sense of purpose and they must also have felt safer. Knowing that a patrol had been coordinated meant that combat support from the rest of the organization would be available, if need be. Heck, at least the command post would know where they were and when they were supposed to return.

I also had to get rid of the bad apples that had been polluting the entire organization: the bad leaders. In the army and in combat, however, it is hard but not impossible to fire people especially at a time when just getting enough bodies to fight was an issue. These bad leaders would not be fired from the army, just from the unit. I could not change the fact that over 30 percent of the soldiers in company where in Iraq because of the stop-loss policy, but I might be able to affect their attitude toward their role. Getting rid of the leaders who encouraged bad attitudes was a big step in that direction. The authority to fire people or to make changes was one of the single most powerful things the battalion commander had given me. I decided to switch the entire 3rd Platoon at JSS Ur with SGT First Class Donovan's 2nd Platoon at JSS Sha'ab with Delta Company. Delta Company put up a fight, but the battalion leadership supported me. They somewhat knew the situation at JSS Ur but did not truly know how bad it was. It was enough that they knew changes were needed and trusted my judgment on those changes. The move happened within just a few days—at lightening speed for a task like that. While the platoon leader in 2nd Platoon was subpar—the battalion commander had even complained to me that he was weak, which is never good—the injection of Donovan's platoon in the company, an example of what "right" looks like, was critical to getting Alpha Company back on track. Yes, I should have felt bad for taking a problem and giving it to another company, but the switch would put 3rd Platoon on a much less complex and risky assignment. The JSS Sha'ab mission was only to secure the JSS and Iraqi operations center. It did not involve going out on patrols. This would limit the amount of damage the platoon's leadership could cause and the medals they would be awarded for causing damage.

Another organizational change I needed to make was to form my own subunit that could move me around the battlefield. Company commanders at the time were a major piece of the operations that were creating stability in Iraq. The commanders went out daily to meet with key local leaders like mayors, police chiefs, and council members. To do so, commanders needed a separate element that could freely move around the battlefield without taking one of the platoons away from their patrols. Since Alpha Company's last commander was so inept and inactive, he did not have such a unit. The soldiers of headquarters platoon that might make up such a patrol were serving as the 1SG's personal work detail. During his absence on leave, the senior mechanic living at JSS Ur, MSG Blake, stepped up to assume 1SG duties, and for the short time he served in that role, he was a godsend.

I put in another request, this one to pull SSG Fincher's squad out of FOB Prosperity. I knew this was yet again a big ask. I wanted the element pulled and I did not offer anything in exchange. Slightly surprising me, the battalion leadership again supported my request. I now had Fincher and his small team to serve as my patrol and security. While these men had not necessarily impressed me when I first met them, Fincher did, and I needed a cohort of strong leaders in the company to support me for daily operations. Fincher not only created the patrol for my missions, he became my right-hand man. He was the guy who would tell me if something was not right, including my own actions, which is crucial. Normally this role would be fulfilled by the company 1SG, but once Ramos, the man in that role, finally returned from his two-week leave, I knew after the first conversation he would be of no help to me or the company. The first thing he said to me was, "Sir, you were not here, it was hell." 1SG Ramos never left the post again until the day we redeployed. I have no idea how traumatized he truly was from the IRAM attack, but for the next ten months, he stayed on post doing administrative tasks. He voluntarily took himself—the senior NCO—out of the fight to get the company back on its feet. He did not actively mentor the NCOs in the company. He did not go on patrols with the platoons to observe the soldiers and NCOs on missions. He mainly kept to himself. I honestly do not know what he did all day while the platoons and I went on missions during the day. In the army 1SGs also serve as the senior enlisted adviser to their officer counterpart—in this case, me. It was clear that Ramos would not fulfill that duty. The lack of Ramos's help made the role of my strong NCOs, including Donovan and Fincher, even more vital to the company's future success.

Within a week of trying to recover at JSS Ur, the company finally got some good news. The entire battalion had a new area of operations. We got word that we would all be moving to a new location. Alpha and Bravo Companies would move to COP Apache to assume command of the COP and the new battle space that included a Sunni-dominated district called Adhamiyah. As I had said in my talk on night one, Alpha needed a new start, a clean slate. The move to a new location, a new battle space, would help create a fresh perspective.

COP Apache had an interesting history. It was a palace of one of Saddam Hussein's sons along the Tigris River. It had only a few structures. During the 2003 invasion, the U.S. Air Force dropped a joint direct attack munition (JDAM), a large bomb ranging from five hundred to two thousand pounds, on the palace. Later the Iraqi army took over the main building for a headquarters. We moved into one small building that had probably been the workers' quarters, along with all the CHUs the army had brought in for us. This was a big step up from JSS Ur. It was an actual facility, not an empty sand lot filled with a bunch of CHUs and a maze of walls. Its location along the Tigris was another reason it was a big step up from the JSS at Ur. It was an instant morale booster for Alpha Company. Except for a few minor gripes, (a complaining soldier is a happy soldier) the troops were happy about the move and took to their new home like ducks to water.

Another unexpected gift, and one of those minor gripes, was the fact that our new home at COP Apache had space for only one company, not two. Our battalion had made the decision to not only move my company there but Bravo Company as well. This meant we had to build special bunk beds inside the insufficient number of CHUs and in the few rooms of the buildings we would occupy. We were forced to shove eight soldiers in CHUs designed for two people. These were the same CHUs in which Alpha Company had one soldier occupied when the men first entered Iraq and were living at FOB Prosperity. Remember, these were the size of shipping containers, about eight feet wide by forty feet long—half the length and half the width of a single-wide mobile home. In other places, we

Conditions for Social Cohesion

had to stick twelve soldiers in rooms that were designed to house four. Talk about getting to know your fellow soldiers! Proximity conditions were in effect, and unit cohesion would benefit from it. Eight soldiers shoved in space designed for two, or twelve soldiers in space designed for four, meant they would practically lay on top of one another in bunk beds stacked three-high, have to crawl over each other to get in and out of the CHUS . . . and the smells, dear God, the smells. It was worse than in 2003 because back then we had at least been outside. Now the soldiers were essentially living in Dutch ovens.

As we were getting set up at COP Apache, Ramos was informed that we were assigned logistical responsibility for the COP. This meant we needed to assign an NCO to look after the daily operations of the COP, such as coordinating all contractor support—like trash pickup, laundry, mail, etc. I asked the 1SG if he would be that person because these were traditionally 1SG functions. He was adamant that it could not be him, that these duties far exceeded the 1SG's job. Why did this not surprise me? He went on to explain that COP Apache needed a mayor and he recommend SSG Delgado. I was surprised because Delgado was not only a senior squad leader but also the SSG whom I had identified during my first few days of inspections as being *the* guy, the one with all the referent power over his squad, platoon, and across the company. He was the NCO I had identified as a negative influence but a powerful figure nonetheless. I was further shocked when the 1SG said that Delgado had volunteered to do it. This meant that Delgado would give up his leadership position over a squad of nine men and his influence over many of the soldiers in his platoon. I could not understand how he would just give up being a squad leader like that, a respected leadership position, so I asked the 1SG to bring him to me to talk about it.

When I asked Delgado directly, his head dropped and he looked at the ground as he explained, "Sir, this is my third tour. I'm done. I can't do it anymore." And just like that he abandoned his men, and COP Apache had a new mayor. One of the two team leaders in the squad, SGT Collazo, was elevated to squad leader. I will never know if it was the IRAM that broke Delgado or if it was the twelve months on, twelve months off rotation as well as the combat experiences during those tours that he had lived through for the past six years. He had seen more combat than many would ever see in a career. My immediate shock was replaced with sadness at the thought of such a giant being broken. Despite my initial impressions about his negative influence on soldiers, he was a good man. Then and now, I hope for only good things for him.

Not only did Alpha Company get a new place to live, we got an entirely new mission and area of operations. The company would no longer just be guarding a balloon and a sandlot yard. We were given three major neighborhoods of Baghdad in the Adhamiya district: Delphia, Qahira, and Wazeriyah, all of which were across the Tigris River from FOB Prosperity and downtown Baghdad, closer to Sadr City. Adhamiya had been one of the most anti-government neighborhoods in Baghdad until just a year before. Heavily Sunni, it was the location of one of the most revered Sunni mosques, Abu Hanifa, and where many former Ba'ath Party officials lived. It was also the last place in Baghdad where Saddam hid before the American arrival. The area our company had been assigned had a combined population of seventy-five thousand people, two police stations, an Iraqi Army battalion headquarters, a highway patrol station, four major Iraqi Army checkpoints, ten local militia Sons of Iraq checkpoints, three mosques, two major markets, three schools, a welfare center, a boys club, headquarters to one of Iraqis biggest newspapers, and the power plant that controlled the power for much of Baghdad. Working with all the Iraqi security forces, government, and businesses, Alpha Company would be responsible for the security, stability, reconstruction, and administration of the entire area, all while fighting against a vicious enemy that included new groups in addition to the Shi'ite JAM. Insurgent groups in this new area include Shi'ite death squads, Al-Qaeda in Iraq (AQI), and many other groups opposed to a stable Iraq. This type of mission set required the entire battalion and company to reorganize. We were ordered to have a patrol in sector 24 hours a day conducting reconnaissance,

Conditions for Social Cohesion

raids, meetings with local security forces and government representatives, or just interacting with the local community.

Keeping a patrol in a sector 24 hours a day was not an easy task. With only three platoons in the company, it required breaking platoons into smaller patrol units. Now platoons would go out with about half their manpower, or two squads, so that they could conduct two patrols per platoon in the rotation. Battalion only tracked the number of patrol elements the company could man, not the number of platoons. Even my headquarters security element was counted as a patrol and included in the rotation. Offsetting this increased requirement was a lesser obligation of base security: COP Apache was mainly guarded by the Iraqi military who lived within the COP with us, so our security requirements were far less than the massive burden at JSS Ur.

The heavy patrol requirements led to the assignment of 2LT Chad Headly to my company. Headly was a brand new lieutenant straight out of the Engineer Basic Officer Course. The battalion wanted me to take this new officer and create another platoon. I was furious, asking: "Sir, what do you mean create another platoon?" I knew they meant I had to cobble together from within my soldiers an additional element that was big enough to patrol, but I had to ask the question as a form of protest. Major MacMillan, being the ever-calm voice of reason said, "John, I understand your frustration, you have to do it. You have the numbers. I'm sorry." This was of course highly irregular. Platoons are not just created overnight. It was another example of how bad off the greater army was, trying to maintain such a massive force in Iraq in support of the 2007 surge. Orders are orders. I called in the other two platoon leaders and their platoon sergeants, excluding 3rd Platoon at JSS Sha'ab, and asked them to help me find the right NCOs and soldiers in the platoons to create a new platoon, green platoon. (All platoons were given a color that became a part of their radio call sign: 1st platoon was red, 2nd white, 3rd blue, 4th green.) Each platoon had to give up their best, not their borderline, soldiers. Headly was straight out of his basic officer training, and he was an engineer, not an infantry officer. He was being thrust into combat operations and would have to start patrolling the next day. The company had to give him our best to make such a thing even come close to working. We decided to make SSG Martinez, one of our best and most senior squad leaders, the platoon/patrol sergeant. We added other strong NCOs like SGTs Rubio, Morgan, and Schetter, and soldiers such as PFC Mazrim, SPC Stafford, and others who were the two platoon's top performers. Headly was getting a stacked deck, hopefully stacked enough to allow him to succeed in a job he had not been trained for.

Aside from their tight living conditions, the previous company actually left us something extremely good: their interpreters. The unit we replaced at COP Apache had rotated back to the United States and its interpreters were transferred to its replacement unit, us. This was lucky for Alpha Company, which had only one interpreter when at JSS Ur. Now we had two per platoon and these guys were seasoned veterans. Nearly all of them had been serving as interpreters embedded with American units for almost six years by that point. Once the U.S. mission changed from destroying Saddam Hussein's regime and military in 2003 to a counterinsurgent nation-building mission, interpreters became the key to everything. They gave Americans the ability to talk to local citizens, analyze information, and catch enemy insurgents as well as to understand all the cultural intricacies so important to building relationships and gaining trust. They became advisors to their soldier counterparts, usually the officers. Each interpreter of course had his own personality, strengths, and weaknesses, just as his American partner did.

For my job as the company commander, I had Ahmed and Brad. Normally, interpreters had made-up names like Brad, Max, and George so that their true identities would be concealed from the Iraqi people. Interpreters and their families were frequently under attack for working with the Americans. Ahmed, who did not care if anyone knew his name, was the oldest interpreter in the company, heck probably the battalion, at over sixty years old. Brad, which was not his real name, was in his mid-twenties. Each provided me with unique capabilities. Age is a very respected attribute in Iraqi culture,

Conditions for Social Cohesion

so I brought Ahmed to any high-level government, tribal, or general meetings. The Iraqis treated him like a VIP and gave me much more respect when talking through him than, say, a twenty-something Brad. On the other hand, when I was doing a high-intensity mission, such as a raid to capture a suspected insurgent, Brad was the man. He was aggressive, loud, and forceful, exactly what was needed during those times. I patrolled every day and when I did, Ahmed or Brad were by my side. I spent more time with them than I did anyone else in my company and we quickly became close friends. Ahmed was like a grandfather figure and Brad seemed like a little brother.

Ahmed and Brad were in combat with me; they were my battle buddies, essential members of my band of brothers. Just like fellow soldiers, social cohesion formed as I relied on them constantly. The interpreters lived with us, and most of the interactions with them were transformational. They were my trusted advisors: I could not do my job or achieve my mission without them. This was similar to how I relied on SFC Donovan and SSG Fincher, or how I would have relied on a strong first sergeant. I depended completely on Ahmed and Brad on all matters related to Iraqis. They were my advisors, teachers, confidants, counselors, coaches, and cheerleaders. They taught me what I should be doing, because they were the experts and had been doing this for six years, over and over again. They were high-level company command interpreters who knew all the people I should meet frequently. I needed them thousands of times more than they did me. We spent all of every day together, which included endless hours in my vehicle. The bonds formed very quickly and deeply. Trust had to be there for me to do my job, and it was there, absolutely. Ahmed and Brad taught me an immeasurable volume about local history, current events, religion, cuisine, culture, entertainment, customs, family traditions, infrastructure, politics, academics, social norms, business, the Iraqi military and police, and every other aspect of Iraqi life. I cannot imagine how I would have had any success in my mission without these two men who had become closer to me than probably anyone else in my life. I was certain we would remain friends for life.

Then the unthinkable happened. One day my driver came running into the company command post. He was frantic. Something was wrong with Ahmed—he had collapsed. We rushed him to the battalion surgeon, also on COP Apache. Ahmed was a notoriously unhealthy eater and also smoked like a chimney. He was having a heart attack and I was terrified for him. The doc did what he could, then called for a MEDEVAC. Ahmed was flown to the next level of care, a larger medical facility not far away. He died before arriving there. It was devastating to everyone in the company, especially the members of my headquarters element but most of all me.

Ahmed had served as an interpreter with the U.S. army for six years. He had completed the process to move to America with his family and start his journey to become a U.S. citizen. His family would now have to stay in Iraq. It crushed me. I had to go to my room to hide my emotions. It was an incredible blow, harder than any other death in my military career. It was the worst I had ever felt about someone's death until my mother died three years later. I was destroyed.

Another setback came from my problem platoon. Although 3rd Platoon was detached to Delta Company at the FOB, they still belonged to me. That meant that when they caused problems, they were my problems. This new problem was senseless and brutal, even for a war zone. PFC Black was a 220-pound, mean-looking soldier. His squad leader, SSG Artez was a small man, weighing no more than 160 pounds, but he carried himself with the bearing of a hardened military man. On this day, Artez walked by the makeshift gym at the JSS Sha'ab and noticed Black bench-pressing over 300 pounds in his flip-flops.

Artez made an on-the-spot safety correction, "Black, go get your tennis shoes or boots on. What are you doing?"

Black put the weight down and looked at Artez with fire in his eyes. "F*ck you," he snarled.

Artez responded in utter amazement, "What the f*ck did you say to me, private? Get up and stand at the position of parade rest."

At this point, Black had turned his back to Artez and began mess-

Conditions for Social Cohesion

ing with the weights. Artez stepped closer and raised his voice as loud as he could, "Hey, motherf*cker, did you hear what I said?"

Like a rabid animal, Black lunged at Artez, driving into him with a full tackle from across the weight bench. The sergeant slammed to the ground and, before he realized what had happened, Black was on top of him beating his face in with a ten-pound weight. Black proceeded to savagely beat Artez unconscious. It was pure luck, and what clearly saved his life, that other soldiers heard the slamming weights, ran into the gym, and jumped on Black. It took five soldiers to contain the monster. But the damage was done. A MEDEVAC was called and Artez had to be evacuated all the way back to the United States. He never fully recovered. Because of the brain damage he incurred, he would suffer from seizures and have a stutter for the rest of his life. He was medically discharged from the army a year later.

Despite the fact that 3rd Platoon was attached to Delta Company while at JSS Sha'ab, I was required to oversee PFC Black while he was awaiting his transfer back to the United States to face a military court. I clearly had to always have more than one soldier watching him. I hated having him around the company—Alpha Company had enough problems to deal with. Sadly, this was the state of things. We had to take all these punches while trying to heal as a unit.

Even as I retell this story, it sounds unbelievable, but it is true. Even more unbelievable, Black claimed PTSD as his defense, knowing that the chain of command or army would walk on eggshells with soldiers in disciplining anything that might be PTSD-related. He received minimal punishment after psychological testing validated that he had mental issues—no surprise there—and he was later medically discharged from the army. I was stunned. This was a gross injustice, in my opinion, and I assume in SSG Artez's too. Unlike the incident in 2003 with SPC Ewell when his fellow soldiers turned their backs on him for disgracing the unit, Black faced no group or institutional punishment for his heinous actions.

Despite these tragic events, I was seeing gradual and steady improvements in Alpha Company. About a month after getting set up in COP Apache, the battalion ordered a health and welfare inspection. "Health and welfare" was a euphemism for the company commander and 1SG going through every room and every soldier's personal stuff to ensure they did not have contraband, such as drugs, alcohol, etc. These inspections ensured soldiers were not only living properly but also ensured they were not hiding anything they weren't supposed to deep in their personal areas. After the huffing canned air incident that led to the shooting of the soldier in the neck back at JSS Ur and other things that had happened, the battalion and higher-level officers wanted more leaders going through soldiers' belongings as a preventative measure. If accountability and discipline were lacking in the unit, it would be aggressively instilled.

With the men of Alpha Company crammed into those CHUs like sardines, at least I would not have to waste time moving to each soldier's individual living quarters. I walked into the first CHU and the stench hit me like a slap in the face.

"Good God, Lieutenant Kane, are the showers not working?" I asked.

"Yes, Sir, they are," he answered.

One of the soldiers spoke up. "Sir, it's Red." All the soldiers in the CHU laughed, including SGT Red.

"Good lord, man," I said. "Lieutenant, look into that. You guys are in here nut to butt. Talk to SFC Tripp (the platoon sergeant) about monitoring personal hygiene."

It was great to see the soldiers laughing, even if it was over something as gross and disgusting as horrible personal hygiene. Moving on to a few more CHUs, I opened a soldier's drawer and it was full of porn DVDs. Porn was on the prohibited list. I did not really understand or agree with the ban. It was all under General Order Number 1: Prohibited Activities for Soldiers, which included barring soldiers from "introducing, purchasing, possessing, transferring, selling, creating, or displaying any photograph, videotape, CD/ DVD, movie, drawing, book, magazine, or similar representation depicting pornographic or sexually explicit material or images."[5] What did the big army think soldiers were, warrior monks? Maybe pornographic thoughts should also be banned. I showed the drawer of porn to the 1SG, who just shrugged. I then pulled a plastic bag filled with a purple gelatin mass from the drawer. What the hell is this? I opened it and touched it. Then it hit me. I dropped it.

"Goddamn it, that's a pocket p***y!" (a male masturbation device).

The soldier whose drawer I was inspecting burst into laughter, as did the other soldiers in the room. I just looked at the 1SG and said, "Umm, he has to get rid of all this."

The 1SG nodded and said, "Got it, Sir."

I did not bother following up to see if he actually enforced General Order Number 1 in this instance. I wished SGT Red's body odor would have remained the disgusting low point of the health and welfare check, but that was not the case.

In just a few weeks of living side by side, this group was getting closer, and morale was improving. Surprisingly, what others might consider poor living conditions actually made these soldiers happier. As with our dismal camp at the water plant in 2003, suffering together helped these soldiers bond. There is a fine line between discomfort and misery of course, so the conditions should never be too bad. In this case, though, it was about proximity to one another, which can be a good thing. Again, a complaining soldier is a happy soldier.

An additional blessing in disguise was that unlike the plush living facilities on the bigger bases, COP Apache did not have a 24-hour cafeteria. The army soldier-cooks (as opposed to contracted civilian workers) served military-style meals during set windows of time for breakfast and dinner (lunch was still MREs). Patrols would come off missions and eat together. At a minimum, squads were eating together, in accordance with their patrol schedule and other priorities of work. "Breaking bread" as a group provides another natural bonding time. This truth has been observed in many contexts outside the military, as well, including construction and factory workers taking lunch breaks together, executive dining rooms, high school cafeterias and college dining halls, church picnics, family holiday dinners, couples' date nights, and craft services on movie sets. All these and countless others are well-known examples of people bonding over meals. It is a tradition that many people feel is nice and good to do but may not know that the event has a long history of fostering social cohesion in small teams. That timeless tradition continued with Alpha Company, the new Alpha Company.

We were off to a good start, as much thanks to the circumstances as to the change in leadership. Whatever the reason, Alpha Company was beginning to evolve from being a bunch of disparate, detached, separate individuals into a congruous, connected, and cohesive unit. Having internet connectivity would soon be less of a priority than the safety of the soldiers to the left and right. Unit pride was beginning to replace cynicism, despair, and fear. Eventually maybe the men might put the emotional damage of the IRAM attack behind them and instead look ahead to accomplishing our missions and returning home safely at the end of this deployment. The next few months would be telling for the company. At the very least they were laughing together.

9

Connected and Fighting

Within a short time after moving to COP Apache, Alpha Company was finally starting to function. Soldiers were living and eating together, doing purpose-driven missions where they understood why and what they would be doing when they went outside the wire everyday, and as a result, they were viewing themselves differently. They no longer felt like the black sheep of the battalion. They eventually became the ones trusted for a majority of the complex missions, such as time-sensitive target raids, missions based on current intelligence, ambushes, and clearance operations. Although the company remained under the heavy scrutiny of our battalion commander and CSM, my senior leaders and I were able to filter most of the heat from the men, which contributed to the improved esprit de corps.

An offsetting factor, though, was the ever-present connection to the outside world. The internet café at COP Apache was a small room in the main building, and every time I walked past, it was full. It did not matter if it was two o'clock in the morning or two o'clock in the afternoon, it was the hot spot of the COP. Soldiers were still constantly going on patrols, doing their required team tasks, such as vehicle and weapons maintenance, and they were eating together, but then they would seek hours of time everyday on the internet to write emails, message friends and family, update their status on social media, or just maintain their online persona. Unlike any other war I had read about or personally experienced, soldiers were leading two lives—their combat life and their online presence. A few soldiers even paid a local national who worked on Apache to run cable from a makeshift internet router to their beds in the cramped CHUS. This included me. Instead of having to wait for a computer at our internet café, we could come directly off patrols, lie in bed, and connect. Even I was not immune to this drug-like addiction. Mail calls were a thing of the past. If you received something physical in the mail via snail mail, it was usually placed on your bunk while you were out. Instead of that anticipation of hearing my name being called at mail call, I anxiously awaited the time when I could go to my room to see if anyone had sent me an email. The sound of the 1SG calling out "Lieutenant Spencer" was replaced by the welcome robotic female voice announcing, "You've got mail."

Dr. Lisa Silvestri, associate professor of Communication Studies at Gonzaga University, produced some of the most groundbreaking research on the new world of communication and combat, specifically the constant access to the internet in combat theaters after 2006. She studied how the transition from letter writing between soldiers and the outside world to electronic communication has fundamentally changed the experience of combat for soldiers. The constant connectivity and immediacy of electronic and social media forums changed the nature of wartime communication. Unlike combat letter writing of the past, communication home does not reflect the remoteness of combat or absence of loved ones but rather emphasizes commonalities and immediacy between soldiers and their external social network.[1]

Admittedly, daily communication with the home front has positive impacts. It allows fathers, mothers, sons, and daughters to remain connected and a part of their loved one's lives and dulls the pain of these separations. It blurs the lines between the stress of combat experiences and the tensions of everyday life at home while establishing a social support network with people the soldiers value at home. Unlike any combat in the past, soldiers can now share each and every experience they have—the good, bad, and ugly—with their loved ones at home on a daily basis. But the blurred lines also cause soldiers to divide their mental resources and energies. Soldiers become fully aware of the daily stresses on the home front, and families are more cognizant of the many experiences the soldiers are having in real time.

I watched the constant connection to the outside weaken unit cohesion. The social cohesion formed in the past through sharing the hardships of combat as the result of soldiers not only going through the experience together but also processing the event together afterward was no longer happening. The mind-numbing hours spent together after a stressful combat experience with soldiers talking to each other about what they just lived through was not happening nearly as much as it had in 2003. Soldiers weren't finding comfort in peers, friends, and trusted warriors who not only just physically survived the same thing they did but who also had to deal with it mentally. They were not recounting the experience to ensure what they saw with their own eyes was what their fellow soldiers saw or perhaps how it was completely different. Instead they jumped online immediately after every combat patrol to share that exact experience with loved ones outside the primary group in their unit. I started to notice or be confronted with the negative by-products of constant connection with the home front more and more.

One day shortly before I was scheduled to head out on a patrol, SSG Fincher came up to me to say, "Sir, Private First Class Hershey cannot go on patrol today. He's all f*cked up. His girlfriend is pregnant with their baby and she's on crack, all drugged up at her mother's house. Private First Class Hershey was up all night talking to her on the phone. She's threatening to overdose and stuff. He is a mess."

I said, "Goddamn. What's he going to do about it? How does not going on patrol help?"

Fincher said, "He's all messed up in the head, Sir, and he is a walking zombie from not sleeping. I do not want him on patrol with us. He would put other soldiers at risk. We need to get him to see someone like the behavioral health guys at Camp Taji. He says his father might be able to talk to his girlfriend. Possibly get her checked into a program, but he can't reach him. He's tried phone, email, and text. If he stays back, he may be able to reach his dad.

He also thinks he'll miss the call if he is out, further making him a hot mess. I can run the patrol without him."

Looking back, I cannot help but contrast this situation with the story from the Battle of the Bulge of the German soldier learning about the birth of his daughter weeks after it happened. PFC Hershey might have been better off during World War II.

I decided to go with Fincher's recommendation. Hershey's distracted state would have been a risk to himself and to his fellow soldiers in a combat situation, so we went on patrol without him. That was not the end of my connectivity problems for the day though.

After I got back from the patrol, the 1SG approached me saying, "Sir, we have to talk. I just received an email from the mother of a woman back home who said SPC White is scaring her daughter." I asked who this woman back home was. Was it someone in White's family? He said, "No, just the mom of a girl from his hometown who told her parents that SPC White is posting awful things about how he loves killing Iraqis, that all he wants is to do it some more." I asked if it was true and the first sergeant answered, "Yes, we checked his Facebook posts, almost every day for the past two weeks he's posted about getting blown up by IEDs, shooting Iraqis, and wanting to kill more people." The strange thing was that I knew White had never been on a patrol that made contact or ever fired a weapon outside the wire.

I called SPC White to my company command post and asked him if he wrote those things. He hung his head and did not look me directly in the eye. He simply said "Yes" and I asked why. He then looked me in the face with a stern expression and stated, "Because that's what I want to do, kill Iraqis." I asked why he would post that kind of stuff on the internet. He could only reply "I don't know." He seemed to want his entire network of virtual friends to believe he was experiencing a war that he was not. His online persona was becoming more real to him than his in-person life. I dismissed him and then met with his platoon leader and platoon sergeant. The 1SG was there as well. We discussed options for how to best handle White, eventually opting to also send him to Camp Taji to talk with the behavioral health specialists and continue to monitor him. This included monitoring his Facebook feed. I also directed them to pay extra attention to him when on patrol to be sure he did not fire on any Iraqis without first making a PID. I was worried about him trying to make his fantasy persona a reality. I could not believe that this was what modern day leadership had come to, but it was the new reality. There were no further incidents or discussions related to SPC White. His imaginary online persona probably continued, but his platoon leadership at least kept it in check with the monitoring.

Even I was pulled in multiple, competing directions, torn between focusing on the battlefield and the home front. I received this email from my sister:

> Hope you got your cookies by now and are enjoying them. Let me know if you didn't get them. I got FIRED from my job yesterday. I was appalled because they attacked my work ethic. If they would have said I don't play well others, I could have handled that, but they were malicious and flat out lied. So, I'm a little upset, but not that much because I wasn't happy and I really didn't like those people. We'll see what happens from here, but don't worry because we'll be fine.

While I was not overly concerned because she was not upset and there was nothing I could do anyway—and I had received the cookies—this was a distraction from where my head needed to be. My family still lived in suburban Indiana where available jobs and median income were not high. It was far less serious than having a pregnant girlfriend threatening to overdose, but I was still concerned about my sister and how soon she would find another job. Her family needed the second income. Should I send her money? Was there any advice I could offer? Could I help her find a new job? What were the right words with which to reply to her email? These were the questions on my mind when I should have been completely focused on my men and the mission. My sister had no way of knowing that I was struggling in command. She had no idea that by this point I had started taking drugs to self-medicate.

Not long after getting to COP Apache, I began struggling with the pressure, what we often call the burden of command. The number of problems that needed to be addressed in Alpha Company while also pushing the soldiers out on patrols everyday, seeing the responsibility of it all, and feeling that everything rested on me just consumed me. I feared what my soldiers were doing and anything that might turn them into bad apples. I also had some long-established ideas regarding all the things I was supposed to doing but was not getting done. My leaders did not tell me outright that I was doing things right or wrong, but the battalion and brigade commanders visited often, with clear messages of the things they saw as important, things I was afraid I may not have been accomplishing completely. Of the two, the battalion commander had a closer eye on the unit because of its previous systemic failures. I'm sure he had a wide view, but during one of his visits around this time, he showed up and nearly lost it over soldiers' hats being dirty. To him it was an example of our lack of military discipline. At the time I thought, "Dirty hats, you have to be sh*tting me." The brigade commander, on the other hand, asked more about what I was doing for my company's area of responsibility, such as finding the bad guys, building the Iraqi security forces, and working with the different levels of local governance to improve essential services (water, sewage, gas, medical, schools). Company commanders basically had to be the sheriff and mayors for their areas but through their Iraqi counterparts. What the hell did I know about being a mayor or running a city? My company's area included three neighborhoods with more than seventy-five thousand residents. I was just making crap up all day, everyday, doing what I thought was best or doing what I thought I should be doing. When IEDs went off in my area, it was my fault. When a police station arrested the wrong guy and a local leader complained to the brigade commander, it was my fault. When a council member one level up from mine complained that the trash was not being picked up on time in my area, it was my fault. These issues are not made up. These are real examples from my tour. At least we fixed the problem of the dirty hats. We also had a working internet.

Connected and Fighting

The brigade commander also ordered that all company commanders had to be out in the sector, patrolling, meeting with local leaders six days a week. He only wanted us staying on the COP to do administrative work one day a week. If he visited the COP and the company commander was in, that was his first question: "How many days a week are you out?" So not only were we required to have a patrol in sector 24/7 but I also had to be personally in sector almost all day, everyday.

Soon I discovered that there was just not enough time in the day. Under the supervision of SSG Fincher and me, our patrol left early in the morning and made the rounds of meeting with one of the three police chiefs, Iraqi Army leaders, the local governing bodies, local tribal or neighborhood bosses, the power or trash company, local shop owners, or stopping in to see one of my platoons on their missions. We returned anywhere from ten to twelve hours later. Thanks to the new digital nature of warfare, I returned to find that I had somewhere between twenty and one hundred work emails. I dropped my gear in my room and immediately got back to work. I had one of our former handymen in the company build my room right next to the company command post, with a door literally leading from it to my bedroom, where all the radios and computers that tracked everything were located, where soldiers of my company on rotating shifts talked to the patrols that were out or to higher command when they called. Unlike the previous company leadership, I felt I had to be readily available to everyone in the company. Even when I was getting a few much-needed hours of sleep, I was only a loud voice and two steps away from being back on the job.

Most days after putting my gear away, I returned to the command post and would begin going through emails. I would try to prioritize the emails from just information to those that required an immediate response. If I did not respond fast enough, a call would soon come. There were, of course, personal emails from home that also needed my attention. I had to determine if those messages from home were urgent or, if not, how long I could go without answering them given our new world of immediate electronic gratification. So I usually wrote, "Yes Mom, I am okay today, like yesterday or last week." I answered as many of the emails as I could and then entered my room to try to sleep. I was also frequently found asleep in my work chair attempting to answer emails. Depending on the soldiers on shift, I might get a nudge and a "Hey Sir, do you want to go to bed?" or sometimes I would just be left to myself. I jerked awake eventually. Once in my room, I got anywhere from four to five hours of sleep if, and that was a big if, nothing major happened in the middle of the night. My guys in the COP were disciplined; they had very specific wake-up-the-commander criteria. As we say, however, the enemy gets a vote: if something blows up, wake up CPT Spencer. If the battalion commander is on the radio demanding to talk to CPT Spencer, wake him up.

It did not take long before my body started to shut down, so I started taking drugs. I say drugs loosely; it was nothing illegal but drugs nonetheless. For some reason totally beyond me, in 2008 the army was issuing energy drinks to soldiers in mass quantities, all across the country.[2] It was as much a staple at feeding time as having a spoon. The energy drinks were called Rip Its. Just the name "Rip It" brings a smile to veterans of Iraq and Afghanistan many years later. There they were, these small, chemical-filled energy drinks— 2-ounce cans of speed. Each can contained 100 mg of caffeine, 500 mcg vitamin B12, 40 mg vitamin B6, folic acid, niacin, taurine, glutamine, glucuronolactone, and other crazy ingredients. Rip It is from the maker of Shasta, Faygo, and La Croix. I started with just one a day, but with my new schedule, constant connected warfare, and the normal process of needing more of a drug the more you use it, I soon required five to six cans a day. I stayed wired on caffeine and the other mysterious chemicals of the energy drinks all day, enabled by the unending supply line. I rationalized that the energy drinks kept me alert and awake, able to perform my duties. The problem with being chemically wired is that I then had to add chemicals to come down off the energy to get any sleep I allowed myself to have. I was too proud to go to our medics to ask for any actual prescriptions, so I ordered NyQuil by the gallon. Thanks again to our digital world, soldiers could order just about anything off Amazon and, poof, there it was. Multiple, gallon-sized, cherry-red Nyquil bottles to take before going to sleep. I was a walking zombie. Photos of me during this time are scary: the bags under my eyes had bags.

Like my sister's employment situation, there was nothing I could do to reverse the hands of time and remove connectivity from the battlefield. It was now just a fact of life and a new leadership challenge. I had to find ways to address the situation and minimize any negative impact, just as I had had to address unit morale and discipline at the start of my command. Until then, real world combat harshness continued to rear its ugly head.

On December 17, 2008, around six o'clock at night, Green Platoon was on a mission to examine the main Iraqi Army checkpoints that bordered the north end of our assigned area of operation. This was the platoon we had just formed and was led by 2LT Headly, our new engineer officer. The platoon had been out for about an hour and was headed to the next Iraqi Army checkpoint, driving up one of the main north-south routes in the area named Route Dover. The road was bordered on the left side by small stores that were basically one-room shacks that served as shops. These included a convenience store that sold cigarettes and small, prepackaged foods; an electronics store; an automobile parts store; and a butcher who sold goat meat. The other side of the road was a long line of concrete barriers emplaced over the years by American forces to stop roadside bombs and to create pseudo-gated communities for the different neighborhoods. Green Platoon had driven along this route probably a hundred times.

As they drove, the new green platoon sergeant, SSG Jimmy Martinez, remembered that it was the road where he had taken a picture of a young child, no more than ten or eleven years old, to send to his own kids. Any time Green Platoon had stopped at these shops, the boy would be there trying to sell packaged sweets resembling chocolate Twinkies to the soldiers. One day it was raining, but that did not stop the kid. He was still out hustling his Twinkies. Martinez wanted to capture the moment as a reminder of perspective, to show his kids to not forget how lucky they were to live in the United States and to have many conveniences.

On this night, as the four vehicles of Green Platoon passed the local shops, a grenade was tossed at them from their right side, where an Iraqi gas station interrupted the concrete barriers. It was spotted by the third truck, driven by SGT Schetter with SGT Rubio in the passenger seat. They saw the stick-like grenade awkwardly tumble through the air. It hit the trunk of SSG Martinez's truck, bounced up, hit the spare tire on the back of the vehicle, and fell to the road directly between the two trucks. The grenade was a Russian-made RKG-3 anti-tank explosive that looked more like a billy club than the familiar round baseball shape of modern grenades. The RKG-3s are shape-charges that are supposed to deploy a parachute when thrown to direct the detonation of molten metal downward, forming a sabot round that can penetrate armor, much like the explosively formed penetrator IEDs common in Iraq at the time.[3] They are a World War II–era device designed to be thrown at tanks and explode on the less-armored tops of the tanks. Fortunately the parachute of this grenade did not deploy, so the blast was not aimed down at Martinez's vehicle. If this grenade had not fallen and bounced off the HMMWV it would have had a deadly effect, despite the armor of the vehicle. Luckily the bounce of the grenade and the speed of the vehicles somehow caused it to explode in the middle of the street. The grenade detonated at a generally horizontal angle and spewed its charge across the other side of the road toward the shops. Unfortunately the blast and molten lava projectile hit a ten-year-old Iraqi boy directly in the stomach. He just happened to be standing with his mom at the small convenience store; it all happened so fast. Schetter and Rubio did not have time to warn anyone or even to scream "Lookout!" Everyone heard the explosion, but it was odd, not as loud, bright, or explosive as the roadside IEDs they had been attacked by so many times before. Martinez did not even know what had made the sound until Rubio radioed, "Grenade, a goddamn grenade just exploded in front of us." Green Platoon continued to drive forward about fifty to seventy-five meters before stopping to clear the nearby ambush zone. Martinez checked on his exposed gunner to confirm he was uninjured. Once they realized what had happened, they returned to the area and tried to do what they could to help. Martinez, Rubio, and Shetter were the first members of the platoon to notice the chaos that was unfolding by the convenience store.

ssg Martinez noticed the brightness of the blood and the limp body in the arms of the crying mother dressed in blue. It shook him to his core. The tiny yellow flip-flop floating in a puddle of blood caught his eye. As a father, he immediately thought of the unbearable pain that he would have felt had it been his young son, almost the same age. He stood frozen, unaware of what to do next. Everyone was screaming—the mother's words in a foreign tongue—but clearly pleading for help. Green Platoon's interpreter, Max, gathered what he could from the mother's screams and moans. On top of praying she moaned in pain that her son was all that she had. Her husband, the boy's father, had been killed the year before during the height of sectarian violence in the area. After just a couple seconds of watching the macabre scene, Martinez snapped back to reality and yelled for spc Watson, the combat medic he always had with him: "Doc! Get over here. Schetter, Rubio, guard Doc while he helps. The rest of you push out, establish a perimeter, stay alert." Doc Watson rushed to the boy and did all he could for him, as the Iraqis watched and Max translated. The security perimeter was focused on the T-wall, where the attack had come from.

I received notice of the attack and moved my convoy directly there. By the time I arrived, the civilians had already left, but Green Platoon was continuing to secure the site. I was told the child had been taken to the local hospital after he and his mother were put in the back of a civilian pickup truck. I was only able to talk to Headly and Martinez. I could tell that both of them were shaken by the attack. It felt like more than the normal post-adrenaline crash. I got the basic information about the attack and told them to finish up the post-attack procedures, such as asking locals if they saw the attacker. (They never do.) Along with the local police, we were able to find pieces of the RKG-3 (the parachute and other remnants) to accurately identify the device. Our vehicles were undamaged, with no sign of the attack except for a little shrapnel from the grenade.

I left the patrol and headed back to COP Apache. After stowing my equipment, I called the battalion commander to give him my update of the incident. After that formality, something inside made me want to go check on the soldiers of that patrol. If Martinez looked shaken, more of the troops must have been too. When I went to the area where Green Platoon vehicles were parked, the soldiers were not there. They had already completed all the post-patrol vehicle and weapons maintenance. I went to their CHUs, but again few of them were around. I then found almost all of them in our internet café. This really surprised me. I expected to see them in small groups talking about what had happened that night, just as we had in 2003. But there they were, sitting silently in front of computer screens sharing their day on Facebook, sending emails, posting updates, and talking about what had happened in that attack with outsiders, not their small group of fellow soldiers.

I did not see Martinez; he was one of the few soldiers who had paid for an internet cable to be run directly into his area of his CHU. I later learned that after the patrol he had lain on his bed trying to process what had happened that night. One of the things that hit him hard was wondering if that had been "Twinkie boy." Could it have been? The images continued to flash in his mind. He was having trouble sorting it all out, trying to compartmentalize that it was just part of the job. This time, though, he could not do it alone. He needed to talk about it. The other guys in the CHU were out, probably at the internet café. So he reached for his laptop and checked to see if his wife was online. Facebook said she was, fortunately. Although he really needed to talk, there was only so much he could tell his wife. He did not want to worry her, nor did he want to look weak in her eyes. He kept it concise: "So, this happened tonight. . . . We had a rough patrol. . . . Don't worry, I'm fine, but I saw an Iraqi kid get killed. It's pretty f*cked up." There was not much she could say to help him, especially because he had

Connected and Fighting

just told her he was fine. When it came to telling his wife about his experiences in the war, his view was "no news is good news," so he did not share a lot of daily war events with his family. Maybe when he got home he would. Maybe. Did this senior soldier get the emotional and psychological support he needed from the conversation with his wife? Although I hoped he did, I seriously doubted it. She had not been there to share the trauma with him. She could not tell him how she was feeling about it. She was limited in how much she could assure him that his emotional response was normal, acceptable, and similar to what she was going through. Only his fellow Green Platoon soldiers could do that, but they were not with him. They were online with their own loved ones, getting the same lack of understanding that Martinez likely received.

Dealing with combat, or living with the combat experience, is a complex practice. While not often discussed, social cohesion is a major part of how soldiers can live with war, how they cope with what might be horrors to civilians. Soldiers need to talk to other soldiers to process what they have seen, hear how others perceived it, understand why it bothered them, and to grasp that they are not alone in struggling to cope. It is also how the leaders and the group as a whole identify any soldiers who are truly having trouble dealing with what happened. Soldiers know one another. They can tell if someone one has been impacted so significantly that he needs additional help possibly because of a string of events in a short time frame or because a single event was more gruesome and tragic than others. It could be a scenario where a grenade was tossed at a soldier and might have killed him if it had functioned correctly. It might be because that grenade bounced twice off the soldier's own vehicle before exploding. The soldier might have seen a mother crying over her little boy's injured body; that the little boy looked like a familiar local kid only makes it worse. If the boy reminded the soldier of his own kids, that could have overwhelmed the soldier.

This process of talking to other soldiers, allowing everyone to process what they have seen, is another critical part of the bonding process while serving in combat. Only the other soldiers with them during the extreme stress of combat and the psychological trauma of a combat situation can fully understand. The instantaneous connection with the home front and support networks back home interrupts that coping process on site. The ability to reconnect with home immediately after patrols and the practice of doing so stops that natural cooling off—the processing, sharing, and coping with combat dynamic. I recognized the damage of this intuitively and its impact on social cohesion within my unit. Some of the hidden impacts might not be seen until soldiers return home and go through the inevitable process of gradually separating from the brothers with whom they had experienced combat and shared hardships.

Global connectedness has altered almost every facet of a soldier's daily life. Sure soldiers still spend time talking to one another, but I saw a measured difference in non-battle time between my two combat tours, and that difference revealed itself in combat performance. In 2003 I saw the bonds between soldiers manifest as greater battle effectiveness. The communication between platoon members was personal; their teamwork under stress was admirable. They were not individuals as much as parts of a larger, single organism. The organism has had many names: family, tribe, clan, primary group, or band of brothers. Just as one hand guided by the brain passes a fork to the other hand with nary a conscious thought, so it was within my platoon in 2003. Yes, our prior unit training and many other known and unknown practices with social bonding contributed to this interconnectedness, but more than that, it was those moments in the shade of the vehicles, talks during meals, and the shared decompression after battles that fostered the symbiotic relationships.

In 2008 I saw individuality among soldiers in battle. They would quarrel over decisions that should have been automatic and instantaneous. At the COP, interactions were much more transactional. Talking consisted more of just what needed to be done, whereas there would have been friendly banter in the past. Teams, squads, and platoons struggled to learn together from their daily challenges.

There was no intergroup policing of individual actions, like when the squad members in 2003 responded to the shooting of the civilian. These discrepancies were more pronounced among the younger soldiers. At least the older ones had lived through those closer years before constant electronic connectivity and had retained some of the good habits of previous times such as eating together and coming together after patrols to talk informally about what had occurred. Unfortunately, there was little inclination to pass these lessons along to the younger generation, and the younger soldiers did not seek to learn the bonding habits of the past; they probably weren't even aware that such traditions existed and if they did, how they would be handed down (verbally, or in ways more familiar to them, such as an email blast, or a Facebook post?).

Studying American soldiers in the early months of the 2003 Iraq War, Leonard Wong and a team of researchers found that emotional bonds of trust between soldiers were what motivated them to fight.[4] Their research highlighted the importance of conversation during noncombat time where bonds of trust, friendships, and group identity are built. Motivation and social cohesion are huge topics for any organization but particularly for the military. Building and leading teams are what the army does best. There is no institution better at this task. Just as an army studies the environments soldiers fight in, it should also recognize changes in the environment they live in, changes that can have good and bad effects. Further research is needed to determine the extent of this potential long-term effect of ever-increasing connectivity.

As a company commander I did not have the luxury of waiting for further research. I had to operate in this environment and do what I could to find all the pieces of the puzzle and solve it in a way that optimized the unit's combat effectiveness and each soldier's opportunity to cope with war. We still had many months left in the deployment. Alpha Company seemed to have turned the corner in overcoming the bad habits of the past. We had to continue that transition. The remaining months gave us plenty of chances to prove we could.

10

Protecting and Building the Full Team

A little while after the child was hit by the grenade blast, I faced a moral dilemma in my efforts to fix Alpha Company. 2LT Headly had a negligent discharge (ND) of his weapon (meaning the weapon fired accidentally) into a clearing barrel at the front gate of COP Apache. Military bases always make soldiers entering a post stop by these barrels and clear their weapons to ensure they are not loaded once inside the base. It may not make immediate sense that in combat the army makes soldiers empty their weapons before entering their own installation, but if you knew how easy it is to have a weapon accidently fire when fully loaded and strapped to your back or just carried 24 hours a day, the rule has real logic behind it. Yes, soldiers should always have a round in the chamber of the weapon when outside of the COP to always be ready to immediately fight if attacked, but that round has to be removed when arriving back on post.

Before Headly's event there had been a rash of accidental discharges (ADs) in the brigade. "Accidental discharge" was not actually the correct terminology. The army had made a new classification: negligent discharge or just ND. The army created the new term because it wanted to emphasize that the weapon fired because the owner was negligent. He or she failed to do something properly. The word "accident" may implicitly lessen the blame. Some staff officer in the Pentagon probably got a medal for this change in terminology. The worst of the recent NDs in the brigade was by a Bradley gunner who accidently fired a 25mm cannon round out of his post, landing God knows where in the nearby neighborhood. The brigade and battalion leaders were furious. They took that fury out on everyone by increasing the scrutiny on NDs. This did not do anything to address the cause of the uptick in NDs, but sometimes leadership attention can lessen the occurrence of a problem. At the very least, and I mean very least, it can make the brigade commander appear to be taking effective action in the eyes of his boss, the division commander.

A more effective and sensible response might have been to determine the root cause of these incidents and if a common thread could be found, work to eliminate that cause. It might be that newer soldiers like Headly committed the NDs since they are thrust into continuous combat operations with little experience—in which case more training of fresh arrivals could be instituted. Another cause could be fatigue due to the high operational tempo and lack of proper sleep, which could require a review of the duty rotations, the kind of missions being conducted, and how many. Whatever the cause, no one was taking the time to investigate it.

It also does not make immediate sense that a soldier who accidently, that is, negligently, discharges his weapon into a clearing barrel would be a bad thing. This was the whole point of the barrels—for soldiers to ensure they do not bring loaded weapons onto the base. In actuality, any ND, even into a clearing barrel was an indicator of a problem. The clearing process was very ritualistic. Every soldier, no matter the rank or position, approached the barrel, removed the magazine from the weapon, pulled back the charging handle to eject the chambered live round, visually ensured the round had been ejected and there were no rounds in the chamber, released the charging handle, moved the weapon firing selector switch from safe to fire, and pulled the trigger. The trigger should make a loud metallic click when this is done properly. Then the soldier charges the weapon again and places the selector switch back on safe. That was the process. Simple, right? But accidents happen and every once in a blue moon when the soldier pulls that trigger into the barrel and . . . BOOM! The weapon goes off because there is still a live round in the chamber, one that should have been spotted seconds earlier. That almost always means that the soldier had not paid attention when visually checking the chamber: he had left the magazine in the weapon so that when a round was ejected another was simply fed into the chamber, or he was careless in some other way—maybe due to lack of sleep. The brigade didn't care why. An ND into a clearing barrel was considered to be as bad as an ND while out on patrol. Carelessness leads to injuries or worse. After the rash of NDs, the chain of command dictated that every ND incident be reported to the division commander, who was the two-star general at the organizational level one tier above brigade. Ours was MG Jeffery Hammond, infamous across the division for crushing soldiers' souls. The soldier who was responsible for the incident had to be taken in front of the brigade commander, if not the division commander and typically received some sort of public punishment.

So when our 2LT Headly had this accident, the word spread like wildfire throughout the company. "Guess who had an ND?"

My dilemma was this: Everything in my value system as a commander and soldier, as well as a strong ethical code deep in my gut, said to follow orders and report the incident. If orders were not followed, it showed other soldiers that some orders can be followed while others can be disobeyed. Do as I say, not as I do. But reporting this incident so soon after the incident of the soldier shooting his fellow soldier in the neck and IRAM attack episode would result in yet another kick to Alpha Company while we were down: "The black sheep f*ck up again," or "Typical Alpha," and likely, "What a bunch of losers." These remarks would be made throughout the battalion and also within Alpha Company. Morale had not yet improved enough to make the men immune to this self-flagellation. They had heard this condemnation and said it themselves for too long for the habit to be so easily and quickly erased. The company would most likely be visited by the battalion and higher commands and told how they continued to screw up and disgrace the greater organization, which is exactly what happened after the IRAM attack. This would be proof that nothing had changed, nor would it ever.

The company's identity and self-esteem were especially important to me at this specific moment. After more than an hour of struggling over the decision, I decided to not report the ND to battalion headquarters.

I called Green Platoon together and explained my decision to them. I insisted that Headly was not above the rules, that this was about Alpha and our team. Headly would be punished at my level. We would keep the matter internal and deal with it within the company. It would not be swept under the rug and he would not be treated differently for being an officer (as too often happens). Headly would be required to meet every incoming patrol at the gate, no matter the time, and oversee the clearing of their weapons. To this day, I still struggle with whether I made the right decision, but at that moment I felt team building and self-respect of the soldiers were at a tipping point. Positive action, not negative, was what we needed. We did not have to air our dirty laundry for the entire battalion and brigade to see. They would not be given more reason to criticize Alpha Company.

It was not that Headly received a light punishment. In fact he might have gotten a lesser punishment from the battalion or brigade commander especially because he was so new. There are plenty of situations in which a soldier who does something wrong will get a harsher or lighter punishment than another soldier who commits the same offense. A commander can take the circumstances and other factors into consideration, such as the soldier's record and past offenses. A first offense, like in this case, often will result in a less severe punishment. Commanders also consider the impact of punishment on the rest of the unit. This is exactly what my battalion commander had done during the incident when SPC Ewell shot the looter back in 2003. At the time, the battalion commander felt a harsh punishment of the soldier would have sent a message to the other soldiers that they could not shoot in stressful combat situations. I assure you that after the tenth time being awoken to greet a returning patrol, Headly probably wished his case had been elevated to battalion, where he might have gotten away with a warning and slap on the wrist. On top of the punishment, Headly now had to deal with his soldiers in the context of making such a mistake. He had to carefully acknowledge his mistake while maintaining his leadership presence and focus on everyday missions. Soldiers know leaders are human. They do care about justice, but they also care about being led by strong leaders who can acknowledge a mistake and drive on. On the plus side, Headly would not continue his time in the battalion with a reputation as a screw-up, as would have happened if the ND news would have spread across the battalion. He would now have a chance to build a reputation based on more meaningful actions, such as how well he led his platoon.

When I made my decision, I did not fear getting in trouble myself for not reporting the incident. I fully suspected that the rumor of an ND at Alpha Company would, despite any effort to contain it, make its way to the battalion commander and probably the brigade commander. When they did not receive a report of the incident from me, they might have wondered why. They may have chosen to believe that the rumor was false, so as not to have to deal with a company commander being derelict in his duties. Or maybe, less likely, they chose to trust my judgment in how to best lead my troops. On the other hand, they might have just had more pressing matters and forgot about the rumor. Whatever the reason, it was never mentioned to me. If it had been, I was perfectly willing to explain the rationale behind my decision and take whatever chewing out or hits to my performance evaluation that the commander would want to dish out. What I was not willing to accept was for my men to feel like a bunch of losers anymore, especially for a relatively minor thing like an ND into the clearing barrel. My company's morale and the rebuilding of its systems were more important than me keeping my ass intact. Whatever qualms I had about my integrity as an officer requiring me to follow the precise letter of this specific temporary rule was outweighed by the good of the men. There's a greater degree of integrity on that side of the equation, so that's the side I chose to err on. And yet over a decade later I still sometimes second-guess that decision.

Just as I never heard any questions from above about the incident by Headly, I never received any reports or rumors of the Alpha Company soldiers questioning my choice. Better yet, no one gave Headly an attitude about his error at the clearing barrel. On the contrary, I heard less about the company being black sheep, the f*ck ups, and the losers. There were signs of esprit de corps taking a gradual swing upward. Rather than the straw that broke the camel's back, this incident was one more like a two-by-four strengthening the structure of our improved unity.

If there was any question about my ethics, I was later presented with another opportunity to demonstrate my integrity. Character and ethics are core to being a soldier, leader, and officer. They are also core to who I am. That's why the ND decision bothers me still, even though I believe in my heart that it was the right decision. It is the thought that someone else, especially any Alpha Company soldiers, might think otherwise and view me in a negative light that nags at me. As an officer, I know that the soldiers were always watching me, not just how I was doing my job, but also the decisions I made, especially the decisions that had an ethical or moral element. This is so very important and could have been a real issue if I demonstrated any behavior that could be considered even a little bit unethical. It is simple: there is black and white; there could be no gray. So one day when an Iraqi man offered me $20,000, there was no question in my mind, or in the minds of my soldiers, what my answer had to be.

It was on a day my headquarters unit and I visited a checkpoint where every vehicle was stopped and searched for anything suspicious or illegal, especially weapons. One of the vehicles was a shiny, spotless new Mercedes Benz, which was very unusual in that part of Baghdad. When the car was searched, we discovered that this Iraqi man had a briefcase containing $20,000 made up of one-hundred-dollar bills, which was twice the limit established by brigade as reportable. There was nothing illegal about having this much money, and he would not be arrested, nor would the money be confiscated. I explained to the man that he had to be escorted to our battalion headquarters to be asked a few questions. The man did not want to do that. Instead his solution was that I should take the money. He told me, "Just take the money, it's yours." If nothing else had been suspicious about the guy—but it was all suspicious—this strongly suggested that something was amiss. The men were watching me with curiosity and some amusement. Of course I showed no sign of indecision, nor did I experience any. There was only one answer.

I escorted the man and his money to battalion headquarters. That was one of the few moments I can point to and say it was a clear demonstration to the men that I followed the rules. If I had hesitated for a second, all the soldiers would have seen that, for soldiers can smell phoniness in an instant. The cascading effects it would have had on the company would have been terrible and irreparable. Just as important, my integrity is worth more than $20,000; in fact, it is priceless. Word of the episode spread quickly through the unit. It was a story told with respect and admiration directed not only at me but at Alpha Company as a whole.

At COP Apache I maintained my focus on task cohesion. This is the degree to which soldiers in a unit work together to achieve common goals. In contrast to task cohesion, social cohesion is how much the men like each other and interact well with one another. Social cohesion seems to be something that happens when the conditions are set for it to develop: proximity, many hours spent together, and shared hardships. But task cohesion requires more direct leader input. I continued to push for every soldier to know why they were going on a mission and what they would be doing while out there. I stressed the military system's mission statements, planning, operations orders, inspections, etc. I also had to create missions of value, something that was nonexistent at Alpha Company under the previous commander. I did not have to do anything special, just my job as it was supposed to be done. I also had to walk the walk. I led my maneuver element, SSG Fincher, and the group that traveled with me everyday. They had to know why we were going out on a daily basis to meet with the wide range of actors in our area. If they did not understand why we were going out, if I were just to show up and tell them to get in the vehicles to drive around, such behavior would spread like poison gas to the other platoons. This was something new in Alpha Company and the men responded well to it. Change is often met with resistance, even outright opposition. Not in this case, thankfully. The men appreciated the difference and rose to the occasion. I appreciated them in return. They had been trained in proper military procedures, they knew what they looked like and that standard procedures had been missing. They wanted to operate in the proper manner.

Operations in Iraq at that time were mainly focused on stability, working with the local Iraqi people and leaders to assist them in establishing legitimate democratic governance, and providing essential services such as water, power, sewage, and education to the population, probably in that order. We were not digging wells and teaching classes, but we were facilitating the establishment of systems that would enable the Iraqis to do so for themselves when there were no more Americans around, maybe with the assistance of international aid organizations. The first step involved communication with local leaders and average citizens. This was very much focused on individuals and required a lot of meetings. It was not really a team sport, not one that involved a large number of soldiers. I had to push the soldiers to understand that this was a part of the end goal, so that we (American troops) could one day leave and Iraq could be stable without us. To their credit the soldiers understood and accepted this. True, they joined the army to fight bad guys, not to hand out soccer balls or drink tea in meeting after meeting. But they understood that sometimes handing out soccer balls could be an effective way to fight bad guys. Just the act of the commander respecting the troops enough to talk with them about the mission, strategy, and tactics greatly improved the situation within the company. My predecessor had possibly never communicated with the company in a positive, respectful, productive fashion. It was like night and day and the soldiers were basking in the sun.

So yes, the big picture was nation-building and the soldiers grasped that. Warrior teams, however, are designed to engage in combat and be proactive in finding, fixing, and finishing an enemy force. We still had the number one responsibility: to establish and maintain security in our designated battle space. Without security the governance and infrastructure conversations could not take place. We were fighting a war against a faceless enemy who used guerilla methods, such as IEDs and base bombs, as their primary tactics, and terrorized local leaders by threatening their families or killing the most influential leaders to send the message that working with the Iraqi government meant death. This all made nation-building extremely challenging but not impossible. The complex situation allowed, even required, us to be creative in designing missions for the soldiers going out on patrols.

We assigned patrols to search houses for any enemy material and equipment, such as weapons and IED-making supplies. Patrols would go out to neighborhoods in our area and do "cordon and knocks," where they would seal off a block or so, then politely go door to door knocking, and then asking if they could enter and search each house in detail. While Alpha Company never found any contraband in these searches, it allowed the leaders of the patrol to talk to the civilians, including the head of the house, and ask vital questions about local insurgent leaders or fighters. Sometimes these conversations provided more benefits than the searches might have. Regardless of the tangible, measurable results, the impact on troop morale and unit cohesion—both task and social—was strongly felt.

As things started to cohere and good things were happening, another demonstration of integrity occurred. This time it involved SFC Tripp. As mentioned previously, the platoons were divided into two patrols. Usually the platoon leader led one of these and the platoon sergeant led the other. When 2LT Kane was not with the patrol, Tripp was in charge of it. He was one of Alpha Company's best NCOs, along with SFC Donovan and SSG Fincher. The platoon's medic was on his mid-tour leave, so the battalion medical platoon had provided a replacement. During one particular cordon and knock, this replacement soldier pocketed some money he had found while searching an Iraqi's house. No one noticed because soldiers were split up into different rooms, leaving the soldier alone. Once the patrol returned to base and were at the clearing barrel performing their weapons checks, Tripp noticed this soldier acting odd. Immediately after clearing his weapon, the medic shuffled hurriedly to the port-a-john. Tripp decided to investigate and checked the port-a-john, where he found the money stashed underneath it. He confronted the soldier and told him firmly, "This is not the way we act, not in this platoon." Tripp brought the soldier to me and reported what had happened, handing me the stolen Iraqi dinars, worth about $300. Tripp's actions were exactly what I wanted to see at this time—an inspiration to the other soldiers and a boost to esprit de corps. The next day, Tripp and I went to return the money and explain to the Iraqi man that a bad soldier, not one of us, had taken it. I reported the incident to the medic's supervisor, battalion physician assistant (BN PA), Doc Riley, another prior service officer, who was furious at hearing about the incident. That soldier never came to support Alpha Company again.

I want to be clear. I did not invent cordon and knock patrols. I actually relied heavily on Bravo Company for tactical recommendations. Bravo Company, whose soldiers were also living at COP Apache, was led by CPT Jensen, who had been in command for three years. Usually captains only get two years maximum in company command. Jensen was a strong leader who earned an extra year in command and was invaluable in that position. He was a true professional and always had time for me and, unlike me, was not learning on the job. His company, practices, and leadership style were an immediate "what-right-looks-like" and I cannot thank him enough for all his time, lessons, advice, and encouragement. Just like 1LT Bernstein back in 2003, Jensen again provided not only peer mentorship and someone I could turn to when I felt I was drowning in the unknown but also personal comfort that there was someone else out there dealing with challenges similar to what I faced.

In the military, leaders have a shared responsibility for the health, growth, and strengthening of the organization. This gets accomplished partially through leaders teaching and training those who come after them. I clearly did not receive (or would have wanted) any mentoring from my predecessor, CPT Niddle, so I was fortunate to have been collocated with CPT Jensen. Even when a position looks to be an individual role, such as a company commander, it truly is a team sport where there are shared relationships of reliance, trust, and support.

Actually, before my arrival in Iraq and after the company post I was supposed to take was filled, the next plan was for me to take

Bravo Company from Jensen because he had been in command for so long. When it was announced that I would get Alpha Company, he and I were both unhappy. I had hoped to take over a very solid company instead of Niddle's dumpster fire, and Jensen had been looking forward to moving into a less stressful role. All the company commanders in the battalion had been in their positions for at least thirty-six months, held over because of the army's personnel crisis and kept in command through the deployment. In the end, maybe it was fate. In Alpha Company I had a chance to really prove my abilities, and the soldiers also got to confirm that they were not the black sheep after all.

It was not always easy though. Our plane, our team, was being built in flight. Even I had to understand that nothing about bringing Alpha Company back from the pit of their former status would be an individual act. Despite all my personal struggles with the weight of it all, I eventually felt team collaboration, especially with my soldiers and NCOs. When I talked to Kane and Tripp, I felt they were doing everything in their power to improve their platoon. I saw them working to establish standards, drilling their tactics, and taking time to take care of each other. I saw it in how Headly's NCOs were building their sense of a team in their newly formed platoon by ensuring everyone knew they were Green Platoon and proud of it. Moving the platoons around, followed by the sidelining of negative leaders and bad influences, had helped.

The new Alpha Company was coming together as a team. Shortly after Headly arrived, MAJ MacMillian called me to let me know I was getting a new executive officer, my second in command, to replace 1LT Slate. I was confused and wondered why he would send me *another* new guy so soon after sending Headly and being told to form a new platoon. Then MacMillian told me who I would be getting: 1LT Otis Ingram. I knew of Ingram from visiting Bravo Company. He was not only the senior platoon leader in the battalion but everyone knew he was the best.

Ingram did not falter in living up to his reputation. He came into Alpha Company and immediately asked, "Sir, what can I do to help?"

I told him about the normal XO things such as assisting in property accountability, working with the 1SG to ensure the company was always supplied (ammo, gas, food, etc.), and working with the battalion XO for all the reporting requirements that come with the job. He took copious notes and then repeated himself, "Yes, Sir, but how can I help you?" Just like that, I had an amazing team player on my immediate core team. The 1SG continued to be an absent leader who never went out on patrols, but now I had 1LT Ingram as a true teammate on whom to rely. While I was out on patrols, he was on COP Apache doing XO duties, monitoring the company command post, checking on the platoons, coaching and mentoring the platoon leaders, and much more. I immediately had an emotional burst of light. The need to be able to trust in others, to rely on them in the stress of combat or everyday operations is a vital part of all levels of the army just as it is in life.

Although cordon and knock was an established method, Alpha Company did manage to come up with one new tactic: "Operation Trunk Monkey." At the time, military units were assigned pieces of battle space—a certain number of neighborhoods. The unit, especially the commander, then owned the security and development of those slices of the overall pie. While fully recognizing that the Iraqis owned their land, the ownership of the battle space by the unit commander came with the responsibility for its security. If something bad happened in our area, the higher leadership looked to me for answers. Specifically, if IEDs exploded frequently along roads in our neighborhood, it reflected poorly on me and Alpha Company. This again goes back to the perception of the unit: "Why didn't you stop the IEDs? Get out there and patrol the roads, do more searches." It did not matter if the bombs and those who emplaced them came from outside our area. If it went "boom!" in our area, it was Alpha Company's fault. Likewise, if it was one street outside of our area, it was the other commander's fault in the eyes of the battalion and brigade. That's just the way it was. Those were the rules of this particular game.

We had major highways or streets that bordered all of our neighborhoods. The real ability to stop the influx of bombs and the movement of bomb-making materials was nearly impossible. The area was as porous as a chain link fence, a one-foot high fence at that. We could search every house, but any insurgent could still drive in from somewhere else and plant bombs in our area. So we started Operation Trunk Monkey. (The name was derived from a series of hilarious car commercials.) Patrols went out on the main roads and two to four of our trucks pulled off to the side of the road while the front of the convoy kept going. Up the road, the front trucks came to a stop and halted the traffic. Then once the vehicle came to a stop, the trucks in the rear pulled into the road, locking civilian vehicles in our security perimeter. Soldiers would leave their trucks and methodically search the vehicles and compare all occupants to our Persons of Interest cards or Be On the Lookout (BOLO) alerts. The soldiers in the front converged on the middle, along with the soldiers from the back. Then everyone got back in their vehicles and opened up the highway for traffic to resume. A well-executed trunk monkey could search one hundred cars or more in just fifteen minutes.

Just as our house searches never uncovered bombs or bomb-making materials, none of our vehicle searches turned up any either. It did not matter. Tactically it served as a significant deterrent for insurgent would-be bombers. The frequent, random vehicle searches caused them to transit by roads outside our area or choose a different target area to bomb. In regard to team building, it gave the platoons something they could do to take the fight to the enemy. It enabled them to engage, even if they were not technically winning games. This allowed the soldiers to practice and improve their skills. By doing it faster we were able to search more cars in the same amount of time. Morale in the unit soared. The soldiers had missions of value. They were no longer just driving around waiting to be blown up by an IED or trying to kill time. They were doing real soldiering. They were making a difference in the war and in the country. A clear sign of the improvement in morale and unit cohesion came a few months into Operation Trunk Monkey. The soldiers found a monkey in a local market and had a great idea for a joke. They asked the owner to put the monkey in the back of a car

Protecting and Building

and took a picture of it. They proudly brought the photo back to me—proof that they found a real trunk monkey. Mission success!

Another funny incident demonstrated that Alpha Company's reputation in the battalion had improved to the point where we could make a small mistake and not get everyone's blood pressure boiling. I was out on patrol and my CP (command post) radioed, giving the message "DUSTWUN" or "Duty Status–Whereabouts Unknown," which means an American has been captured and we had to immediately implement certain procedures. Upon receipt of this urgent message, everyone launched and locked down their area. We had intel at the time that the enemy was trying to capture an American soldier, so there was already a heightened state of alertness. When the CP radioed that message, I launched to my predesignated position and called my platoons, telling them to lock down their assigned positions. I then called battalion and told MacMillan, who was the battalion operations officer, that Alpha 6 was in blocking position 4. He replied, "What are you talking about?" I explained that I had gotten a DUSTWUN. He said, "No, all CPs were told BPT." The acronym "BPT" means "Be prepared to." At this particular time, I had our headquarters medic SGT Rice manning the CP, and he was not as familiar with the prowords (procedure words). Battalion had sent a message to "BPT DUSTWUN." The medic did not know what BPT was, a subtle but important distinction, so he left it out of the message. No action has to be taken in response to BPT, so if he had relayed the correct message we would have all just been ready to respond, alerted, if you will. No real harm was done. Everyone was already out in sector, so it was not a big deal. Everyone else just laughed it off. The fact that we could was a huge step forward for Alpha Company.

Some of the most stressful but motivating operations were the raids on enemy personnel. These were mostly capture missions, not kill-or-capture. They were more reminiscent of police raids, where use of deadly force is limited to self-protection. They were stressful because it was extremely hard to surprise an enemy in the dense urban terrain. If they were not surprised, they could get away before we arrived or even be prepared to fight. Fortunately we

5. Photo of a monkey in a trunk, taken by soldiers of Alpha Company.
Courtesy of author.

mainly encountered runners, not many fighters. We did have one
target explode an IED on our team as we closed in on him, so the
threat and seriousness of the operations were never taken lightly.
These were time-sensitive targets, meaning the operations had to
be executed very quickly, based on current, real-time intelligence.
We would get a target packet sent via secure email, radio call, or
secure chat room (at this point we had secure chat rooms like Facebook messenger) with the information. This included a photo or
description of the target individual, his reported location, and a
few other sparse bits of information. We were given a short sus-
pense (deadline) to start movement to the target; a few times, that
requirement was as little as fifteen minutes. We then had to figure
out how to get to the objective location as fast as possible before
the neighborhood caught wind that we were coming and the person we were trying to catch escaped.

These were very technical operations that required immense

teamwork. Each element of the operation, the navigators in the front, the vehicles and personnel that established the outer cordon around the target block, the inner cordon that sealed off the immediate vicinity of the target house, and finally the raiders that entered the building (by breaching, which means kicking or knocking the doors down, if required), secured the target guy, confirmed his identity, searched the house and secured anything that might be of intelligence value, and then rapidly got out of the area. This was not an operation Alpha Company had practiced before the deployment, which made it even more gratifying for the men when they did it well. They were learning something new and important, all the while excelling at it. I went on every one of these missions, not because I was a super leader or micromanager but again because the brigade commander required it. I let the platoon leader control the entire operation, but I was there as a buffer between the platoon and the constant calls that would come from higher up about the status of the mission, all because they were micromanagers. In battalion and brigade's defense, many of these patrols did quickly exceed a platoon's ability to control multiple moving parts. Brigade, trying to help, would push any assets that were available at the time of the raid, such as attack helicopters, drones, or even other patrols in the area. If this happened, I assisted the platoon leader in controlling those assets. Sometimes I even used my vehicles as blocking positions for him. For the first few times, all our platoons were horrible, unsynchronized, slow, and often off target, giving the people we were after plenty of time and routes to evade us. We rarely caught the guy we were going after, but we steadily improved and it was only a matter of time before we scored.

I did not realize it at the time, especially amid the remaining frustration and criticism from higher up, but this operation was key to forming cohesion in the platoons. A team needs to practice with feedback, such as the information received from an opposing team in a sports game, or in our case, an enemy. Whether or not we got the enemy personnel we were targeting, the feedback from our missions let the team know if what they were doing was working. Most importantly this practicing and learning in real time showed each individual that he (1) must do his part or the team suffers and (2) that even if an individual does his part, everyone else in the team must do their part or the team fails. A true sense of team reliance must be built here. There is shared hardship in a loss, or in this case from never getting the bad guy, which can build unity. On the other hand, if there are no existing bonds, it can also become demoralizing or fuel soldiers' resentment toward each other or the team as a whole. The men have to believe that they can win, even get a few wins in a row. In peacetime the army fosters this team reliance through simulated combat and training exercises, controlling the results, and, if need be, adjusting the complexity. In combat I had to do it in real time with no control of the outcomes.

The upward trajectory that the company had established served us well here. Rather than giving in to resentment, frustration, or self-criticism, the men bounced back each time our quarry got away. The shared experience drew them together and hardened their resolve to do better next time. Each individual learned his role and his tasks. Each team was comprised of individuals who were determined to get that group win together. There was even a sense of intracompany rivalry. It mattered which platoon would be the first to snag their target or who arrived faster at the objective. It was important who collected the most useful intelligence material.

Until we scored the big win, we celebrated the smaller ones. Eventually we would capture our target and savor that win. We were getting steadily closer, progressively better. It was only a matter of time—we could all feel it. That helped our task and social cohesion as well. The men knew that each time we were given a time-sensitive target it was higher command trusting us as a fighting force. Unlike Alpha Company's existence at the beginning of the deployment, someone viewed them as valuable and they all recognized it. As 2LT Kane observed, "We improved from the black sheep of the battalion to the ones trusted for a majority of the complex raids, ambushes, and clearance operations. Holy Sh*t, we're infantrymen again. What a f*cking concept!"

11

A Winning Team

On December 29, 2008, we received another call for an immediate raid to capture a high-value target who was believed to be in the local area, a man linked to numerous IED attacks against American and Iraqi security forces. I received the call from the battalion operations officer, Major MacMillan: "John, I'm emailing you the target packet now, we do not have much time. Your team needs to move immediately."

I said, "Sir, I can get them moving in thirty minutes." I always asked for at least thirty minutes to notify the platoon. That allowed the platoon leader to initiate the quick reaction force procedures, such as getting the vehicles staged at the front gate, engines running, with all men positioned in the vehicles, weapons loaded, and completely ready to go. Then the platoon leader would meet me in the company headquarters, so I could give him the target packet, a clear task and purpose, and leave him time to get down to his vehicles, brief his squad leaders who would in turn brief their soldiers, and then move out.

Major MacMillan said, "We don't have time, I need you moving in fifteen."

I replied, "Sir, Fifteen!?!"

"Yes, brigade wants you rolling now, I bought you ten and I'll stall for you for five more. I know you can do it."

I loved Major MacMillan. He was a soldier's soldier, always kind, calm, and empathetic. He knew I had been given a massive pile of crap from CPT Niddle and was being asked to do a lot. He was always on my side. From those first few months while working with him in the operations center forward, he was not only my leader but always my mentor. Like me he had been previously enlisted. Maybe that is why we had a close bond, a mutual respect. I am not a religious man and never found comfort in talking to the military chaplains assigned to all units in the army, but I found when I talked to Major MacMillan when I needed support or comfort, I always felt better. That is powerful. So when he said he knew we could do it, I knew it too.

2LT Kane quickly met me in the company command post, where I told him we did not have time. I said, "Let's talk on the way down." Moments earlier I had called SSG Fincher and instructed him to get our vehicles positioned near but not intermixed with Kane's platoon. Kane called his platoon sergeant and squad leaders to his vehicle and gave them what we call a Humvee top brief, which meant giving out information using one of the HMMWV hoods as a briefing table. Kane briefed them on who the target was: Abu Omar. We had an old picture of the man, a grid location to a house, and photo images of the street. Kane did not need to go into great detail on the order of vehicles designating which men would get out of the vehicles and who would be staying in the vehicles to form the perimeter. They had developed a standard way of doing this exact type of urban raid over the recent weeks. Kane pointed to the map, quickly discussed direction of travel and the route, and noted how the vehicles would all move simultaneously to form the four-pointed perimeter around the block as shown on the photo imagery, which we had received in the target packet. He only had five trucks in his convoy: four gun trucks and one military intelligence truck from brigade headquarters equipped with what was needed to positively identify Abu Omar if we did capture him. Kane finished his briefing and was about to give his squad leaders a chance to explain things to their guys, but he knew from our talk on the way to the trucks that there most likely was not enough time left for that.

He looked at me and asked, "How long do we have, sir?"

I looked at my watch and answered, "Two minutes to launch."

He turned to the sergeants, who had already heard me, and

directed, "Load up, brief your guys on the way." That was not ideal, but a well-trained team could convey the necessary details to everyone during the ride to the objective: mission, location, target person, distance to target, what role they had, and special things they needed to do or be aware of. Kane could also give out any further instructions over his platoon's radio net.

First Platoon moved through the secure gate of COP Apache and headed to the target, which was located in a dense urban area only about a mile away. As the convoy approached, the streets got narrow and were so constricted we had to pull in the side mirrors on our HMMWVs. As the lead vehicle approached the street that was supposed to contain the target house, it slowed down.

"STOP!" the lead vehicle radioed Kane, "I think the target house is a construction site."

"What?"

"Uh yeah, and there are like a hundred dudes working on it. It's a big open area. It appears the photo imagery was not recent. Two houses on the block have been demolished and one is being reconstructed." A few minutes went by, or what felt like minutes, but it could have been seconds. "What do you want us to do?" came the call to Kane.

Normally I would not hear all of these radio communications, but when I traveled with a platoon on a mission like this I maintained one of my radios on the platoon's radio channel. That made a total of three channels I had to listen to: the battalion, the company, and the platoon. I needed the battalion link so that I could answer all the requests for information that would come, despite MacMillan's efforts to shield me and my company. He had the next level up brigade usually breathing down his neck as well. My company radio channel was used to maintain communication with my command post back at COP Apache and the primary place where I talked with Kane. The platoon net helped in that I did not have to bother Kane for updates on the operations. I could gather a lot of what I needed from his platoon's talk.

As 2LT Kane was deciding what to do, the men of the construction site noticed the lead vehicle. The message to Kane commented on these workers, "Sir, they see us and are starting to talk and move around."

Kane reacted quickly: "Lock it down! 1–1 take the northwest edge. 1–2 northeast. I'll take southeast. 1–4 take the rear sw block." This was an audible and not the standard flow or positioning of vehicles that the platoon would have used during the mission. The unique situation on the ground required Kane to adapt at lightning speed and he did.

All the drivers stomped on their gas pedals and the HMMWVs bucked up. Within seconds the vehicles were closing in on their destinations, dust flying, trapping the large crowd in their perimeter. All the soldiers except for the driver and gunners jumped out and faced the crowd with their weapons ready, pointed down but easily raised if a threat appeared from the crowd of military-aged males working on the site. Without orders, the men of each truck fanned out and tried to expand their ability to at least appear to have the site locked while trying to prevent anyone, what we call "squirters," from leaving. In just two minutes the platoon had control of the site. The gunners provided additional oversight from their vehicles. To put their actions in better context and show how impressive they were, this was only the fifth or sixth time this platoon had conducted such a raid. They were quick learners and were now acting in unison instinctively.

The first platoon radio telephone operator SPC Cyrus Simmons and driver SPC Jeremy Bedola, from Kane's vehicle, stared at the crowd. Bedola stepped out of his vehicle to support Simmons. They noticed two Iraqi men looking very uncomfortable. "Sh*t. They look like they want to run," Simmons said to Bedola. As soon as he said it, the two Iraqi men started running across the large distance separating the construction site and other houses. Simmons only screamed "sh*t!" and started running after the men. Bedola responded instinctively and followed Simmons almost before he realized who Simmons was chasing. The two Iraqi men wore nothing more than flip-flops and the typical full-length shirts. Simmons

A Winning Team

and Bedola had body armor, helmets, full kit, boots, and their weapons. How they were able to run fast enough to catch up with and capture the two squirters baffles my mind even today, but they did. I guess all their fitness preparation back at Fort Carson had paid off. Maybe drinking all the Rip Its did too. The two Iraqi men were brought back within the perimeter.

Seeing the chaos of the Iraqis trying to spread out beyond the limits, SFC Tripp advised Kane to have the soldiers start collecting everyone in the middle, forming a tight perimeter around just the people and not the entire site. They did that and I saw the soldiers moving all the construction workers into the middle. They then put them in lines. "Holy sh*t, they are putting them in formation," I thought. But what they were doing was preparing to search every one of them systematically. Once corralled they pulled five guys out of the crowd at a time, had them empty their pockets, looked for identifying marks, and let the intelligence crew do their thing to identify the right guy. It was no surprise to anyone that one of the two runners was, in fact, Abu Omar. Jackpot! First Platoon had done it. They placed plastic flex cuffs around his wrist, what we called zip-tying him, and took Abu Omar back to COP Apache where he was handed off to the battalion intelligence team.

We later found out that Abu Omar was not just any high-value target, he was HVT No. 5 on the division's list, a major leader and part of a bomb-making chain of al-Qaeda in Iraq. In fact, several special task forces made up of the most elite soldiers had conducted raids to capture him and failed. That made Alpha Company's win even sweeter.

Just like bad news, good news traveled fast. I received a call from the brigade commander that night congratulating us. I made sure the entire company received the accolades that were coming in. Alpha Company had transitioned from the black sheep to one of the best companies in the brigade. The capture of Abu Omar was not the only display of improved performance. The platoons were succeeding on multiple fronts: on the quantity and quality of joint patrols with our local police, the number of vehicles searched, our response times, and more. I started to receive ribbing—the good kind—from my peers, specifically CPT Jensen in Bravo Company: "Damn John, you're making us look bad." The raid was probably our most important win. It was a victory against a recognized and cunning adversary. It required the entire platoon to work instinctively as a team, for every individual to do his part, with the brotherhood of one soldier willing to face adversity for his brother, like when Bedola followed Simmons in chase. These stories spread across Alpha Company and the rest of the battalion and brigade, and it felt great for all of us.

That high would not last long, however. Just a month after Abu Omar's capture, in January of 2009, we began to transition our responsibilities in Adhamiyah to another unit. This happened across Iraq on a more or less yearly basis. It is not true to say American forces fought in Iraq for eight years. They fought one year over and over for eight years. This replacement was a routine process, where over a few weeks an incoming unit from stateside learned from the outgoing unit. That new unit would in turn start its own system of conducting operations. It is also the start of their process of building new bonds and the formation of teams to execute combat just as the outgoing unit had needed to do when it arrived in country.

In February 2009 we transitioned swiftly from the war zone to the home front. Thanks to the advancements of modern day transportation, it only takes days for a military unit to go from the combat zone to their stateside bases. Over just a few days, more than five thousand soldiers returned home to Fort Carson, Colorado, on contracted commercial airplanes. We stopped in Kuwait, as most units do. Once there soldiers received classes on preparing for the dramatic transition out of the war zone. They were warned that it would likely be a shock to their system. They were instructed on how to deal with going from conducting operations everyday, with the fear of being blown up by an IED or a hidden enemy trying to kill them, to driving their own car down the streets of Colorado Springs. It is also where soldiers filled out questionnaires to see if they were mentally at risk. Surprisingly, none of them reported problems, even if they had them.

I always found these questionnaires to be a joke: "Did you see any dead bodies?"; "Did you engage in firefights?"; "Did any of this bother you?"; "Do you have trouble sleeping at night?"; "Do you self-medicate?" I cannot speak for all soldiers, but I found these surveys to be funny because everyone knows if you mark anything negative, if you self report having an issue, you must talk to a behavioral health specialist about your problems. This specialist would be someone who was not there with you during the hard times. That should not matter in the bigger picture of their expertise, but at that moment, it just does not work. Everyone also knew if you checked one wrong box, you would spend more time at that stage of the process, rather than just continuing on with the other tasks required to get you home. The behavioral health check, at that moment, was set up to fail. We all just wanted to finish the necessities to be cleared to go home.

Heck, my own mental state was questionable. It was not so much that I was traumatized by the horrors of combat. It was that I had overwhelmed myself with the stresses of command, doing things to my body and mind with self-medication and sleep deprivation. One of the reasons I still question my decision related to the negligent discharge was the state of mind I was in during that time. I was a walking zombie, and maybe I had assumed too much risk to my entire team. I was not about to put any of that on a survey or questionnaire. I did not mention my breakdown after the death of Ahmed, my troubles holding things together, or my nighttime visits by an outstretched hand holding a pair of bloody dog tags. Those were my burdens to carry. Call it compartmentalization or denial, but it was my reality.

I am not sure what it will take to fix this cultural inclination to keep emotions inside. There will have to be a cultural redefining of what strength means in the military. Seeking help or acknowledging mental struggles is not weakness, but there will always be a problem in the system if specialists from outside the warrior's tribe are considered to be the solution. This is why social cohesion and the communal and historical attributes of the primary group are so important. They provide the coping and alert mechanisms that do exactly what the Kuwait surveys and questioning was attempting. That is why any threat or weakening of social cohesion in combat is a major issue.

While going through the redeployment process in Kuwait, we had a couple days waiting for an air force aircraft. This was still only days from our combat experience at this point on the way to the home front. For most of the war, everyone knew upon deployment when they would generally be returning home, but it could easily be argued that the speed of the return from combat actually has a detrimental effect. In World War II the trip home on a boat took weeks or months. This allowed for another period of decompression for the soldiers. But now trying to reintegrate and decompress has to be done simultaneously, making the adjustment process much harder. It is a second order effect of modern war that is still not well understood.

Returning home was bittersweet. All soldiers find happiness in the freedoms of being home: showering whenever you want, walking barefoot on carpet, wearing clean clothes, eating good food, going out with friends, dancing, and drinking. Most of all we found happiness in just reconnecting with loved ones. Everyone missed their family, spouses, girlfriends, kids, and other loved ones. Being reunited was the sweet part of coming home, at least at first. The bitter part is what we bring back from combat. The transition can be dangerous: The simple act of driving a car becomes a stress-filled adventure for the first few days, depending on the soldier and his experiences. Every piece of trash on the road or guard barrier is scanned for bombs. Every building-lined avenue looks like a sniper alley. Feeling a lack of control when in crowds or around a lot of people is unsettling. For most soldiers, this all goes away fairly quickly, although the thoughts can linger in the back of the mind for extended periods. Some soldiers continue to struggle with what they saw and did while they were deployed—the stress, gore, and killing weighing them down. This is all going on while new stresses are introduced, including the friction of walking back into a home of loved ones who have figured out how to live without you as they learned new daily routines. It is not easy facing a wife you have not been intimate with for fifteen months, kids who are a year older and have spent that year without you, people who have changed for good and not so good. Suddenly there are bills, kid activities, and decisions about what to do on the weekend.

My return was a little out of the ordinary and bittersweet. 1LT Emily Shockley had redeployed two months earlier. We were able to stay in touch thanks again to the advantages and disadvantages of connected warfare. She was able to meet me at the reintegration center on Fort Carson. Although this was very different from being greeted by a wife and kids, it was also . . . complicated. When I had rushed to Colorado from Georgia to hurry up and deploy, I had simply lived in an extended stay hotel until it was time for me to leave. I put my few belongings into storage and departed. Now that I was back in Colorado, I was basically homeless. So when Emily came to pick me up there was a little bit of, "Ummm where should I take you?" Luckily, she opened her house and couch to me. One additional welcome aspect of being with Emily immediately after returning was that, as a recently returned veteran, she understood what I was going through. Unlike many people on the battalion and brigade staff, her job as an EOD officer took her outside the wire almost as much as an infantryman. She was a hands-on leader. She led from the front and was very often on site for the EOD (or detonation). She too had been shot at and faced the constant risk of direct fire, IEDs, mortars, and IRAMs. She had seen wounded or dead bodies and had friends who had been wounded and killed. I did not need to explain to her or avoid explaining to her that I was still on high alert and on the lookout for snipers and IEDs. She was more supportive and understanding than most spouses knew how to be. We also did not have to deal with any history of household decision-making or family finances. So despite a somewhat unclear personal situation, I came back to a less bitter, much sweeter homecoming.

Usually the transition chaos calms in time, at least for the most part. For the army's part, it tries as an organization to ease the transition. A series of mandatory reintegration classes are required once soldiers get back home. Slowly, soldiers and their families find a new normal; most soldiers find their way and continue life. They still go to work every day, so seeing the soldiers they served with helps in that reintegration. But it is short-lived because they are either quickly moved to another post, transferred out of the army, or all their brothers are transferred to other posts and replaced by different soldiers.

A new practice is to ship most people out of the unit soon after they return. That can be as short as ninety days after their redeployment. Officers, NCOs, and soldiers are transferred to new military bases. The army thinks this builds diversity, variety, and depth in military education, and overall team-building skills. For Alpha Company, this did not happen as planned. All the "stop-losses" were finally allowed to get out of the army and they exited en masse. Others got out of the army because their three- or four-year commitments were up. Within four months, all of the platoon leaders were gone as well as most of the squad leaders and soldiers. All that remained were two platoon sergeants and me. I stayed because I had joined the company while they were on their combat deployment and still had time left in my two-year assignment as company commander. Alpha Company was completely new. In the blink of an eye, it was a different organization made up of new team members. Everyone who had bonded over the shared hardships of war were scattered to all points of the compass. That brotherhood was now just a memory from the other side of the world.

For many of the soldiers who get out of the army, it is as traumatic as for those who stay in and is often cited as worse than being in combat itself. Ideally the shared bonds of combat and social cohesion, thereafter, tie the members of the small group to each other. On leaving the military, though, that deep feeling of brotherhood was likely never felt again. Once soldiers separate and reenter civilian life, they do not feel that anyone in the world understands what they have been through or what they have suffered and experienced except the brothers that were there with them and fellow veterans who have walked similar paths. They also feel an emptiness from no longer having a mission or purpose, an objective to achieve, side by side, each day.

There are very few professions that bring that sense of communal effort and mutual support. Professional sports are one possible exception, but not many people can make a career at that level and there is no threat of death. Law enforcement and firefighting are the most similar organizations that rely on small group interdependence. They have daily high-risk situations, teamwork, and cohesion, but there are still differences as they often face danger only occasionally or with a limited number of comrades. There are just a select few situations in life that require each person of a group to rely on the person next to them to do their job well in order for everyone to survive and succeed. Few careers bring the adrenal rush that soldiering carries with it almost every day, except on the days when we were bored stiff.

SSG Jimmy Martinez left the army in 2016, seven years after our combat tour in Iraq. After leaving Fort Carson and entering society far away from military personnel, he fell into a deep depression. He felt alone in the world. I will not pretend that I can psychoanalyze him and explain what caused his darkness. The important fact is that depression is very real. In part, Martinez was down because he went to war, formed a band of brothers to survive the horrors of combat, and then traumatically separated from that family. Four years after his retirement, he still has good days and bad days. He continues to struggle every day. When he meets another veteran, even a stranger at the grocery store wearing a "veteran" cap, it gives him an overwhelming connection of comfort, like a family member rediscovered. It is usually brief and just in passing, but it feels good. It brightens his day and makes him feels less alone.

He told me in a recent phone call that to this day there is a lot of that stuff that he does not share with family and friends. It is not that he tries to keep it bottled up, but they just could not understand. He told me, "I had felt alone for so long. Those experiences were a part of my life that I've learned to kind of put away. If you came to my house, you couldn't tell that I was in the army, unless you saw some of the stuff in my garage. It's always been easier for me to talk to the guys who went through it. There were just some things that I saw over there I don't like to talk about."

He described some of the things that we had seen as the worst that humanity has to offer: nasty, vial, inhuman things. Now that he is out, he uses social media infrequently. He said the only reason he even stays on social media, keeping his Facebook page active, is so he can be available if someone from his past army life wants to connect. When someone messages him, he is there. It has come in handy too. He had a few guys contact him when they were having a hard time. He continued,

> It's nice that we can reach out to each other via social media, but I think for some of those guys, they are very connected, always on social media. Sometimes there is a negative aspect, too. I really want to talk to so-and-so because a particular memory is bothering me, but you see them living their lives through their social media persona and do not want to bother them. You think, I do not want to burden them with my problems, they are happy. They are married and have kids, the last thing they want to hear about is my problems. With my experiences over there and after coming home and not really having anybody I could talk to face-to-face, somebody who understands what I am talking about, it is like I am surrounded by people but I am completely alone. There's definitely a wanting for a lot of us.

Recently Martinez was visited by one of his fellow sergeants from the 2008 Iraq tour. "When Sergeant Johnson came to visit," he recalled, "we had some beers and talked about Iraq. Our connection was instantaneous. It was honestly one of the most pleasant moments I have had in years. Just to be around an Alpha Company guy in flesh and blood sitting there, talking sh*t, drinking beer. It just felt like home, a different type of home because I had felt alone for such a long time . . . I think the generation of soldiers who are enlisting right now will struggle to achieve the emotional connection to the soldier to their left and right because of social media . . . They will have too much connectivity. It will be detrimental to any mission."

SSG Martinez tried to keep in touch with as many Alpha Company soldiers as possible, especially those from Green Platoon, like SGT Schetter, SGT Rubio, SPC Mazrim, and others. He particularly kept in touch with Schetter. He checked on Schetter frequently on Facebook, saying, "You still have my phone number, call me." On January 24, 2018, SGT Schetter posted on Facebook celebrating his eight years of friendship on Facebook with Martinez.

On February 18, 2018, less than a month after Martinez reached out, SGT Ryan Schetter committed suicide. He died in his mother's home at the age of thirty-one. No one knows which demons plagued Ryan. There is no way to now know if it was what he saw in 2008, when he was the driver of the third truck of the Green Platoon convoy the night they were attacked by a grenade and the Iraqi child was hit by the blast or if it was any other event in his twenty-six months of deployment. After serving two tours in Iraq, Schetter returned to his hometown to continue his military career as a recruiter. He was honorably discharged in 2014 and had been studying at Southeast Missouri State University, where he was a member of the Student Veterans Organization and volunteered at the Veterans Transition Home.[1] When he died, he was engaged to his lifelong friend Vanessa. Her daughter, Kyra, recently joined the army, the career Ryan had encouraged.

I was happy to hear that SSG Martinez had tried to be there for Ryan, even messaging him, "I am here for you brother." Maybe SGT Shetter felt less alone for the moment, seeing those words. Maybe a virtual connection was not what he was looking for. Again, I cannot pretend to know. It also made me happy to hear that several of his Alpha Company brothers were able to attend the funeral.

Veteran suicide is a complex problem. From 2007 to 2017, the rate of suicide among veterans jumped almost 50 percent, reaching twenty-two suicides a day. Veterans are 1.5 times more likely to die by suicide than Americans who never served in the military.[2] While soldiers can sometimes be helped by talking with the people they served with, they often do not want to bother that person, the ones they see on social media who seem to be doing okay and living a good life. They do not want to be a burden to that friend. Of course that other soldier would usually love to hear from a battle buddy, especially one who needs help, one that they can help. These bonds forged in war are often stronger than even connections with family. Societal norms seem to push us to believe our wives and kids should be the people we feel closest to, not some guy we have not seen in ten years who was with us at war for twelve months. This can cause the soldier to feel guilt over something he cannot control, even when what he is experiencing is normal.

Do not get me wrong—what happened to the soldiers of Alpha Company is not all bad news. Yes many have struggled, but many have also flourished. 2LT Kane got out of the army after he returned from Iraq, went into corporate America, and is now a very successful construction project manager with a staff and large team. Tripp, Donovan, and Fincher stayed in the army and became either first sergeants or command sergeants major, most doing multiple additional deployments. We all shared one thing: a connection from our shared experiences.

Instantaneous connection made possible by the telecommunication explosion has a role even in the process of soldiers returning home. While in war, soldiers are together but connected to the outside world. When they return from battle, they are still connected through the internet to those with whom they experienced, but many are still alone, like Martinez. They are typically connected to their band of brothers solely through electronic communication. Sitting at the barstool of a VFW or American Legion, like I remember from my childhood, is arguably not as frequent a practice for returning veterans of today's wars. There are pockets of strong post 9/11 veterans' groups with active and frequent meetings at locations like the American Legions or VFWs, but they do seem to play a different role than they did for the post–World War II generation who returned en masse to their communities. The numbers are just different. After the end of World War II in 1945, almost eight million allied military personnel were sent home. In September 1945, two million American army personnel began transitioning home.[3] Many of these soldiers returned to find large groups of veterans with similar experiences in their own communities. War changes and so does society. Now soldiers returning to society will see similarities or shared experiences with less and less of the population.

Veterans today have social media to stay connected with private Facebook groups for their units. Martinez did that, as did I. We looked to social media to keep us in touch with those soldiers with whom we had formed the bonds of such remarkable strength. But virtual connection is not the same as in-person communication. The human desire to connect in such a personal way will not be diminished any time soon. We as a society and/or military know more about how to override human biology as a prerequisite to fight (the need for training, conditioning, a sense of control, and the awareness of fellow soldiers with you in the battle) in combat than is known about how to deal with combat and return to society after a war. It is all about forming social, emotional bonds. The need to establish the environment for bonds of friendship, trust, and love to form will be as critical today as it was in ancient warfare. Cohesion and lasting connections are the very essence of what is needed to send men and women to war, and it is the vital component to bringing them home—for them to live with war.

The war correspondent and author Sebastian Junger accurately describes why many soldiers miss war:

> I've been covering wars for almost 20 years, and one of the remarkable things for me is how many soldiers find themselves missing it. How is it someone can go through the worst experience imaginable, and come home, back to their home, and their family, their country, and miss the war? . . . I think what he [the soldier] missed is brotherhood. He missed, in some ways, the opposite of killing.

What he missed was connection to the other men he was with. Now, brotherhood is different from friendship. Friendship happens in society, obviously. The more you like someone, the more you'd be willing to do for them. Brotherhood has nothing to do with how you feel about the other person. It's a mutual agreement in a group that you will put the welfare of the group, you will put the safety of everyone in the group above your own. In effect, you're saying, I love these other people more than I love myself.[4]

Combat is arguably the worst environment and human experience imaginable, but soldiers would rather be there united with their comrades, an attachment formed under great duress, than return to a society wherein one does not know who they can or cannot count on. They miss their tribe, the band of brothers that slept together, ate together, and trusted each other unconditionally.[5]

A Winning Team

12

On the Other End of Connected Warfare

In May 2018 I retired from the army after twenty-five years of service. I had served eight years as an enlisted soldier and seventeen years as an officer. A lot had changed since my 2008 Iraq deployment, and the deployment in 2003 seemed like a lifetime ago. In 2009 I married 1LT Emily Shockley, whom I had met in that God-awful COP Callahan. The local cell phones we both carried in Iraq allowed us to stay in touch when I moved to COP Apache. When we both made it back to Fort Carson, Colorado, we started dating. It did not take long before I asked her to marry me—and she said yes! We began a new life together.

At the time of my retirement and after nine years of marriage, we had three beautiful kids: Isaac, Isabel, and Maggie. Emily also survived breast cancer. We had spent four years each teaching at the United States Military Academy and then Emily returned to an operational unit as a battalion executive officer with yet another combat deployment on the horizon. I then became a work-from-home parent.

Emily and I approached everything as a team, especially parenting. I am not sure if it was due to our upbringings or the fact that we had both been in the army for so long that we assimilated fully to this new life. It was probably a combination of the two. Our military backgrounds also made us adamant about being strong, independent individuals. We both like to demonstrate our ability to do whatever the mission, task, or job calls for while also approaching every task or mission as a team. It is a tough combination, but we made it work.

Now I say that we were a team, but that really is not true. Before we had kids it was much less complicated. We both woke at five-thirty in the morning and went our separate ways to do exercises with our units. Emily occasionally surprised me at work by bringing me coffee. Then we would both work a full day and try to make it home to eat dinner together. Children changed everything, as they always do. I actually called Isaac, our firstborn, the game changer. From the moment he took his first breath, all the priorities in my life changed.

For team Spencer, there were things I just could not do, such as breastfeeding, and there were a few things we each did more often than the other. Emily prepared almost all the dinners. I did almost all the yard work, but we really tried to share all the duties of parenthood. Of course we were both in the army and we were at the mercy of our jobs and immediate supervisors. For the first two years of Isaac's life, I worked at the Pentagon, which was more than an hour from our home. Emily was in company command less than fifteen minutes from our house. That meant if anything happened with Isaac, the expectation was that Emily would have to handle it because she worked ten minutes from our child's day care, even though she was in a more stressful position at the time. She was Wonder Woman and I hated the burden she had to bear because I had to leave before Isaac woke and often did not even make it to dinner due to evening commutes in Washington DC.

We knew when going into a life with kids that being a dual military family would be very difficult. We still did it, and we added a child every two years. Isaac was our first, Isabel was born two years to the day after Isaac, and then Maggie came two years later. As expected, dual military life was challenging but even more so than we imagined. The commitment between the army and our family, to be there for our kids, was a daily struggle. We dropped the kids off at day care at six o'clock in the morning, and one of us, usually Emily, picked them up after four thirty in the afternoon. This would be just in time to feed them dinner, possibly go to an after-school activity like gymnastics or soccer, and then it was time for baths, to read books, and put them to bed. We were really only spending two to three hours a day with them plus weekends if we did not have to work. We were actually lucky. Many soldier parents we knew on other posts or with different jobs than ours had to drop their kids off before six o'clock in the morning to make the typical army exercise formation, and picked them up when the day care closed at six o'clock in the evening, usually running in the door to avoid the by-the-minute extra monetary charge. That is not what we wanted. Although we appreciated the support we received from family, and we loved our day care teachers like family, we did not want other people raising our children.

The stress of managing work and being there for the kids was always present. In general soldiers do not get to call in sick to work and they do not get to take days off if a child is sick. If one of our kids became ill—typically every few weeks for babies—and was banned from day care for no less than forty-eight hours (like someone with a contagious disease) it caused the enactment of the real and feared problem of "Who is not going to work today?" Luckily we had some amazing bosses who always understood, but even then, we had to deal with the perception of not being at work or requiring special exceptions. The guilt associated with the perception of not performing well frequently sparked disagreements between us, often targeted at the person who got to go to work.

The plan was always for me to retire at twenty years, which is the magic year a soldier can retire and immediately start receiving retirement pay; however, I did not. There was nothing really forcing me out. Emily and I were still making it work, sort of. At around the twenty-year mark, Emily and I were reassigned together—which is not always the case when married couples are both in the army—to teach at the United States Military Academy in West Point, New York. The work hours and flexibility were much different than a typical army job or location so there was no real reason for me to get out of the army.

The first indication that something would need to change involved Emily taking a high-profile job. She was selected to work as the xo for the dean of the West Point Academic Board, who was a one-star general. Before Emily accepted the job, we discussed what it meant. We knew that working for a general officer meant Emily would lose much of her previous flexibility. She would have to work longer hours and have much less predictability with her schedule. We knew that for the first time I would have to take primary kid duties: I was in the batter's box. Emily quickly started to miss dinners. Shortly thereafter came cancer. I was thrust completely into the primary caregiver role. But neither work nor cancer stopped Emily. She still found a way to keep up her share of the teamwork and the shared roles we had in place. She was planning dinners for us while getting her radiation treatments. She rushed to get the kids during any free moment she had.

Even through cancer and Emily's high-profile job, there was still no reason for me to get out of the army. Emily's boss and the entire West Point team were amazing. Within a few days of her diagnosis and a few days before surgery, Emily's boss brought her into the office to ensure her that she still wanted her as the xo. She and the entire West Point community bent over backward to help us out. Our military service is a part of our identity. We did not know what would happen with Emily's cancer or how it would affect our family, but she did not want to lose her place in the army at this point.

As Emily kicked cancer's ass and she returned fully to her military job, we knew the time was coming for me to decide about the military. As the saying goes: all good things must come to an end. Soldiers are usually only allowed to stay in one location for two to three years. So when our time at West Point was coming to an end, and the army was asking for our preferences on our next move, we knew my time had run out. I notified my assignment manager, human resources of the army, that I would retire.

I will not lie; my retirement was a sad day. I barely let Emily celebrate it, although we did go through with the normal ceremony. We had friends and family come from all over and there was cake, but it was not a happy day for me. If I was not a soldier, what was I? I had been a soldier since I was seventeen years old. My mom actually signed me in—we joke that she signed me away—at sixteen. I joined the army before fully maturing and was literally re-raised in the military. I was taught how to eat right, take care of my body, talk to people, respect others and earn respect, build cohesive teams, and so on. To say I was institutionalized is an understatement. Being a soldier was at the core of my self-identity.

At my retirement ceremony I gave a small speech. I put on a good front, and yet it actually felt more like a funeral than a retirement. I told the small crowd of family and friends that for all of my adult life my identity was founded in being a soldier. As time passed, I took on other related identities: sergeant, ranger, officer, commander, brother to other warriors, and husband. Still, none of those identities was as important to me as being a father. I said that being a "daddy" was my most important identity. I meant that deeply.

What I did not say, what I would not say in public, was that I was leaving the army because I did not think I could be a good father while still being a soldier. The military life completely works for some families. We met some amazing families during our time in the army that seemed to not only make it work but loved it. It just was not what we wanted. The army is founded on ground-based soldiers of small teams who rely on putting the unit, the team, the fellow soldiers first. I had done that in combat and for my entire career. I cherished those times, being in a band of brothers. But I personally did not think I could continue to do it while my kids watched from home; once I thought that, I knew it would not be fair to my men, my brothers, to continue.

You see, my dad left when I was about six or seven years old. My mom raised three kids while working three jobs. I had absolutely no adult male influence my entire upbringing. My mom did the very best she could, but aside from that, I was left with little male guidance, mentorship, or dreams. The military became my ticket out. I started a new life, one where I was determined to never repeat the past. I would be there for my family, unlike my dad was for me.

Within a month of my retirement, we left West Point and moved back to Fort Carson, Colorado, where Emily and I had started our lives together. We knew before getting assigned there that Emily would have to deploy to a war zone only six months after our arrival. Luckily she deployed to Kuwait instead of Iraq. United States military forces have served in Kuwait since Operation Desert Storm. The bases and amenities are very nice. The base she deployed to, Camp Arifjan, made the old FOB Prosperity look like a slum. Camp Arifjan had its own post office, Starbucks, Baskin Robbins, Taco Bell, two post exchanges, 24-hour gyms, swimming pools, community centers, single-person CHUs for officers, and strong Wi-Fi access across the base.[1] Emily was required to visit her subordinate units in Iraq and Afghanistan, so it was not all cotton candy and roses, but we both knew from personal experience that it could be much worse. She would be gone for nine months, and I would take care of the kids and the home front until she returned.

We had just moved to Colorado but all of our family was on the East Coast. We lived too far north of the military post for me to get to know anyone she worked with, and to be honest, I did not feel right joining her unit's family readiness group (FRG). The FRGs were made up mostly of the spouses of soldiers; the military commander met with them from time to time to establish lines of communication between the command and the soldiers' families. The groups also conducted activities like parties and afternoon coffees to let the spouses become friends, talk about their concerns, and share what they knew. They are a great resource, but I just did not see them for me.

Immediately after leaving the military, all of my daily interactions with people who understood my situation and had experienced the things I had experienced, ended. I do not drink and I could not see myself hanging out in bars, so the VFWs and American Legions that were so important after World War II and that I observed when I was young were not for me. Through Facebook, I stayed in touch with many of the brothers I had served with. By "in touch," I mean I watched their lives evolve through what they posted, and occasionally made a comment or two on a military-related post, remembering our time on days like Memorial Day or Veterans Day. I would not call that "connected," and they could not help me in my current situation. Operation Homefront was a solo mission.

A few months before Emily's deployment, we decided to tell the kids she would be leaving to work overseas. Each kid processed the news differently. Isaac, our oldest at seven, took it the worst. He cried and asked, "Why can't Daddy go?" I thought, but did not say, "Oh boy, would I! Put me in, coach!" My silence did not stop Emily from saying, "I wish he could go, too." I fully recognized this was counter to my desire to be a dad, but that warrior part of me was not dead; it was just a lesser priority. Isabel, five years old and our consummate stoic, smiled at Isaac and said, "Oh well, at least you have your mommy doll" (a doll Emily had bought for each kid with a full picture of her in uniform on it). Maggie, our youngest at three, really did not understand but smiled anyway. At that moment, the worries started. I was concerned about how the kids might cope without their mom, both in the short and long term. To be sure, thousands upon thousands of military families have replayed this scene in the last decade and throughout history, but this was my family.

Some research shows that military children often become more resilient through the constant moving during a military life.[2] It supposedly enables them to make friends quickly, accept change, etc. That may be true. But if you dig enough, you will find other studies that show that deployments that have been a staple of military life for over seventeen years have been associated with poorer mental health in military families, behavioral problems in children, and higher risk of divorce.[3] Trauma is trauma and I personally did not think children should have to be without their moms or dads for extended periods of time. The military is not alone in this; plenty of professions require parents to travel, some for extended periods. Most of the U.S. Army had been on a nine-to-fifteen-month deployed and a twelve-to-twenty-four-month home rotation since 2002, with little end in sight. Some army families—I often think of SSG Delgado, SFC Tripp, or SFC Donovan from 2008, who had all been deployed for over four years of their children's lives—had been dealing with an absent parent for a very long time. I recognized all this but also fully understood that it was our chosen profession. Nevertheless, this was my family and I hated the situation.

I did not have a solution in mind. The all-volunteer U.S. military could not simply be an army of single people. If I think back to early in my career as a soldier, I might have actually believed that, but that is not reality. Hundreds of thousands of parents had gone before Emily or stayed at home like I did to raise the kids and continue life, but it still royally sucked.

Emily built a "deployment wall" in our main family room. It was a wall with the words "Our Deployment Wall" scrolled across the top; two large clocks, one marked "here" and the other marked "there"; a mailbox and dry-erase board for messages to mom, and a chalkboard countdown that allowed the kids to change the numbers daily.

I was torn about the dolls and the wall. Thanks to the army and war, I had learned to compartmentalize. I preferred putting anything reminding me of her away, finding a new normal, and then rejoicing when she returned. None of this was about me, however. It was for the kids, and really, I think it was for Emily. She did not want to be forgotten.

"Store my ring," she said. Just like that. She said that if anything happened to her, she did not want it to get lost. In my head I reworded her statement to be: "Take this, if I die I don't want it lost." Either way I took her ring and stored it safely in our fire-safe box. It was a somber realization of the reality of where she was going. Even though she would be in Kuwait most of the time, I knew she would still be traveling to other more dangerous combat zones.

Emily made Thanksgiving dinner on the eleventh of November because she would not be home for the actual holiday. It was good and yet an early reminder that she would be gone during all upcoming holidays. I had a strong feeling that despite telling the kids that she would be leaving soon, none of them realized why we were doing the big meal early. Of course we discussed it with them, but what do you do? Keep talking about it to ensure they get it? They had never been more than a week or two without either their mom or dad. Did they really understand what nine months would be like?

Doing a mock Thanksgiving made me think of all the holidays I would have to do by myself. Emily, super mom, had been amazing and adamant about establishing family holiday traditions. She did it all: special things to eat, like turkey, corn, whipped potatoes, and cabbage for Thanksgiving and Christmas, and all the special gifts and unique practices for holidays like getting new clothes for Easter and making 4th of July American flag cake. I wondered how the hell I was going to pull off birthdays, Christmas, and summer vacations without her. Those are all multiple-phase operations with extreme planning. I would rather plan a full combat mission against an enemy city. For seven years, Emily had always been the one to meticulously lay presents out early to ensure each child was more or less equally covered, with no one given too much or too little, equal amounts of money being spent on each kid. Some presents were wrapped and others were not. I was usually in the garage assembling something. She did the lion's share of the holiday decorating. I just did outdoor decorations or activities, like hanging lights. Now it would be all me: every holiday, every tradition.

On the last day before her deployment, Emily had to go to work just to show she was alive, but other than that she had the day off. While she was out, I decided to watch Netflix while ironing. I chose a new series called "Medal of Honor." That was a mistake. Watching scenes of combat in Afghanistan cut too close to my own experiences and thinking about Emily being "over there."

Later that day, Emily and I attended the Veterans Day recognition ceremony at our kids' school. She and I were seated on the stage of the school's gymnasium among the guests of honor. There were probably about twenty to thirty veterans on the stage. All the kids were seated on the gym floor in front of us. At one point they burst out with a spontaneous chant of: "U.S.A, U.S.A, U.S.A." Emily and I were very moved. Who would not be? But I also wondered if this was a Veterans Day ceremony or a parade to say good-bye to Emily. It was weird that it felt like some type of ceremony to send her off. After the chanting was silenced and the guest speaker gave his talk, one child from each fifth grade class, the ones who had won a writing assignment on what Veterans Day meant to them, was called up in front of the assembly to read their essays. One girl read an essay she had written describing being a military child—how her mom was deployed right now and how hard it was having to spend Thanksgiving and Christmas without her. Great—this was all I needed a day before Emily was scheduled to leave. I did not want to look at Emily, not even in my periphery. Eyes straight I thought. But after an elbow and a soft voice in my ear, she said, "Isaac is crying." Damn. How fitting with my own feelings. My child is in the crowd crying; he later said it was because it made him think of Mommy leaving. I could not get to him or console him in any way. I realized how I felt about being there for my kids while their mommy goes to war for nine months: helpless.

Later that night as Emily packed her bags and stacked them by the door, it really set in that she was leaving. I called to have her phone suspended, something we could not see ourselves without. It was hard to imagine her disconnecting from the real world, our family world, to enter another world, one with war at its center. Based on my two combat deployments, I knew that is exactly what needed to happen, an eerie disconnection from our life. Luckily times had changed and she would be entering that other world in a new connected type of wartime environment.

Our last few hours were spent like every other night, except Emily let the kids sleep in bed with her. I did not look forward to breaking them of that. The last thing I remember hearing is Isaac telling her how he did not want her to leave and something about someone farting in bed.

Early in the morning of her departure, before the kids woke, I took Emily to the place where she would load bags and ship off. We did not speak many words, and then we took a quick photo and said good-bye. Long gone were the days of me being a stoic. Having children and the love I had for Emily had turned me into a giant softie. I tried to keep my emotions in check, nonetheless. I had no idea what the right words were to say in that moment. "Stay safe" was all I could come up with. We had debated taking the kids to the send-off. The timeline really prevented it, but once the soldiers checked in, the families had a chance to hang out a few hours while the soldiers waited for their transportation. Neither of us wanted that. Emily said she did not want to "ugly cry" in front of the kids and her soldiers; I agreed. Taking Emily—my wife and mother of my kids—to go to war felt more like a military task: drive to base, get the car unpacked, and say good-bye. And that is about how I tried to handle it, despite all my emotions. We both had eyes full of tears, but we held it together. I am not sure if we were trying to help the kids or ourselves. I know that if the kids had been there, if the tears in their eyes had started to roll, it would have been "ugly" crying all around.

I also could not help thinking that we had robbed the kids of the good-bye. As parents we wanted to protect our kids from trauma. But we did not spare them the sadness; that came no matter what. One of the youngest memories I have as a kid is standing by my dad's faded blue four-door sedan as he was driving away. He was leaving to supposedly find work in Florida. We lived in Indiana. My parents had been divorced for a few months, but I think they had some type of arrangement to still live together for me and my two sisters. I cannot remember how old I was, maybe my son's age as when Emily was deploying, but it's a vivid memory. I also remember the day my mom got the phone call a few months later when my dad told her that he had found a girlfriend and was not coming back. I think we kids all knew when he left that he was not coming back, but not my mom. I am no child psychologist, but I have to believe both of those memories shaped me and contributed to the development of my personality. Should we have shielded our kids from those real family events, from processing scenes and dealing with them? Clearly, we chose to be protectors. If it was overprotection, we will probably never know.

It finally hit me as I drove away after dropping off Emily. The car was silent on the long drive home. It hurt really bad. I did not expect it to be that painful or so immediate. For God's sake, I was veteran of two wars and a ranger. It felt like I was in mourning. It felt similar, though not as extreme, as when my mom died a few years earlier. Why? Emily was not dead; she just was not here. Nevertheless, the emotion was nearly overwhelming.

I actually got tired of hearing people say, "Oh, it won't be that bad, you have social media and other forms of communication." No, actually it was terrible. No amount of technology replaces physical presence, the feeling of someone there. Some things are irreplaceable: the touch of a mother, my wife's smile when I do something crazy, the laugh of my best friend, and the ever-present feeling of someone else alive in the room with me. Because telecommunications are a part of our existence, that's what people said; somehow they thought that keystrokes were a substitute for having Emily there. That is what we said to the kids, though: "Mommy will be able to call often; we can always FaceTime her; you'll see her almost every day." We said those things, but we really did not know if it would be true or how much it would help.

We had a friend come to the house to watch the kids while I executed the drop-off mission. The friend was retired LTC Rob MacMillan, who had officiated our wedding on top of Pike's Peak mountain, and was also godfather to Isaac. Isabel, the devious one, convinced him that they were allowed to drink Gatorade and eat cookies for breakfast. Oh well, at least they were all happy! I tried to be stoic and hurriedly finished getting them ready for school; within fifteen minutes, I had them out the door. To be honest, I did not want to face them. I did not want to see their pain. As I walked Isaac into school, he looked at me about to cry, "I miss Mommy." All I could say was, "I know buddy, me too." He continued to walk and faded into the crowd of little people. I did not know it at the time, but I would say that phrase a thousand more times over the coming months..

When I got home, I just sulked for almost the entire day. I was in mourning. How was I going to raise three kids for nine months? I had already learned that parenting was not like combat. There is no training for parenting. You just jump right in like a paratrooper but without a day of training. Yet here I was, jumping in again. Just like being a brand new company commander in Iraq, I learned on the job. I of course had many years of on-the-job training to be a parent, lots of experience. But parenting with my best friend and partner was completely different than doing it alone. I had to learn and experience doing things solo rather than as a team. There was also no immediate feedback, like there is in combat. In battle the enemy lets you know quickly if you do something wrong. With kids, I may never know. I think all parents worry if they are doing the "right" things. I really worried about whether I would or if the experience might, in some way, harm them through something I would say or a moment of need I would miss.

For the rest of that day, I tried to immerse myself in work, dishes, laundry, but I struggled to concentrate on anything. Despite all the mental preparation, knowing this day was coming for months, it still hit me like a ton of bricks. I felt lost. And then I panicked, "What the hell am I going to make for dinner?"

My plan after picking the kids up from school was to keep them as busy possible. As I was pulling into our driveway, Maggie saw Emily's car in the garage and asked, "Mommy home? Mommy home tomorrow?" It broke my heart. How do you explain to a three-year-old that Mommy is not coming home for two hundred and eighty-four days when they have no temporal sense of time?

That night, Emily called. Unlike during my two deployments, Emily was living in an even more connected world. She was making her way to Kuwait and had stopped in Germany. Since she had an iPhone and we had Verizon service that had not yet turned off, she had phone service just like she was traveling in our town, although a little more costly. Each kid got to speak to her, but only for a few minutes. After ten minutes, Emily said she had to go. For some insane reason, I was angry after the call. Why could she only talk for ten minutes? It only upset the kids more. I also knew it was insane to be upset: she was deploying to a combat zone. I should have know better, but having to deal with three distressed kids steamed me, despite a career of military service and knowing she had no control over her schedule.

The first day finally ended as I was putting the kids to bed. Each one explained how they missed Mommy. For the girls, all I could say was, "Me too, honey." What were the right words? For Isaac, I told him to "try to be strong." It is probably not right to expect a boy to be different but again I was doing what I felt was right. I have struggled with this concept of what it means to be strong ever since Isaac was born. I was raised by a single mom in a house full of women (her and my two sisters), and I did not play any sports in school. There was not a single male influence I could emulate until I joined the army. I felt completely in the dark as I tried my best to be a good father to my son.

I approached each day as the first. Stay as busy as possible. Keep the routine. Wake at 0615 hours, get the kids dressed for school, brush their teeth, fix the girls' hair (do not forget a cute bow), feed everyone breakfast, and move out for school drop off. Then it was time for the grocery store. How do you plan and buy food with one less adult? I soon learned. I was adamant to not slack off on dinner meals. I did not resort to "single guy" pizza and hot dogs. It's especially tough with picky eaters. I swear Maggie is a vegan. No matter what I cooked, she only ate well if it was pasta and milk (ok, maybe not a full vegan). So we stuck to the schedule: I picked the kids up from school, went to an after-school activity (usually soccer), made it home in time to cook dinner, gave baths, brushed teeth, read books to the kids for twenty to thirty minutes, and then put them to bed. My twenty-five years of military service was showing up with schedules and strict routines.

Before Emily left for her deployment, she spent hours recording herself reading books to the kids in front of a camera. She usually woke up early every day and recorded a book or two. She eventually did about forty of them. Amazing! Now that she was gone, each kid watched and listened to Mommy reading them a book. Emily really did everything she could to make sure she was still a part of their daily lives.

A week or two went by. The schedule and busy routine were working well. Even on the weekends, I kept the children active. I replaced school with activities at the pool or the local trampoline park. As I got braver, I took the kids out to eat once a week just as a treat. The only real challenge was when Isabel needed to go to the bathroom during the meal. I could not leave the kids at the table to take her. Telling her, "Look you're going to have to hold it" did not work. So I roused everyone up and off we went to the men's restroom. I always hoped the waitress did not think we had left and would start clearing our table. The next challenge was when Miss Independent (Maggie) decided that she was too big to go into the men's restroom with me. She wanted to go into the girls' bathroom. Usually I would not let her go in somewhere like that by herself, but I would learn in many ways that what I used to be comfortable with would have to change.

I turned to music to calm me. Over the years, I had rarely listened to music. In the car we played *Kidz Bop* for the kids. When I worked out, walked the dog, or drove by myself, I listened to audiobooks, not music. But on my first deployment in 2003, I found that music was my refuge; I had an old-school discman and listened to CDs to help me fall asleep. Each night I fell asleep to the music, and every morning I woke up with the cord to the headphones woven around my ears or, worst case, my neck. The lyrics really did not matter much. It was the voices; they calmed my mind. After my 2003 deployment, I immediately stopped—or felt I did not need—the routine. On my next deployment to Iraq in 2008, I found I needed to have music again. One of my favorites was Kid Rock and Sheryl Crow's "Picture." I must have played that song a thousand times. It probably served as a coping mechanism for my brain from extreme stress. Once on the home front as a house dad, my mind spiraling in a thousand directions, I returned to my music. After the kids went to bed I found myself just watching music videos, YouTube singers, and singing competition shows like *The Voice*.

When Emily had made it to Kuwait and was established in her CHU and work schedule, she was able to get Wi-Fi set up in her room. This meant that she could call the kids without having to leave her bed. Because of the time zone, Emily woke up at four o'clock in the morning to FaceTime with the kids everyday around seven o'clock at night our time which was just about the time I was finishing bath time in our routine. I handed one of the kids the iPad and continued the routine, brushing teeth, and reading books. After she worked through each kid, we said goodnight and told her we loved her. After I made sure the kids had fallen asleep, I continued to text with her for the next thirty minutes to an hour as she did her morning exercise and got coffee before heading into her tactical operations center (TOC).

During this time, I found myself on the other end of connected warfare. I was the home life intertwining with her war routines. Her experiences were also finding their way into our home life. I consciously tried to refrain from adding stress to her life. Although she was mainly in Kuwait and I knew when she was in other places, not necessarily exactly where, but at least another country, I still wanted to shield her from the daily anxiety of the home front since I knew from personal experiences how that could impact soldiering. I wanted her mind focused on her missions and on returning physically and mentally healthy. And yet I found she was having none of that. She wanted to be a part of our daily lives, and modern technology allowed it. I think her greatest fears were that we would forget her, that her influence would change, and we would create a new normal without her.

Even if I wanted to shield her from the tensions at home, it was nearly impossible. Every night she wanted to know the good and bad. She asked the kids how their day went. What was the funniest part of their day? What had they learned that day at school? Even I did not know what was going to come out of their mouths. Sometimes, it was crazy things. Maggie explained, in the way only a three-year-old can, how she scared Daddy. I sleep very hard once I nod off. Emily had always been the first person to be awoken by the kids. With her gone, I was the magnet for late night escapades. Maggie walked into my room one night, stood a few inches from my face, and then screamed, "Daddy!" I must have jumped three feet off the bed. By the sound of the scream, I thought she was hurt. I scooped her up and blurted out, "What happened? Are you ok?" She said, "I lost my button." Yeah, all the kids enjoyed telling Mommy that story. They also enjoyed telling Mommy any time I raised my voice or had to correct their behavior. Emily was usually a great sport, listening to their list of complaints but not commenting to me. One day she mentioned to me, "Make sure you don't burn them out on routine." In hindsight, it was a fair comment, but in the moment, it upset me. Don't burn them out on routine? That was the only way I was surviving. I did not let her know it bothered me. Again, I tried my best to keep her anxiety low.

It was a bad situation, no matter where she was. Kids want both of their parents. They missed her, and it showed. There was nothing that could be done. I missed her too, so while I was supposed to be the strong one, it still hurt. I had a sinking feeling in my stomach, an achy pain that I tried to keep at bay. I would notice something of Emily's, like her hairbrush, and I was almost shocked by her absence. Sometimes it felt so bad that it increased my breathing. This was not to the point where I could not breathe, but where my heart raced and I struggled to breath normally. Perhaps I was experiencing actual anxiety. Some days I could work at night, others I could not. Getting things done during the day was also hit or miss. In the early weeks, I had an extreme sense of vulnerability, a heightened sense of risk. What would I do if there was an emergency with one of the kids? The closest friend was thirty minutes across town. Our family was all on the other side of the country. It did not matter. I had to be strong for the kids and I never let them see my doubt, fear, or pain.

One day Emily and I were discussing things we would do when she got back. We were only two months in. An irrational thought hit me: this was going to last forever. This was obviously not true; that is just how it seemed to me.

It did not take long for the signs of the emotional toll to show up in the kids. Each one processed and struggled differently. Maybe before technology, I could have hidden that from Emily, but not only did she not want me to do that, she told me directly to never hide things from her. It did not matter anyway because she was seeing it in real time, live every night through FaceTime. Isabel started to rebel. I had to correct her behavior and send her to her room more and more each day. It started with little things, like saying rude things to Maggie: "Get out of my room" (they shared a room), or "Mom can't understand your writing." One night I corrected her and sent her to her room right before Emily called. Emily asked to talk with her, so I put the iPad on Isabel's bed. Emily kept asking her to talk and explain why she was making poor decisions. After a few moments of silence, Isabel just started crying and said she did not know why she was being mean or disrespectful. She just sobbed. Emily had to watch on the screen a situation that demanded a personal, physical touch—a hug from a mom and words of encouragement: "It'll be okay." A hug from her dad at that moment would not have been the same, especially since I had just sent her to her room.

I could usually see that Isaac was having a bad day or night because he wore his emotions on his sleeve. A few months into Emily's absence, though, Maggie started to have urinary problems. She had to go pee more and more frequently. It eventually got so bad that she would go to pee every five minutes and cry that she had to pee; only a drop or two would come out when she did. As a guy, I had no clue about girl problems. I consulted Emily every night. Did she have a urinary tract infection? She had no fever and was drinking plenty of fluids. I gave her cranberry juice, yet the problem continued. I took her to urgent care. The doctors tested her for a urinary tract infection but found nothing. After more internet searching, we found out that frequent urination in young children can reflect stress, emotional tension, and change.[4] The thought of my baby experiencing so much emotional stress that she was in physical pain just about killed me. What could I do? Take her to counseling? The thought of that was also devastating. I felt like I was failing.

There were, of course, many ups and downs throughout this time. Emily often sent letters home. I tried to save any school crafts or things we would make for her at home and mail them together every few weeks. The kids were ecstatic when there was mail from their mom. Emily was even able to continue recording her reading books. At the United Service Organization (USO) in Kuwait, there was a shop where soldiers could come in, select from a variety of kids' books, and go into special rooms to record themselves reading the books. The USO then boxed up the book and SD card with the video, and mailed it to the soldier's family. Despite the videos and daily FaceTime, the kids wanted the actual letters, the physical pieces of paper. Each visit to the mailbox was a major event. When a box or letter from Emily came in, each kid visibly lit up; it was the highlight of their day or week. I often found Isabel sleeping with a letter or hand-drawn picture from her mom.

The down times were still frequent. I felt horrible the first time the kids did not want to talk to Emily. Isabel was the first one to refuse. I asked if she wanted to talk, more of a procedural thing than a question, so she recognized it was her turn. She replied, "No," and Emily heard it. That could not have made Emily feel good. I tried to explain to the kids how Mommy needed to talk to them as much as they liked talking to her, even if it was only for a few moments. I told Isabel to let Mommy know you love her. Next it was Isaac. He wanted to play the "text game" rather than talk through FaceTime. The text game was just him texting Emily. That usually entailed Isaac sending a string of emojis. Emily complained to me that he was not talking to her. She threatened to call less frequently. I knew what a day in a combat zone was like, but I did not know what it was like waking up and calling home to try to talk to your kids, only to discover that they were uninterested or having a bad emotional day, struggling without you. I imagined how those thoughts would sit with anyone the whole day until the next call, which would set anyone on edge, wondering whether it was going to be a good call or not.

One of the worst experiences was, surprisingly, Christmas. Such a big holiday without a complete family was just a major reminder of all the downsides of Emily's absence. For the first time in our family, I did almost all the shopping myself, although Emily bought things online and shipped them to the house. Maybe that played to the kid's advantage, as my guilt kicked in during selection time and any normal price limits were stretched way beyond anything in the past. I did my best to replicate the joy and traditions of our previous experiences. I decorated the house to the extreme, again something Emily usually oversaw. Wrapping presents without the kids seeing was a challenge, so I took care of most of the gifts late into the night. Without a lookout, I felt like I was sneaking into an enemy base trying not to make a sound. Each sound I made caused me to fear that a potential enemy was about to walk down the stairs into my hideout; it made my heart race.

The plan for Christmas day was that I would set up an iPad of Mommy for the big reveal and for the opening of each present. Emily had to wake up in the middle of the night her time to make that happen. Each present was opened and shown to her: "Look Mommy, Santa brought me a karaoke machine!" I thought it went well, despite the awkward futuristic and sad feel of a chair with an iPad on it showing Emily's smiling face the whole time. We finished opening all the presents and said good-bye to Mommy. The kids began their daylong toy-playing ritual. And yet, as well as it seemed to have gone for us at home, it had gone horribly for Emily. She laid in her bed crying for over an hour. The experience had torn her apart. The inability to be there to hold the kids, to physically witness their innocent joy and belief in Santa's magic just crushed her. She had missed a major family event. She could not cry for too long because she had volunteered to take a shift in the operations center so that other soldiers could call their families on Christmas, so back to war she went. When I learned how hurt she had been, it was devastating for me as her husband. Was I failing in that role, too? Just as she wished she could have held her children in their joy, I yearned to hold her in her sadness. That was my job, along with all the rest, but I could not do it from seven thousand miles away.

Now that I was seeing the connected battlefield from the homefront perspective, I could not know exactly how it was impacting Emily's bond with her unit. In truth I was not even able to assess how it was helping or hurting our family unity. I just knew that this was the way the world was now and there was nothing I could do to change it, for better or for worse.

Conclusion

War is constantly changing. Weapons, enemies, and political environments are always evolving. The world, our civilization, is also constantly in flux. Our way of life, values, culture, and technologies morph rapidly. War is never fought in a vacuum. What changes the world also alters the way wars are fought. This applies to everything from the type of men and women who serve in the military to technologies used to fight battles. The people who serve in the U.S. Army today are in many ways different than those who came before them. They have a full range of motivations for serving: patriotism, financial interest, tribal bonds, family tradition, and countless others. But in the mind of soldiers, why they fight—for the love of their fellow soldiers—has not changed.

From the beginning of armed conflict, militaries have learned how to develop effective combat teams. That development and the keys to success for military combat performance involve an interdependent set of systems that really has not changed since the early 1800s, arguably much earlier in history. Dr. John Lynn's model describing the components that lead to combat effectiveness (e.g., interests, the motivational system, and the military system) is as accurate for analyzing a modern day unit as it is an army from the past.

One of the key aspects of the military system required for combat effectiveness is cohesion—both social and task cohesion. The bonds developed through shared hardships and during the thousands of hours that span the time while fighting are widely referenced military attributes. They are highlighted in most military movies and books, from Shakespearean plays to box office hits like *Saving Pri-*

vate Ryan or the HBO mini-series *Band of Brothers*. But the details of cohesion, how it is formed and sustained, how exactly it helps soldiers face combat and to live with their actions, is less discussed.

War is first and foremost a collective endeavor. It demands teamwork. It requires small groups to rely on each other and to function as a unit to accomplish their task or mission. Combat is also a human psychological and physiological trial. It necessitates a physiological ability to override the natural human response of fear to face danger and kill other humans. It also requires psychological resilience in order to live with the horrors of combat, the acts committed or events observed, for the rest of the soldier's life.

Task cohesion is self-explanatory, for the most part. A group must agree to an assigned task and work together to achieve it. It requires leadership and constant monitoring to ensure that the team understands what it should be doing, unlike what I found in Alpha Company before I assumed command in 2008.

Social cohesion on the other hand, is much more mysterious. There are, of course, theories about it, studies that have validated it, but I believe there are many known, unknown, or at least some components of it that are taken for granted. Once present, the bonds within a small team allow it to form what is known as a primary group. These groups become almost tribal with their friendship, trust, loyalty, love, and extremely protective feelings members have for one another and the group overall. This love for each other and the team allows each individual to see himself in combat as a group, not as an individual. This collective body is the one fighting the war, facing danger, not the individual soldier. It gives each soldier courage while each is experiencing fear. They know their fellow soldier will die for them if needed, as they would for the other. They know all the members of the group are there for them, doing their part, both physically and mentally.

Social cohesion not only allows the primary group to function as an effective combat team but it also provides the soldiers with a support system that helps mitigate the psychological trauma of their combat experiences. Each soldier knows that their brothers and sisters experienced the same that they did. They can confide in their fellow group members regarding what they saw and how they are dealing with it. The social support of the group is one of their strongest coping mechanisms.

The military and other organizations such as those for police, firemen, and professional sports teams know social cohesion is important but often assume it just happens automatically. I found in my experience in both 2003 and 2008 that the bonds between soldiers absolutely do not happen automatically. They require the right conditions to develop and endure. The right environment must be established and monitored. Soldiers must not only experience combat together, they have to spend hours together getting to know each other, becoming closer than friends—brothers. They need to know that as a group they can accomplish the task they are given, understanding that when they work together, it will lead to not only the success of a mission but enhance their safety as well.

The complex military system that makes up an effective fighting team is a network of critical components that must be maintained by active leadership and course corrections when needed. Getting to a point where members of small groups will die for each other requires real bonding, which is founded on trust. The members of the group must have confidence that each member will do his part and be there for the other soldiers, putting the needs of the group above those of the individual. This cannot be done with words. It must be experienced and demonstrated publicly to each member of the group as they validate the value of both each other and that of the unit as a functioning entity.

Shared hardships are one distinct way to rapidly develop cohesion. Another method is having soldiers spend hours and hours together, training, discussing their thoughts and stresses, or just congregating. That is why any change to how members of a group interact with each other, how they spend time, or how they live in general, has to be assessed against how it will impact the bonding process. This is especially true in the military where cohesion and teamwork can have life or death consequences. That is why every aspect of a soldier's life in combat from the internet and its connection to the outside world, to the living quarters, eating arrangements, daily routines, social dynamics, and the influence of members of the group on each other, are not minor aspects of combat, they are critical data points to combat effectiveness.

The problem of our society's move to connected individuality versus in-person relationships and community life is not the military's alone. A 2016 front page story in the *New York Times*, for example, documented how NBA players were not listening to their coaches' halftime talks or talking to their teammates but rather were glued to their phones, texting and tweeting, seemingly oblivious to the team around them or to the second half they were about to play.[1] Similar dynamics play out in war, except the stakes are higher and the team is more than just twelve athletes.

There are many similarities between team building in the military and in other parts of our society, such as in sports. There is a long-standing exchange of leadership and teamwork practices between the military and many areas of professional sports, but the cohesion needed for combat is very different from sports.[2] Cohesion in war is not just about what is needed for a group of soldiers to fight. It is also about what is needed for them to live with what they have done, what they have experienced. If soldiers are mentally and emotionally distanced from each other immediately after each day of combat, connecting instead with the home front, cohesive bonds with their fellow soldiers and the coping processes are weakened, potentially to the great detriment of the individuals and the broader army.

The military is what management scholars call an open system.[3] It must contend with how its internal systems interact with the larger environment. Open systems theory predicts that changes to any one of the internal or external elements of an organization's systems will cause a change to other elements. This implies that to understand the performance of an organization, one must view it as a system of interconnected and integrated influences or choices.[4]

Similar to an organization's internal factors, external factors will influence an organization's key internal systems. During the 2007 surge, the modern military saw the effects of being stretched thin to save Iraq from spiraling into civil war. To the soldiers fighting it year after year, it seemed like a never-ending war. The stress on the army and its systems of organizational behavior, from the institution to the small unit, was very clear. New personnel mandates, such as those that relaxed standards for recruitment and the stop-loss of those soldiers who had already served their commitment, had serious impacts on soldier morale and unit health. These personnel changes, combined with the gradual quality of life changes that were made in an effort to make the soldier's combat experience better—to include increased digital connectivity between the soldier and home life—caused massive visible and invisible influences on the army's internal and external environment.

In 2008 I saw technology further opening the military system. Because of the internet and social media platforms, soldiers frequently talked to their families, friends, loved ones. They could rely on them for social support on a daily basis, just as they had their entire lives. This did not prevent social cohesion from forming within the unit, although it did seem to slow the process. Alpha Company in 2008 did eventually show the positive outcomes of both task and social cohesion near the end of our deployment. Those were only the outwardly visible signs, however. What we cannot truly know is how soldiers' frequent communication with the outside world, with their loved ones at home, impacted the soldiers' ability to deal with what they experienced each day, transitioning from war to home and, for many, from military to civilian life. Context always matters, so I do not think my experiences provide all the answers. I do hope that my experiences at least give us an idea regarding the questions that we should be asking.

Soldiers must have a way to process the psychological impacts of combat in near-real time. In the past this occurred around the campfire or in small groups, with soldiers huddled around their vehicles, passing the time cleaning their weapons or eating meals. In 2008 I observed an absence of this natural but vital process. Watching the soldiers of Green Platoon immediately seek connection with their external support networks through social media and the internet after the grenade attack that killed an Iraqi boy was just one example. I am sure this break in coming together as a group after a traumatic patrol occurred more than I was able to witness. I should have done more to change this. I could have required more discussion, time together, or decompression after a patrol. A patrol debrief could have formalized the process. It also needs to be natural, however, like it has been through the history of combat. The process of coming together as a primary group to discuss a stressful or traumatic event is critical. It allows the soldiers to process what they witness, what they thought they saw, to hear from the other members of the group that it is okay to be bothered by it, and to identify those who are showing signs of compounding mental stress or an inability to deal with what happened.

Soldiers, like all people, are social beings. They need physical human interaction on a daily basis and they need social support from others to cope with stressful situations. Our bodies respond both physically (release of chemicals) and emotionally to physical touch, verbal and nonverbal communication—a smile, a nod of assurance, the right words—from our friends, families, and other support networks. Soldiers rely on that daily interaction with their friends for social support to conduct and endure the trials of combat. Social media has had massive advantages on our society. It has allowed social connection to continue, but we also know face-to-face interaction is vital to our human needs; especially in combat.

Constant contact with social support outside the primary group in or outside the military tribe presents further complications. It slams war and home lives together. It adds new levels of stress to the experience of the soldiers and their families, stresses that had never been a part of war in this way. It requires the soldier to split mental ability and resources between war and home unlike ever before. The same is even more true of their emotional and psychological abilities and resources. Because this type of connectivity has never been present in war before, the army does not have the knowledge or systems available to assist troops in dealing with these new stresses and challenges. In 2018 I became the other end of the military's open system where the links between home and war were fully open. I was the family connected on a daily basis to the soldier and what she was experiencing in war. I saw the influence of home on the soldier, my wife. I also saw the impact of constant access to the soldier at war on my children and me. It had both positive and negative impacts. At times it lightened her load and feelings of guilt for not being at home with her children. In other moments the struggles from home spilled over to her and were heaped onto the challenges of war. Just as news of my sister losing her job had distracted me from my military responsibilities, many of our calls to Emily left her in tears, which could not have helped her combat readiness. I have no way of knowing if the pluses outweigh the minuses. This is the new reality and we have to better study, understand, and adjust to this connected warfare.

What has been done in the past to create cohesive, effective combat teams still works and is extremely important. Despite the rapidly changing external environment in which the military exists, many tried and true, tested practices of team and organization building still apply. This is what I saw in Alpha Company in 2008. Despite the efforts to make soldiers' lives more comfortable—such as living, eating, and spending their time separately—the company did respond to the changes reversing those new practices so their daily lives were more conducive to forming task and social cohesion. They started living, eating, and spending more time together. In the future the military (and in some ways any organization) has to not only understand its key internal systems (their people and their teambuilding and operating practices) that have worked for decades and longer but also how changes to these processes and to external factors such as connections to people outside the environment will impact group and individual behavior, performance, and resilience.

Telecommunication technology—the internet and social media—has changed the combat experience in unexpected ways. It has changed the soldier's personal experiences in war and the small group dynamics that are key to combat effectiveness. No matter what, the military must not forget that social cohesion is critical to combat. It must be cognizant of actions related to the military's internal systems and to the things outside of the military influencing them. In this way, the military can better ensure the right environments and practices are in place to best allow cohesion to form. It must deal with the ever-increasing connection between the war front and the home front while still ensuring that the cohesive bonds between soldiers aid in effective combat performance and allow soldiers to process and cope with the wars they experience.

The key is to understand what past practices need to be saved or even brought back in the modern world. The answer is not to eliminate external influences such as connectivity. That is not possible and may not be desirable, even if possible. While I saw modern factors influencing and slowing the team building and bonding processes in 2008, I believe that leaders can make changes to establish conditions that are better for fostering social and task cohesion. Creating routines for eating, living, and decompressing together is one option that does not eliminate time spent connecting with home; it just reduces or reschedules it. I witnessed the positives of modernity, the constant ready-access to social support networks outside of combat. The soldiers' families are another important cooperative that has its own norms and offers its own kinds of support. This domestic primary group has yet to be examined in regard to how it might have a beneficial influence on the soldier's primary combat group or how it might ease the soldier's transition back to family life at the end of the tour or into civilian life after the military. In the longer term, alliance with the families while at war may also help the veteran deal with the emotional and psychological effects of war when they return. We just do not have enough information yet to make these assessments.

Alternatively, the connective habits, the daily use of social media and electronic communication for social and emotional support developed while at war might potentially assist veterans in staying in touch with their battle buddies over the years and therefore with the people who understand their shared experiences. This could conceivably help soldiers cope with their demons. I have not personally witnessed that yet. Instead I am aware of the kinds of burdens that ssg Martinez, sgt Schetter, and others of Alpha Company have borne and wonder if it might have gone better for them without so much battlefield connectivity and instead more cohesion and hardship sharing with the soldiers afterward around them as well as decompressing or having access to a physical veteran, a battle buddy, once they were back in society.

No matter if it is the soldier at war, the family at home during war, or the soldier coping with war later in life, we still prefer to see someone face-to-face rather than what can be provided virtually. Studies of the impacts of constant connectivity and social media on young adults has showed that it leads to experiencing higher levels of anxiety, depression, loneliness, and suicide risk than seen in prior generations. [5] This is obviously not what we want for our soldiers, families, or veterans.

Among other things, this book highlights how communications between the frontlines and home have evolved over recent times, and how the modern era is unique when it comes to the immediacy of communications and the sheer amount of modern distractions at a soldier's fingertips thanks to advances in telecommunications. The implications of this change on the combat experience, on leadership, and the process of forming bonds among soldiers, the critical aspect of how and why soldiers fight, is important not just for would-be soldiers thinking about enlisting one day but also for anyone, military and civilian alike, who cares about the strength of our national defense. The ways to improve battlefield cohesion, methods of infusing social media and other technological advancements in a manner that makes our military stronger, and finding techniques to make soldiers better on and off the battlefield still matter. War does require and produce bands of brothers, but now they are connected soldiers.

Epilogue

Emily returned from Kuwait in late summer 2019. We all survived her deployment one day at a time. There continued to be good, bad, and ugly days. We faced each challenge as a family and literally counted the days until Mommy came home. Our daily connection to Emily by email, calls, text, and video chat stayed constant. When it was all over, I do believe that constant connection with Emily was, for the most part, a good thing. But I also still believe there are negative side effects from that persistent and instant communication on the solider, family, and combat teams. As I have hopefully shown in this book, I am left with more informed questions than answers.

I am not sure what Isaac, Isabel, and Maggie will remember from Emily's deployment. As time has passed, many of the memories have begun to fade. That is one of the reasons I was sure to record many of my experiences with journaling in real time while Emily was gone. Time does soften some of the daily mental struggles soldiers and their families face. That is why I believe the study of the complete combat experience must be done in real time. It must be viewed from the collective moment of battle to the individual soldier's mental struggles before, during, and after combat.

When Emily returned, I knew to take it easy during the reintegration phase. I understood from firsthand experience that the transitional speed of a soldier going from his or her combat routines to the everyday schedules, environment, and challenges of home life can be very disturbing. That is hard to explain to kids, of course, but I think they all intuitively understood and eased themselves into the full all-out chaos that is normal for young kids. That didn't stop them from constantly saying the phrase that I knew was like nails on a chalkboard for Emily: "Well, that isn't the way Daddy does it." We quickly reconfigured and within a few months were getting back to Team Spencer. The kids had a new glow. Bigger smiles. It felt right.

Seven months after Emily returned, a global pandemic hit. The 2019 Coronavirus (COVID-19) forced all of our communities to take drastic measures to reduce the spread of the disease. Social distancing became the ever-present requirement. We had to stay at home, delay any family gatherings, and not meet in any large groups no matter for work, school, or kid sports. Every aspect of daily life was pushed to virtual settings. Work was moved to telecommuting, school to e-learning, church to online forums, even family and friend interactions pushed to virtual hangouts using the latest technologies of our day.

COVID-19 taught the world what I had discovered in war: that we (humans) are social beings. We need connections. We need them physically as much as emotionally. Under extreme stress, especially in close combat, no amount of virtual time can replace the human need of physical social presence and community.

I do not miss war. As William Tecumseh Sherman said, "It is all hell." I do feel, though, that there is a small hole in my consciousness. This tear was caused by the absence of the community of brothers and sisters that is the core of military life. This community of people makes you feel, as soon as you meet them, like you can talk about anything and understand each other on a very personal level, despite varied pasts and lives. I miss the bonds of brotherhood that I formed in war with the soldiers close to me. The connections were forged with soldiers whom I came to know and depend on through a unique combination of uninterrupted time spent together and shared experiences of extreme situations filled with stress, fear, excitement, hardship, and most of the time success. I miss soldiers like 2LT Mike Kane, 1LT Otis Ingram, and SSG Fincher. Years can pass between us, but when I talk to them it is like we had spoken just yesterday.

I also miss the feeling of being given a very high-risk mission against a worthy opponent where death or injury are possible. Being given the operation with full trust, autonomy, and confidence from my superiors while knowing that my team and I were fully trained, ready, willing, and extremely capable of succeeding was a challenge and an honor. When this happened, when all systems were fully functioning to superior combat effectiveness, it was near euphoria.

I have learned from my study and years of reflection that this personal feeling of confidence and being a part of a functioning team in war is a very complex phenomenon. Each individual soldier has different motivations, thoughts, and beliefs. The soldier's mind is present in the moment but also full of many other thoughts, stresses, and concerns. A team is not just a collection of individuals but a collective body relying on practices, tactics, and constructs, such as cohesion, that are centuries old. I have also learned from reflection that there was a lot I did not know about how war would affect my team members or me individually. I have discovered that there is a lot that we know about the human requirements of close combat and how to cope with many different types of stresses both in battle and during its aftermath; yet there are things that the army and society also take for granted and often leave unquestioned.

Ultimately I do believe there are changing aspects of war that we do not yet fully understand, such as the impacts of modern connectivity between the soldier and their external networks (friends, family, loved ones) on his experience in war. That new reality does impact the development and functioning of teams. It deserves more study and attention.

There are many consistencies in my two combat tours and my time as a stay-at-home parent with a deployed spouse. One of the biggest is that I made a lot of mistakes. If I could do it all over again, I would do many things differently, but that is not how war or the army works. I can only hope that my experiences may help others see a situation differently, inform future decisions, or simply encourage them to ask their own questions.

NOTES

1. What We Believe and Know

1. George Santayana, *Soliloquies in England and Later Soliloquies* (New York: C. Scribner's Son, 1992), 102.

2. "Audie Murphy's World War II Heroics, 70 Years Ago," History Channel Online, https://www.history.com/news/audie-murphys-world-war-ii-heroics-70-years-ago.

3. Deputy Secretary of Defense Speech, Medal of Honor Ceremony for SGT Shemin and PVT Johnson, June 3, 2015, as Delivered by Deputy Secretary of Defense Deputy Secretary of Defense Bob Work, Pentagon Hall of Heroes, https://www.defense.gov/Newsroom/Speeches/Speech/Article/606677/medal-of-honor-ceremony-for-sergeant-shemin-and-private-johnson/.

4. Leslie Zenleny, "Morale and Leadership," *Journal of Applied Sociology* 9 (September 1924–August 1925): 207–15.

5. John A. Lynn, *The Bayonets of the Republic: Motivation and Tactics in the Army of Revolutionary France, 1791–94* (Boulder CO: Westview, 1996) 23.

6. Lynn, 26–36.

7. Lynn, 36–38.

8. Lynn, 22.

9. John Hayes, *The Theory and Practice of Change Management* (London: Palgrave Macmillan, 2002), 130.

10. Most of these works are examined in detail in Edward Coss, *All for the King's Shilling: The British Soldier under Wellington, 1808–1814* (Norman: University of Oklahoma Press, 2010), 191–210.

11. Samuel A. Stouffer et al., *The American Soldier: Combat and Its Aftermath*, vol. 2 (Princeton NJ: Princeton University Press, 1949), 107.

12. S. L. A. Marshall, *Men Against Fire* (New York: William Morrow, 1947), 42–43.

13. Marshall, 161.

14. Edward A. Shils and Morris Janowitz, "Cohesion and Disintegration in the Wehrmacht in World War II," *Public Opinion Quarterly* 12 (Summer 1948): 281.

15. Mikael Salo, "The Relation Between Group-Level Characteristics and Group Cohesion," U.S. Army Research Institute for Behavioral and Social Sciences, November 2006, https://apps.dtic.mil/dtic/tr/fulltext/u2/a460547.pdf.

16. Roger W. Little, "Buddy Relations and Combat Performance," in *The New Military: Changing Patterns of Organization*, ed. Morris Janowitz (New York: Russell Sage Foundation, 1964), 221.

17. Charles C. Moskos Jr., *The American Enlisted Man: The Rank and File in Today's Military* (New York: Russell Sage Foundation, 1970), 146.

18. Lenard Wong, Thomas Kolditz, Raymond A. Millen, and Terrence M. Potter, "Why They Fight: Combat Motivation in the Iraq War," GlobalSecurity.org, July 2003, https://www.globalsecurity.org/military/library/report/2003/ssi_wong-kolditz -millen-potter.htm.

19. Eduardo Salas, Armando X. Estrada, and William B. Vessey, *Team Cohesion: Advances in Psychological Theory, Methods and Practice* (Bingley, UK: Emerald, 2015), 11.

20. Salas, Estrada, and Vessey, 11.

21. Stephen E. Ambrose, *Band of Brothers: E Company, 506th Regiment, 101st Airborne from Normandy to Hitler's Eagle's Nest* (New York: Pocket, 2002).

22. Lynee Messer, "Natural Experimentation," *Encyclopedia Britannica*, October 7, 2016, https://www.britannica.com/science/natural–experiment.

2. Welcome to the Platoon

1. Lenard Wong, Thomas Kolditz, Raymond A. Millen, and Terrence M. Potter, "Why They Fight: Combat Motivation in the Iraq War," GlobalSecurity.org, July 2003, https://www.globalsecurity.org/military/library/report/2003/ssi_wong -kolditz-millen-potter.htm.

2. John A. Lynn, *The Bayonets of the Republic: Motivation and Tactics in the Army of Revolutionary France, 1791–94* (Boulder CO: Westview, 1996), 30.

3. Lynn, 23.

4. Mind Tools, "Forming, Storming, Norming, and Performing: Understanding the Stages of Team Formation," https://www.mindtools.com/pages/article/newldr _86.htm.

5. Anthony King, *The Combat Soldier: Infantry Tactics and Cohesion in the Twentieth and Twenty-First Centuries* (Oxford: Oxford University Press, 2014), 238.

3. Jump Right into It

1. Kyle Jahner, "Key Moments in Army Airborne History," *Army Times*, February 29, 2016, https://www.armytimes.com/news/your-army/2016/02/29/key-moments -in-army-airborne-history/.

2. Andrew D. Robinson, "Operation Northern Delay: The Evolution of Joint Forcible Entry," US Army Command and Staff College, Fort Leavenworth, 2018, https:// apps.dtic.mil/sti/citations/ad1084521.

3. Edward Coss, "The Vicissitudes of Violence: Fear, Physiology, and Behavior under Fire," in *Technology, Violence, and War: Essays in Honor of Dr. John F. Guilmartin, Jr.* (Boston: Brill Academic, 2019), 286.

4. Home Away from Home

1. Lisa Silvestri, *Friended at the Front: Social Media in the American War Zone* (Lawrence: University Press of Kansas, 2015), 54.

2. Lenard Wong and Stephen Gerras, "CU@ the FOB: How the Forward Operating Base Is Changing the Life of Combat Soldiers" (Darby PA: Diane, 2006), 8, https://publications.armywarcollege.edu/pubs/1748.pdf.

3. The Meaning of Mail, National Association of Letter Carriers, the Postal Record, December 2011, https://www.nalc.org/news/the-postal-record/2011/december-2011 /document/12-2011_meaning.pdf.

4. Michael Goldfarb, "Meet the Fobbits," *Washington Examiner* (Washington DC), June 13, 2007. https://www.washingtonexaminer.com/weekly-standard/meet -the-fobbits.

5. Wong and Gerras, "CU@ the FOB," 3.

6. Lenard Wong, Thomas Kolditz, Raymond A. Millen, and Terrence M. Potter, "Why They Fight: Combat Motivation in the Iraq War" GlobalSecurity.org, July 2003, https://www.globalsecurity.org/military/library/report/2003/ssi_wong-kolditz -millen-potter.htm.

7. Wong et al., 12.

8. Eduardo Salas, Armando X. Estrada, and William B. Vessey, *Team Cohesion: Advances in Psychological Theory, Methods and Practice* (Bingley, UK: Emerald, 2015), 4.

5. I Can't Leave

1. Steve Liewer, "In Iraq, Some Service Members Live Like Princes while Others Sleep in the Sand," *Stars and Stripes*, October 17, 2003, https://www.stripes.com/news/in -iraq-some-servicemembers-live-like-princes-while-others-sleep-in-the-sand-1.12783.

2. "My Lai Massacre," History Channel, updated April 17, 2020, https://www .history.com/topics/vietnam-war/my-lai-massacre-1.

3. Edward Coss, *All for the King's Shilling: The British Soldier under Wellington, 1808–1814* (Norman: University of Oklahoma Press, 2010), 195.

4. Mark Schone and Matthew Cole, "Calvin Gibbs, Leader of 'Thrill Kill' Soldiers, Guilty of Murder," *ABC News*, November 10, 2011, https://abcnews.go.com/Blotter /leader-thrill-kill-soldiers-found-guilty/story?id=14924863.

5. George W. Bush, *Public Papers of the Presidents of the United States* (Washington DC: U.S. Government Printing Office, 2010), 1316.

6. Chester County Hall of Heroes: Honoring the Sacrifice of Heroes, "Bernstein, David Richard," https://www.chescoheroes.org/297/Bernstein-David-Richard.

7. Chester County Hall of Heroes, "Bernstein, David Richard."

6. A Different Army

1. United Nations Security Council, "Iraq Stands on the Brink of Civil War, 'Violence Seems out of Control,' Special Representative Tells Security Council," accessed December 11, 2006, https://www.un.org/press/en/2006/sc8895.doc.htm.

2. "Occupation and Continued Warfare," Iraq War 2003–2011, *Encyclopedia Britannica*, accessed October 5, 2019, https://www.britannica.com/event/Iraq-War /Occupation-and-continued-warfare.

3. Alan McLean and Archie Tse, "American Forces in Afghanistan and Iraq," *New York Times*, http://archive.nytimes.com/www.nytimes.com/interactive/2011/06/22 /world/asia/american-forces-in-afghanistan-and-iraq.html?hp.

4. Lolita Baldor, "Army Misses Recruiting Goal for First Time Since 2005," September 21, 2018, Military.com, https://www.military.com/daily-news/2018/09/21 /army-misses-recruiting-goal-first-time-2005.html.

5. John Spencer, "The Military's Real Problem: Fewer Americans Are Joining," Politico (Washington DC), December 15, 2015, https://www.politico.com/agenda/the -militarys-real-problem-fewer-americans-are-joining-000005.

6. Bernard D. Rostker, "I Want You!: The Evolution of the All-Volunteer Force," RAND, 2006, https://www.rand.org/pubs/research_briefs/rb9195.html.

7. Eric Sundstrom, Kenneth P. De Meuse, and David Futrell, "Work Teams: Applications and Effectiveness," *American Psychologist* 45, no. 2 (February 1990): 120–33.

8. Lenard Wong and Stephan Gerras, "CU@ the FOB: How the Forward Operating Base Is Changing the Life of Combat Soldiers," 1, https://publications.armywarcollege .edu/pubs/1748.pdf.

9. Wong and Gerras, 24.

10. Wong and Gerras, 13.

11. Tom Roeder, "Official: Troops OK in Noncombat Roles," *Gazette (Colorado Springs)*, August 22, 2008, https://gazette.com/news/official-troops-ok-in-noncombat -roles/article_f3ea163c-c510-5625-96e7-9457729aaaf5.html.

12. M2 Bradley Infantry Fighting Vehicle, *Encyclopedia Britannica*, https://www .britannica.com/technology/m2-Bradley-Infantry-Fighting-Vehicle, accessed January 8, 2020.

13. Steven Hurst, "U.S.: Raid of Baghdad's Sadr City Kills 49," *Washington Post*, October 21, 2007, https://www.washingtonpost.com/wp-dyn/content/article/2007 /10/21/ar2007102100159_pf.html.

14. John A. Lynn, *The Bayonets of the Republic: Motivation and Tactics in the Army of Revolutionary France, 1791–94* (Boulder CO: Westview, 1996), 22.

15. John R. P. French Jr. and Betram Raven, "The Bases of Social Power," in *Studies in Social Power*, ed. D. Cartwright (Ann Arbor MI: Institute for Social Research, 1959), 150–67.

16. Conrad Crane, "The Future Soldier: Alone in a Crowd," *War on the Rocks*, January 19, 2017, https://warontherocks.com/2017/01/the-future-soldier-alone-in-a-crowd/.

17. Edward Coss, "The Vicissitudes of Violence: Fear, Physiology, and Behavior under Fire," in *Technology, Violence, and War: Essays in Honor of Dr. John F. Guilmartin Jr.* (Boston: Brill Academic, 2019), 285–87.

18. Noah Shachtman, "Superbombs 101," *Wired Magazine (New York)*, March 6, 2007.

19. John Spencer, "To Understand PTSD, Send Scientists to War," *Wired Magazine (New York)*, December 18, 2017, https://www.wired.com/2017/01/understand -ptsd-send-scientists-war/.

20. Coss, "The Vicissitudes of Violence," 288.

21. "PTSD and Shell Shock," August 21, 2018, *History Channel*, History.com, https:// www.history.com/topics/inventions/history-of-ptsd-and-shell-shock.

8. Conditions for Social Cohesion

1. Robin I. M. Dunbar, "Coevolution Neocortical Size, Group Size and Language in Humans," *Behavioral and Brain Sciences* 16 (1993): 681.

2. Dunbar, 725.

3. John A. Lynn, *The Bayonets of the Republic: Motivation and Tactics in the Army of Revolutionary France, 1791–94* (Boulder CO: Westview, 1996), 22.

4. William Golding, *Lord of the Flies* (New York: Berkley, 1954).

5. "General Order No. 1—Prohibited Activities for Soldiers," https://www.nytimes .com/interactive/projects/documents/general-order-no-1-prohibited-activities-for -soldiers.

9. Connected and Fighting

1. Lisa Silvestri, *Friended at the Front: Social Media in the American War Zone* (Lawrence: University Press of Kansas, 2015), 54.

2. Eddie Jackson, "When the Combat Switch Is Broken: The Dangerous Effects of the Military's Embrace of Energy Drinks," *Modern War Institute*, March 16, 2017, https://mwi.usma.edu/combat-switch-broken-dangerous-effects-militarys-embrace -energy-drinks/.

3. Dan Shea, "RKG-3 Hand-Thrown Grenades," *Small Army Defense Journal*, August 17, 2011, http://www.sadefensejournal.com/wp/rkg-3-hand-thrown-grenades/.

4. Lenard Wong, Thomas Kolditz, Raymond A. Millen, and Terrence M. Potter, "Why They Fight: Combat Motivation in the Iraq War," GlobalSecurity.org, July 2003, https://www.globalsecurity.org/military/library/report/2003/ssi_wong -kolditz-millen-potter.htm.

11. A Winning Team

1. Obituary of Sgt. Ryan Patrick Schetter, Crain Funeral Home and Cremation Service, https://www.crainsonline.com/obituaries/Sgt-Ryan-Schetter/#!/Obituary.

2. Leo Shane III, "New Veteran Suicide Numbers Raise Concerns among Experts Hoping for Positive News," *Military Times*, October 8, 2019, https://www.militarytimes .com/news/pentagon-congress/2019/10/09/new-veteran-suicide-numbers-raise -concerns-among-experts-hoping-for-positive-news/.

3. Elly Farelly, "Bringing Home the 8 Million Boys After WWII; Operation Magic Carpet," *War History Online*, June 29, 2016, https://www.warhistoryonline.com/world -war-ii/brining-home-8-million-boys-wwii-operation-magic-carpet.html.

4. Sebastian Junger, "Why Veterans Miss War," TEDsalon (New York), January 2014, https://www.ted.com/talks/sebastian_junger_why_veterans_miss_war/transcript#t-802402.

5. Sebastian Junger, *Tribe: On Homecoming and Belonging* (New York: Twelve, 2016).

12. On the Other End

1. "Camp Arifjan Army Base in Arifjan, Kuwait," MilitaryBases.com, https://militarybases.com/overseas/kuwait/camp-arifjan/, accessed November 2, 2019.

2. Patty Barron, "Military Children are Resilient but Still Face Challenges," Association of the United States Army, April 1, 2012, https://www.ausa.org/articles/military-children-are-resilient-still-face-challenges.

3. Sarah Meadows, Terri Tanielian, and Benjamin Karney, eds., "How Military Families Respond before, during and after Deployment: Findings from the RAND Deployment Life Study" (Santa Monica CA: RAND, 2016), https://www.rand.org/pubs/research_briefs/rb9906.html.

4. Cindy Gellner, "Why Does My Child Always Need to Go to the Bathroom?," May 25, 2018, https://healthcare.utah.edu/the-scope/shows.php?shows=0_oj2ugrvb.

Conclusion

1. Andrew Keh, "Trending at Halftime: NBA Players Checking Their Phones," *New York Times*, April 20, 2016, https://www.nytimes.com/2016/04/21/sports/basketball/nba-players-checking-phones-at-halftime.html.

2. Mike Krzyzewski, *The Gold Standard: Building a World-Class Team* (New York: Business Plus, 2010).

3. John Hayes, *The Theory and Practice of Change Management* (London: Palgrave, 1988), 130.

4. Hayes, 130.

5. Jean Twenge, *iGen: Why Today's Super-Connected Kids Are Growing up Less Rebellious, More Tolerant, Less Happy—and Completely Unprepared for Adulthood—and What That Means for the Rest of Us* (New York: Simon & Schuster, 2017), 292.

INDEX

skills, 176, 190; organizational, 117; relationship, 109; tactical, 20; technical, 48
Skype, 104
Slate, 1LT, 105, 174
Smith, PVT, 45, 46
social media, 94, 104, 149, 192, 194, 208, 221, 224, 226; connection through, 195, 222; immediacy of, 150; impact of, 225; unauthorized, 193
social norms, 61, 194
social support, 219, 222–23, 224
Socrates, 10
SOF. *See* Special Operations Forces (SOF)
soldier's heart, 115
Soliloquies in England and Later Soliloquies (Santayana), 2
Somalia, 52
Sons of Iraq, 102, 140
Southern European Task Force (SETAF), 14
Special Air Service (SAS), 18
Special Operations Forces (SOF), 18, 32, 74
Spencer, Isaac, 197, 198, 203, 206, 208, 210, 214, 227; text game and, 215
Spencer, Isabel, 197, 198, 203, 208, 211, 214, 215, 227
Spencer, Maggie, 197, 198, 203, 209, 210, 211, 212, 213, 227
Spencer, Sara, 56, 58–59; deployment and, 25–26; divorce from, 96; letters from, 57; stress and, 71
squad leaders, 16, 106, 139, 182
Stafford, SPC, 142
standards, 17, 106; army, 116–17; enforcing, 134; minimum, 110; recruitment, 221
Stanford, SFC, 45–46
stop-loss, 91–92, 110, 136, 190, 221
Stouffer, Samuel, 9
stress, 6, 64, 81, 108, 114, 130, 150, 162, 188, 196, 214, 229; adding, 51–52, 129, 222–23; coping with, 11, 71, 222, 223; extreme, 45, 228; home front, 199; leadership and, 110; mental, 222; psychological, 94; simulated, 46; surviving, 50
Student Veterans Organization, 193
suicide, 225; attempted, 42–43; veteran, 193–94

Sunnis, 65–66, 140
surge, 91, 95, 141, 221
systems: command, 7, 80; communication, 71; establishment of, 171; failure of, 154; gaming, 98; internal, 220, 221, 223, 224; military, 7, 112, 132, 134, 135, 212, 219, 221. *See also* open systems theory

tactical operations center (TOC), 102, 126, 212
tactics, 6, 7, 17, 79, 134, 135; primary, 171; training on, 18, 21
targets, 149, 179; "do-not-shoot," 18; time-sensitive, 178
team building, 6, 10, 167, 174, 180, 186, 201, 220, 224; conclusions about, 11; development models for, 17; skills for, 190
teamwork, 16, 106, 134, 150, 186, 220. *See also* combat teams
technology, 6, 8, 11, 54, 178–79, 213, 217, 221, 228; modern, 212; telecommunication, 224
telecommunications, 194, 208, 224, 225
telegrams, *54, 55*
texting, 212, 215, 220
Thanksgiving, 204–5, 206
Tigris River, 60–61, 69, 138, 140
TOC. *See* tactical operations center (TOC)
To Hell and Back (movie), 5
training, 10, 21, 42, 45, 46, 47, 56, 173, 195, 209; airborne, 15–16; basic, 2, 68, 141; behavior and, 26; bonding and, 17; deployment and, 25; enter-and-clear-a-room, 18, 19–20; live rounds for, 20; officer, 78, 132, 141; on-the-job, 23, 24, 76; ranger, 2, 3; unit, 22, 133; weapons, 79
transitions, 26, 27, 188, 193, 194–95, 227
trauma, 122, 161, 190, 203, 207, 218–19, 222; psychological, 122, 162
traumatic brain injury (TBI), 102
tribes, 162, 187, 218, 222
Tripp, SFC, 146, 172–73, 174, 185, 194, 204
trunk monkey, 176; real, 177, *178*
trust, 180, 195, 196, 229; bonding and, 72, 163, 219
Tuckman, Bruce, 17